No, It Is NOT In My Head

The Journey of a Chronic Pain Survivor from Wheelchair to Marathon

NICOLE HEMMENWAY

Dr Collier,
Thank you for being
part of my recovery journey,
and making a difference in my
life.

Believing in Miracles,
Nicole

M·J

New York

No, It Is Not In My Head

The Journey of a Chronic Pain Survivor From Wheelchair to Marathon

ISBN 978-1-60037-699-3

Library of Congress Control Number: 2009935648

Cover Design by: Rachel Lopez - Rachel@r2cdesign
Photograph by: Hyde Park Photography
Location: Barr Mansion, Austin, Texas

MORGAN · JAMES
THE ENTREPRENEURIAL PUBLISHER

Morgan James Publishing
1225 Franklin Ave., STE 325
Garden City, NY 11530-1693
Toll Free 800-485-4943
www.MorganJamesPublishing.com

In an effort to support local communities, raise awareness and funds, Morgan James Publishing donates one percent of all book sales for the life of each book to Habitat for Humanity. Get involved today, visit **www.HelpHabitatForHumanity.org.**

For Mom, Dad and Dan,
Thank you for keeping my hopes and dreams alive. I love you with all my heart.

For Rick,
Thank you for making me feel like Wonder Woman. You are my everything.

Contents

In Gratitude

There are so many people to thank. I know my journey to wellness would not have been possible without the support and encouragement of my many friends and family.

To My Family—
Mom, Dad, Dan, Rick, Nonnie, Nonno, (Gramsie, Poppa), and all my aunts, uncles and cousins who make up the Hemmenway, Ruo, Mazzeo, Marovich and McEvoy Families…thank you for holding me up when I could no longer stand, and showering me with unconditional love. I owe so much of my newfound happiness to you. You are the wind beneath my wings.

To My Friends—
Meredith, Dylan, Emily, Kristin, Meghan, Nadine, Angela, Brendan, Emily, John, Kerry, Chris, Pat, Molly, Annie, Tim, Tricia, Liz, Megan, Jim, Erin, Maureen, (Bobby), Dan and Marie… thank you for being my shoulders to lean on, and my friends for life. Without you, I would have never made it out of the darkness!

To My Dear Family Friends—
The Callaghan, Kelber, O'Brien, Moriarty, Quinlan, Gulbengay, Murphy, Linebarger, Sarlatte, Kilroy, Capurro, O'Donnell, Bonnici, Buchanan, Gannon Briggs, Minicucci, Krouse, Roscelli, Topic, Holz, Fake, Tischer, Garcia, Fitch, Backes, McPherson, Thomas and Elbogen Families… thank you for supporting my family and me through the bleakest days. Your unending prayers, kind words and strength helped me persevere; I was able to hold on to hope because of you.

To My Large Medical Team, the National Pain Foundation and my Healing Friends…all I can say is thank you one hundred times over. Thank you for your endless dedication in seeing me well. Your encouragement and advice allowed me to continue searching for my miracle.

To My Friends I Met Along the Journey—
Ann, Nancy, (Sue), Jon, Keith, Mike, Erin, Sara, Patrick, Seth, Sara, Ruben, Maureen, Myra, Pat, George, Ann, Jamie, Lamar, Burt, Ariel, Celeste, Alexa, Ambrose, Ares, Erica, Patti, Sarah, Marissa, Amber, Ann, Mick, Mary, Steve, Savanna, Amanda, Candace, Amy, Patricia, Melissa, Sara, Paula, Sonny, Judy, Lee, Julie, Nicki, Kelsey, Terri, Steve, Cathy, Nathan, Paul, (Irene), (Jack), Katie, Laura, Collin, Suzette, Patsy, Connie, Michaela, Patti, Will, Anne, Kathi Lowe,

Scott Drees and the entire Rhodes Family…thank you for entering my life, and walking the courageous road to recovery with me. To my fellow chronic pain survivors, I wish you happiness, health and blessings.

To Carondelet High School, Creighton University, St. Isidore's School Community, Nestlé USA and San Ramon Valley Unified School District…thank you for your patience, concern and overwhelming willingness to help my family through a difficult time. I am indebted to each of you.

To Brad at Hyde Park Photography…what can I say. You are the best at capturing the essence of who I am on film!

To Tom…words cannot begin to express my appreciation and love. Thank you for showing me that I can express anger, fear and pain while still being a pillar of strength and hope. You helped me find the author within, and I am eternally thankful.

To David, Rick, Lyza and Jim at Morgan James Publishing…you have made my dream come true. Thank you for believing in me and allowing me this wonderful opportunity to help and inspire. I am very appreciative of your dedication, time and support. It has been a pleasure to work with such an incredible team, and I look forward to our future journey together.

Harbor Half: Starting Line

I awkwardly make my way amongst the lively group. I feel my heart beating faster as the hairs on my arm stand on edge. Today will be the ultimate test of my healing.

In three hours, I hope to be able to put the past behind me. After a horrific nine-year battle with chronic pain, I want to say the war is finally over and I prevailed. Yet in order to do that, I must risk all the improvements I have made.

Every previous doubt and insecurity festers to the surface making it difficult for me to maintain composure. While I yearn to live a carefree and pain-free life, I know what is at stake. I understand that my decisions today may cause me more pain and tears tomorrow.

I feel like an imposter timidly moving amid a crowd of confident swaggers and boisterous energy. Although it is still dark outside, beads of sweat fall from my temples and down my cheeks as butterflies flutter in my queasy, unsettled, churning stomach. Looking up to the sky for a reassuring sign, I see the iridescent radiance of the moon shining down. It will soon guide me on the initial steps of my journey. *I cannot go back to the days confined to a wheelchair.*

With a fleeting pulse, I tune out Taylor Swift blaring from the crackling radio speakers and ignore the racers talking, laughing and warming up around me. Soon I move toward the back of the starting line, which is just a large makeshift metal apparatus placed in the middle of a blocked-off deserted road. Grateful for the fall weather, crisp temperature and decrease in humidity, I stare in disbelief at the bright, bold banner proudly hanging from the scratched rafters. I wonder what I am doing here.

My lungs tighten and constrict fearing the consequences of pushing myself too far. When it becomes hard for me to breathe, I gasp for air and feel a deep pit swell in my stomach. A lump forms at the back of my throat. There is no turning back. *I have to succeed.*

This is my chance to prove anything in life is attainable. People do have the potential to move past limitations and achieve dreams. Struggling for years with the ravages of chronic pain, I repeatedly heard doctors say I would "never have use of my limbs; that I needed to make the best out of my situation by accepting my disability."

Instead of viewing my determination and ruthless pursuit to recover as an asset, most specialists mocked my perseverance. Western medicine even gave me the cold shoulder when the trained specialists were unable to help me. Like a stray alley cat searching for food, I had to fend for myself when the medical field pushed me aside.

Yet I never gave up. Even with the cards stacked against me. Without mobility of my right hand and at times bedridden, I still refused to give in. Finding a way to look beyond the hurtful remarks, darting glances and hushed whispers, I was determined to beat the hell that had become my life. I always held onto hope—*hope in a miracle, hope in a cure, hope in a better, happier, pain-free life.*

Now I no longer want to live life from the sidelines. I must take a stand and escape the label of "sick and disabled." This is my rebirth, my opportunity to show myself that fear, pain and uncertainty do not control me. I am running for my right to live.

Thinking about being normal again sends shivers down my spine as I also consider the alternative: what if I am not ready? *Is it possible to overtax myself and then suffer another catastrophic setback?*

Not wanting to spend another decade battling the demons and destruction of pain while coping with the torment of being unable to dress, feed or bathe myself, I wear a two-sided mask: outwardly oozing confidence and enthusiasm in my upcoming endeavor while inwardly crumbling to pieces.

Although I know I spent the last four months vigorously training, now that I am here, I wonder if all my sweat and tears were enough. I fear losing the life I have worked so hard to attain. I do not want to fail.

I am out of my comfort zone watching the other runners stretch quadriceps, hamstrings and calves along the beaten sidewalk in small mesh shorts and bright singlet tops. A novice to the running scene, I wonder if tiny, slitted shorts and small, sleeveless shirts are mandatory for running. For I am wearing the complete opposite: Lululemon Athletica inc. custom-cropped black running pants and black high-support tank, and a CamelBak hydration pack holding two liters of water with its side pockets filled with electrolyte-enhancing gels and chews.

While I am a fish out of water, sticking out like a sore thumb, I know all too well that pain knows no boundaries and affects us all universally. Looking around the ironically mixed group of endorphin-hungry, health-conscious, muscularly-toned athletes and barbeque-loving, beer-drinking, softball-playing regular joes, I question what may have happened to them in their lives: *what pain, tragedy or obstacle had they faced and overcome?*

Overwhelmed with emotion, I reach for Rick, my boyfriend and my personal coach for this occasion. I quickly squeeze his strong, callused hand and immediately feel calm. He is my light. After suffering for so many years and wondering whether anyone would ever love me, I had found my true companion. Love saved me, and as life begins to come full circle, I can almost see the end of the road. *I can almost envision a life of normalcy...*

I hear a voice come over the loudspeaker as I take another long, deep breath to quiet my tense nerves. *This is it—my life-changing moment—has arrived.* The earlier anxiety and worry dissipate as my time of triumph nears. I am no longer going to be the pitiful victim or the frightened little girl. Now I am a resilient survivor: the strong, beautiful woman proud of her past and proud of whom she had become.

It doesn't even phase me that running can worsen my condition by flaring my pain and inhibiting my ability to walk. From here on out, my life will not be ruled by medicine or misery. Letting go of the shame-ridden mindset, I am able to see my new life of happiness, health and love.

"Are the runners ready?" Cheers, whistles and claps erupt through the thinning crowd as a rush of adrenaline warms my entire body. Easily spotting my parents' proud, glowing faces, I realize I am doing this for them. They are my heroes, and this journey is my way of thanking them for their undying love, unwavering support and unswerving patience.

"On your mark." My heart palpitates faster as I begin to tune out the outward distractions. My attention is on Rick and me, the smell of the musty gulf and my desire to run. This is my chance to prove chronic pain does not define me as a person or control my hopes and dreams. Refusing to let my disability put limitations on the way I live, I am here to show that through faith and hope, recovery is always possible.

"Get set...," I still cannot believe this day is finally here. I cannot believe it has been over nine years since my world first fell apart and the pain took over. It is unfathomable that six years have actually passed since the medical community considered me untreatable and told me to make the best out of my current situation. Moreover, I especially cannot believe it has been five years since I came to South Texas to work with the doctor who saved my life...the man who refused to give up, lose hope or believe I could not heal.

"Go!"

I crank up my iPod to hear Luther Vandross singing "One Shining Moment." I first heard the song seven years ago while driving home from the hospital after my first attempt at forgoing morphine-derived medications. My parents and I were crossing over the Bay Bridge when I looked across the choppy waters at Alcatraz and Angel Island. It was then that I knew I would be happy again. *That someday I would smile and laugh, and it would mean something.*

With the lyrics giving me the comfort and drive to persevere, I make my way down the street, putting one foot in front of the other. Running would parallel my nine-year battle with chronic pain.

Chapter 1

The Incident

Leaving the starting line, my thoughts drifted to August 28, 1998. The Junior-Senior Welcome Dance was supposed to have been a highlight of my senior year in high school. Instead, it became the infamous evening that my life changed course.

I remember the dance itself was nothing out of the ordinary. I stood in the warm courtyard of our brother school giggling to my best friend Meredith as we heard our favorite new song. I was just so excited to be a senior. This was going to be my year to shine, live and be happy.

Even today, the memory of raising my right hand to give her a "high five" haunts me. Where did it all go wrong? How had our hands missed causing my ring and pinkie finger to make direct contact with her palm?

I felt the throbbing in my hand immediately. While I tried to shake off the pain, it continued to burn as my hand changed colors. I knew I was in trouble once it became difficult to move my fingers. To see my hand turn tomato-red and close into a claw-like position within thirty minutes was horrifying. I went into shock: this could not be a good sign.

That evening I hardly slept. Instead, I tossed and turned while praying for the burning to end. By morning, my eyes were puffy and red from all the crying…and the pain was worse. The next few days were extremely tough on me as I struggled to juggle school and doctor's appointments. Even though I had understanding teachers, I could not manage the stress of classes and a pain that worsened as the day progressed. Life as I knew it was over.

It was hard to comprehend how a span of seconds could change my life. How had I gone from being a normal teenage girl attending football games and dances to an agonizing pain patient visiting specialists and therapists that quickly? I felt as if the world had collapsed on top of me. Soon I started coming to school with my shoes untied and my hair undone. With the sharp pains making it difficult for me to complete homework or study for upcoming tests, my grades plummeted. I could no longer deny the toll the pain was taking on my entire body.

Even if I found a way to manage the searing agony, I could not compensate for the lack of my writing hand. Not being able to participate or complete my mandatory workload forced me to drop Calculus and Physics. The school graciously assigned me *filler* classes like study period and library knowledge so I would still be able to graduate. While I should have been grateful for these changes, I was devastated. I saw myself as a failure. The carefree person who weeks earlier had been naively unaware of the ways of the world was gone. *I felt lost among the healthy.* My life had fallen apart.

∞

As I started to visit a myriad of doctors in the long and dreadful search for answers, every visit seemed to follow a similar pattern. It began with me sitting for what seemed like an eternity filling out tedious paperwork that mostly went unread by the doctor. Waiting became a huge part of my life. I spent hours in cold, unwelcoming waiting rooms with year-old magazines scattered on chipped coffee tables. It did not matter that my swollen hand looked as though I suffered an allergic reaction to shellfish. It did not matter that I had to live with the pestering and tingling sensation of a pack of bees swarming under my skin. I still had to wait with the other weary patients while dreading what was to come.

"Thank you, Dr. X for squeezing me in and seeing me on such short notice." A nod in my general direction was the only acknowledgement I received as they quickly glanced at my chart.

"What seems to be the problem? I hear you are experiencing a lot of pain in your right hand?"

Finally looking up, Dr. X would zone in on my arm and approach the cold table to reach for my hand. Because no one ever asked if it was all right to touch my hand, I found myself hitting them or pulling my arm away so I would not be hurt. While I viewed these swats as a protective measure to keep the agonizing pain at bay, they did not.

I could tell by the doctors' condescending tones and apathetic manners that my antics annoyed them. It seemed they had pre-determined my problem even before entering the examining room. Therefore, I did not look forward to explaining the incident, the unrelenting pain and the loss of mobility. Nevertheless, I described how Meredith and I tried to give each other a high five at the dance, but our hands had missed.

An uneasy silence filled the room as Dr. X looked perplexed. "What do you think is wrong with me?"

While I waited for an answer, I mindlessly thought about the pain that would not go away. Ever since the moment my right index and pinkie finger smacked Meredith's left palm, I had been in extreme pain and unable to move my fingers. It had been weeks since the incident, and the pain kept escalating. Panic now took over, as I would rock back-and-forth on the steel table. I wondered how my life got so far off-track. *This was my senior year.* I was supposed to be having fun with my friends instead of attending numerous doctors' appointments. I was supposed to be a teenager and not having to deal with grown-up issues.

What would I do if my hand never opened? There was no way I could go to college and expect my roommate to button my pants or tie my shoes. I was scared. With the stress becoming more than I could handle, I prayed this doctor would be able to help me. Frightened by the quietness of the room and the possibility of being ill, I would always ask one last question—"Was this RSD?"

Reflex sympathetic dystrophy (RSD), now known as complex regional pain syndrome (CRPS) was a neurological and chronic pain disorder that affected the nervous system. It had been four years since my life turned upside down due to an ankle sprain. I was in the seventh grade playing a recess game of basketball when I went up for a rebound and accidentally landed wrong on my left ankle. The doctors believed the sprain would heal quickly but after three months of painful suffering and limping, I received the RSD diagnosis. Luckily, the disease went into remission two months later after one epidural nerve block. Yet the unusual symptoms and unexplainable pain were two huge red flags that it returned.

RSD had already changed my life forever. It was the reason I could no longer play sports and why my body responded differently than most people. A simple stubbed toe or sore throat would cause me agony. Knowing it could take me twice as long to recover from a simple cold or flu made me constantly conscious of the disease. However, I was adamant the RSD would not change my dreams and aspirations. I could not play sports but I still could have fun. Despite this mysterious disorder affecting my life, I was not going to sit back and watch life pass me by. Except, what if it had returned? *Was it possible this was RSD?*

The anticipation of a diagnosis was nauseatingly painful for me. It was all that mattered and my life hung in the balance. As soon as I heard the doctor clear his throat, my heart would stop beating. I prayed this visit brought me answers.

"From the symptoms you manifest, it is too soon to diagnose this as RSD. You probably sprained some tendons and the combination of swelling and discomfort is causing the immobility in your fingers."

Receiving no helpful information left me emotionally and mentally wounded. Why was I hurting so badly and unable to move my hand? Feeling the problem had to be more serious than some sprained tendons, I could not let the issue go. "So you really do not feel this is RSD? I keep asking because the pain feels a lot like nerve pain, and I just don't want…"

It was then that I would be abruptly cutoff mid-sentence to hear a drawn out monologue about how pain was a normal response to many different ailments besides RSD. *He* was the specialist who studied these problems. *I* would just need to trust his assessment and continue occupational therapy for a couple more weeks.

While there might be a few slight variations, all my appointments ended this same way. There were no concrete answers or end in sight. Doctor after doctor would ignore my symptoms and write off my complaints as a simple sprain and a low tolerance for pain. For the next six weeks, I continued to visit doctors without receiving adequate help. I became discouraged that no one believed me; I just needed the unrelenting torture validated.

Chapter 2

Held Suspect

I now became desperate for answers. I needed an explanation as to why the burning, stabbing pains grew worse by the day and why my hand had frozen into a tight fist. I wanted assurance this agony was not the neurological and chronic pain disorder I had successfully overcome four years prior. I needed to know I would be okay.

Therefore, when I finally saw an orthopedic surgeon in mid-Fall, I believed he would rally around me with support. Dr. Gloom—my nickname for him because he always spoke in a monotone voice—was a middle-aged man known in the community for being knowledgeable in the field. While his apathetic and indifferent demeanor made him unlikable, I had hope he could shed light on my pain.

Dr. Gloom had a large ego and a strange bedside manner. He would enter the room ignoring the patient only to focus on the afflicted limb. I remember that first visit vividly. With his full attention directed toward my right hand, he immediately grabbed my arm to examine. Poking a sharp metal apparatus against my inflamed skin caused me to squirm and wince on the table. It did not bother him that I moved wildly back and forth while pleading for him to stop. He would not let go. Not until I started banging on the table with my left hand did he withdraw his strong grip.

Obviously displeased with my outburst, he questioned my pain like every other doctor. While he agreed I had some of the more common symptoms associated with RSD, Dr. Gloom felt it would be a premature diagnosis. In order to observe my progression he requested more physical and occupational therapy. To help ease the pain, he decided to conduct a series of nerve blocks.

I was living a nightmare. All I wanted to know was why my right arm felt as if it were on fire. At least if it was RSD, I knew I would eventually get better. Sadly, no one in the medical community was willing to hear me or validate my pain. *My life was spinning out of control and I did not know how to regain order.*

I knew I had to stay strong and positive because the nerve block had been a success for me in the past. It was a simple procedure by medical standards. An anesthesiologist injected an anesthetic into the ganglion nerve to block the firing of pain fibers. These blocks were quite common in the pain world so I really had no reason to worry…but I did. It did not matter that I had undergone a similar procedure once before. Thinking about a foot-long syringe inserted in my neck still petrified me.

∞

I thought my heart was about to beat out of my chest when I put on the hospital gown. *Why did they make such sheer gowns when the rooms were so cold?* Seeing two men in stiff white coats appear at the door sent chills up and down my spine. As they begun using unfamiliar phrases to explain the procedure, I became more paranoid and confused.

They would need to press on my neck in order to locate the stellate ganglion nerve. After marking the spot with a permanent pen, they would inject an anesthetic along the surface of my skin to numb and dull the area. Then they would administer the block, a mixture of lidocaine and bupivacaine, known to ease nerve pain and temporarily slow the firing of the nerve fibers. While I might feel a slight burning sensation, find it difficult to swallow or feel deep pressure, these were normal responses and I should not worry.

I continued to sweat as the IV attached to my left arm released a muscle relaxant. There were so many questions I wanted to ask but did not know where to start, so I just stared at the bright fluorescent lights on the ceiling. My mind raced as the anesthesiologists opened all the sterile packages. *Why had I agreed to this?* To think the slightest twitch could lead to catastrophe made me hold my breath and refrain from moving. A rush of heat flowed through my veins and I felt my body become heavier. This had to end my pain; this had to be the answer.

As one of the doctors cupped the back of my neck while using his other hand to locate the ganglion nerve, I looked at my parents. They stoically stood in the back corner of the room with permanent half-smiles etched on their faces. It was obvious they were trying to be strong for me, which made me feel guiltier. *I was the cause of their grief.* I returned my attention to the doctor who nodded to his colleague for the needle. *This was it…*

I felt as if rose thorns had just pricked me, and then the most unexpected thing happened. My once tight, swollen fingers loosened to resemble a baseball mitt. Color returned to my face when I looked at Mom and Dad's true smiles. I believed my nightmare would soon be over. The block had worked…*or had it?*

The doctors stared at each other in disbelief, but neither spoke. It seemed as if they were both downright puzzled by my unusual response. The second doctor grabbed the large needle resting on the metal tray and injected it into the nerve. I instantly felt a deep-rooted zing travel up and down my spine.

Just as I was about to celebrate the procedure's success, I learned of the doctors shared concerns. While glad to see partial mobility return to the hand, they had reservations about the diagnosis in question. Since my hand relaxed *before* I received the block, they thought I had clenched-fist syndrome.

It was possible some sort of stress caused my problem. Whether it be an undisclosed issue, an unmanageable problem, post-traumatic stress disorder or even not dealing with the past, they no longer felt my symptoms were RSD. That had merely been a theoretical diagnosis. With this being my senior year of high school, they believed I might not be ready for the future.

I was in shock. *Were they saying I was doing this to myself? How could a person who did not know me believe he had the right to judge and belittle me because he had read my medical chart?*

"Isn't it correct that the actual incident occurred on August 28th?"

I glaringly nod.

"And isn't it also correct that a year ago, on that same day, your mom was diagnosed with stage-four breast cancer?"

I felt an explosion take place inside my body. Parts of me broke into tiny pieces and scattered into space. It was too late to try to piece together my self-worth, respect and character for the atomic bomb had already hit. Mustering up the courage to respond, I hastily explained that was correct, but my mom was cancer-free now. *Were the doctors' implying my pain had to do with my mother's disease or me going to college?*

Tears formed in my eyes as my voice begun to shake. Unable to look directly at anyone, I stared at my hand while biting down on the inside of my cheeks. I wanted to escape that room, that conversation, that life. *No one believed my pain.* I wondered whom my parents believed: this Dr. Know-it-All or their daughter.

Dr. Know-it-All did not want to upset me. It was just his job to explore all avenues to find out what was happening. As stress played a considerable role in the efficiency of the sympathetic nervous system, it was a legitimate answer to those unexplainable symptoms. With insufficient evidence pointing to RSD, he wanted a psychologist to determine the emotional and mental triggers behind the pain and immobility.

My follow-up with the orthopedic surgeon was only four days after the procedure. By then the pain had already escalated and the limited function I had obtained from the block was gone. I felt trapped in a never-ending black hole, which I did not know how to escape. It did not matter how loud I screamed because no one could hear my cries.

I panicked as soon as I entered the consult room. This would be the appointment when I would hear Dr. Gloom's interpretation of Dr. Know-it-All's report. My skin turned clammy, and I became nauseated. I feared the worst as I firmly pressed my arms into my abdomen. I was not ready to hear another person blame me for my own suffering. *Maybe Dr Gloom would not agree with their findings…*

When Dr. Gloom opened the door, he was smugly reading over the report while fumbling for a pen in his coat pocket. He jotted down notes without ever acknowledging my parents or me. I never knew if it was intentional, but it sure annoyed me. Everything he did seemed slow and drawn out. It worried me that my future rested in his hands. If he confirmed Dr. Know-it-All's findings, I would see a local child psychologist.

"Just like I originally suspected, this does not seem to be RSD. I agree with Dr. Know-it-All and feel a child psychologist might be able to shed light on what is happening."

I was upset. Everyone believed I was embellishing my symptoms and causing this disability. *Why would I make this up? Why would I do this to myself?* While I tried to explain that I was not crazy, it was useless. He had made up his mind, and I could not convince him that the pain and loss of mobility were real.

"Try not to be hysterical. Give counseling an honest attempt and continue with occupational therapy. While I would like it if you could stick to Tylenol, if the pain becomes too severe, take your prescribed medication. The nurse will hand you the psychologist's number on the way out, and I will meet with you in three weeks to re-evaluate the problem."

Then he was gone.

Two days later was my first appointment with The Shrink. My consultation was set for 5:00pm so Dad would be able to drive me. I did not want to go. Since I refused to let another person sum me up in one sitting and judge me, I decided to throw a five year old's tantrum when Dad knocked on my bedroom door.

"I hate to break it to you kiddo, but you don't have a choice. You are going. He is fitting you into his schedule and we are not canceling. The faster you get going, the quicker you will be able to leave."

We did not speak the entire five-minute ride as I stared outside the passenger window huffing and puffing. I hated the dumb doctors who thought I was insane, and I was angry my family had not stuck up for me. While it frustrated me that God dealt me such a lousy hand, I was equally upset at myself for not portraying clear-cut symptoms that would lead to any diagnosis. I was pissed at the world, and no one understood.

I started to yell when Dad pulled up to the building. I felt betrayed by my parents. *How could they force me to do this?* Feeling as if I had no one on my side, I debated whether to enter the gray Victorian building. Yet I knew I had no choice. Whether it be today or tomorrow, I would have to attend this meeting.

I remember taking a seat on the dull, drab, uncomfortable couch in the waiting room and looking around. The mismatched, non-feng shui room with neutral browns and dreary gray color tone made me uneasy and agitated. Why was I here again?

When The Shrink finally came to greet me, he shook my hand and introduced himself. I estimated his age to be early-forties after taking a quick note of his appearance and demeanor.

Although he looked relatively healthy with an average build, I thought he was overly confident and a bit self-righteous by the way he arrogantly puffed out his chest. My first impression was that I was going to hate him.

As we entered his personal office, I noticed The Shrink's grand built-in bookcase. It covered the length of one wall and overflowed with textbooks, journals, abstracts and reports. In front of the wall of words were his mahogany desk and personal chair. Residing on the other side of the desk were two chairs. A couch rested against the wall parallel to the bookcase where he motioned me to sit. As I sat down in complete silence, I fixed my attention on his massive bookcase. *Had he really read all those manuscripts?*

The Shrink began by talking in a trained and much-too practiced voice about how "my problem" was similar to that of a kindergartener manifesting stomach cramps so he could stay home from school. While I had not wanted to give off the impression of being overly emotional or easily agitated, I lost my composure when I heard this comparison. *Was he serious?* Did he really think comparing me to a five year old would make me feel better or want to be here?

I immediately lashed out without thinking. Feeling as though the entire medical community thought I was mentally unstable aggravated me. Instead of looking for alternatives to end my pain and misery, I had to discuss my feelings with a psychologist. The Shrink was just like every other doctor I had encountered; he too questioned my inability to move my right hand and downplayed my pain because of my age.

The room got quiet. Even if The Shrink believed me, it was his job to explore all the avenues of psychology. Because that included numerous psychological tests and hypnosis, he did not want to waste anymore of my valuable time. The faster I could help him, the quicker he could uncover the root of the issue.

"So, Nicole, will you work with me?" I stared through him. There was nothing left to say. While his structured, rehearsed speech led me to distrust him even more, I knew I did not have a choice. I had become powerless, a victim in the healthcare system. Realizing I would have to do whatever he said, I muttered under my breath, "I guess."

The Shrink perked up seeming quite proud of himself and his winning efforts. He then explained the next step would require me undergoing psychological tests. These multiple-choice tests involved answering hundreds of pointless questions like "Do I feel depressed always, sometimes, never or I do not know?" While I saw this as a complete waste of time, he reassured me this was typical protocol in order to determine my mental stability.

However, that did not end the probing. Even after the tests were analyzed and deemed normal, doubts surrounding my pain and my hand's immobility still existed. Now The Shrink wanted me to undergo hypnosis. I was furious. It was apparent he did not believe me either.

I went to that following appointment kicking and screaming. It was not fair that I had to do this. The Shrink was treating me like a five-year old even though I was almost a legal adult. I wanted to punch him or shake him to make him understand I was telling the truth. I was in the worst pain of my life and scared that I could not move my hand. I needed real help and spending critical time talking about my feelings did not give me pain relief. Yet he did not get that…he was too focused on proving I was crazy than helping me get better.

As I found myself again sitting on his stupid couch waiting for the hypnosis session to end, a problem arose. It turned out he was unable to hypnotize me. He kept trying for forty minutes but nothing changed: he could not hypnotize me. With no other tests available to determine my emotional state, The Shrink had to report our sessions as inconclusive.

Dr. Gloom seemed exasperated when I went back to him without any answers or clues to the cause of my symptoms. He did not know what to do considering I had not fit into his pre-established diagnosis. Not having many other options, he haggardly suggested another type of nerve block called the bier block.

Instead of worrying about the upcoming procedure, I found myself relaxed the afternoon of the block. Not even the bright lights or unusual hospital smells bothered me. It was as if watching a nurse organize various tools and needles on a medical stand beside me was a typical part of any day. In fact, I felt ready until Dr. Know-it-All entered the room.

Learning Dr. Know-it-All would preside over the procedure instantly made my temperature and blood pressure rise. I began to shake as he came close to me. My legs swung up-and-down while beads of sweat formed near my temples. *He was the last person I wanted to see.*

I watched the size of my forearm shrivel like a prune while blood and fluid drained from the limb when he securely wrapped the tourniquet around my arm. Tears streamed down my hot face as I observed my lifeless right arm change from opaque to beet red.

The pain was excruciating and intolerable. My parents tried their best to distract me, repeatedly telling me to breathe and this would be over soon. I kept looking at Dr. Know-it-All who never took his eyes of the big, round clock on the wall. I was in pure agony. *How could he stand by and do this to me?*

He finally released the tourniquet after five minutes and an agonizing rush of blood returned to my tiny, disfigured limb. My poor, pathetic hand looked as if I had been in negative-thirty degree weather without gloves. Yet it felt like I was resting it in a hot, crackling fire. My life had become a nightmare I could not escape.

I broke down the following afternoon in my appointment with Dr. Gloom. I was unable to handle the uncertainties of my life any longer. I could not deal with the lightning bolt electrical shocks that besieged my very existence or the paralyzing pain that held me captive. I was frustrated and completely alone. While I wished Dr. Gloom were a physician who sympathized with patients, he was not. Therefore, I did not receive any assurances or condolences.

Instead, he scheduled another stellate ganglion nerve block and ordered me to move my fingers. He told me movement was now a necessity. If I did not start stretching the hand, the atrophy and built-up scar tissue forming around the joints would worsen. Then I would lose mobility forever.

I was aggravated with him and tried to explain I was not doing this on purpose. It was not my fault that my brain could not send the proper signals to my right hand. Dr. Gloom was unconcerned with my feelings and harshly said, "If you don't do it, then your parents will have to do it for you."

Shifting his attention to my parents, Dr Gloom continued. "After speaking in depth to Dr Know-it-All, we know the fingers can relax and move. You need to stretch her right hand three times a day. Is that understood?" Dad was the first to speak. He said 'yes' in such an authoritative tone that I became nervous. *What was going on here?*

To make sure we all understood what was at stake, Dr. Gloom approached the table and asked for my hand. When I refused to give it to him, he grabbed for my fist and begun to pry it open. He did not even flinch as I screamed and clawed at his arms with my left hand. Rather, he just yelled for his nurse and my parents to restrain me to the table.

Anchored down, I continued to bawl and fight back but the four of them were too strong for me. They were torturing me. *How could anyone be so cruel to another human being? How could **my parents** stand back and allow this happen?*

Three more excruciating minutes of hell passed before he released his grip, and I experienced the most intense burning sensation—like the inside of my hand had touched the core of the sun. With knees that trembled and arms that quivered, I stared at my hand as it molded back to its fisted position. I hated him and despised my parents for taking his side.

I stormed out of the office, and screamed the entire car ride home. There was no way I was going to let anybody near my arm. Finally, Dad had had enough. He put a stern stop to my tirade by saying there would be no room for discussion. They were not going to let my problem progress any further; they would follow Dr. Gloom's orders.

I woke the following morning excited not to have school or doctor's appointments. Since I did not want to be around Mom or Dad, I made plans with Meredith. The past eighteen hours had been overwhelmingly hard on me. I did not know whom to trust. With my hand more inflamed and the pain unbearable, I felt abandoned. *I just needed to escape the drama that had become my life.* However, I had no idea World War III would erupt in our living room with the news of me leaving.

As I closed my bedroom door, I hollered for my parents. The house was silent. I walked down the hall toward the kitchen and looked out the kitchen window. Mom and Dad were in the driveway carrying groceries from the farmer's market. Knowing Meredith would be there in less than five minutes meant I had little time for chitchat. I waited until both of them placed bags of produce on the kitchen countertops before blurting out that I was leaving.

Their bodies instantly stiffened. Neither of them moved as they glanced back and forth at each other. Then Dad spoke. "You are not going anywhere until we stretch that hand."

Frightened by his demeanor, I backed out of the kitchen to get away. I thought everything would be fine once I saw Meredith. I even breathed a sigh of relief as I grabbed my bag from the floor and walked to the front door. Yet Dad would not give in. I was not leaving until he had stretched my hand.

I was shocked and in no mood to handle the situation. The feelings of betrayal caused me to retaliate. My intention was to hurt my parents as they had hurt me. Just thinking how my parents firmly held me down on that table made me sick and enraged. *They were my parents: how could they do that to their daughter?* As I continued to shout spiteful remarks, I knew I had no choice but to leave. I needed space to heal the deep emotional wounds.

I spent the next three nights in the guest room at Meredith's house. Instead of discussing what happened with my family, we rented movies from the 1980's, ate pints of ice cream and gossiped over the boys we liked. Being with her was a nice break from my life. I did not need to talk about my pain or crippled hand. Yet even as I pretended to be a normal teenager, the white elephant never left the room: I could run away from my parents, but I could not run away from the pain.

While my time away was supposed to heal my emotional scars, it only intensified them. I felt all the more helpless as I constantly worried who believed me. Although I knew my parents were only trying to help and were acting out of love, I had lost faith in my support system. My pain was real, and it was ruining my life—why would people think I would do this to myself?

I realized at a certain point I had to return home. It was as if I knew the longer I sulked, the longer I would be in pain. This disagreement had gone on long enough—it was time to pack up my tiny duffle bag and go home. Yet I returned to a very different household. Not only did we never mention my running away, but my parents also never tried to stretch my hand again. Instead, we all continued with our daily lives as if it never happened…

I saw Dr. Gloom following my next nerve block. Within thirty-six hours, the pain came back with vengeance and did nothing to help my immobile hand. Dr. Gloom did not want to move forward with my case. He tentatively concluded RSD while referring me to Children's Hospital for more tests and a proper diagnosis. Due to Children's acclaimed work with obscure cases, he felt they would be better able to assist me. It was time for other specialists to get involved.

Chapter 3

Tedious Testing

I was relieved to walk out of Dr. Gloom's office for the last time. Even though I knew I would never have to see him again, it bothered me that he disbelieved my pain and had put me through such hell. *Had I given off the impression of exaggerating my symptoms? Did I look like an unhappy person who needed attention?*

Now that my health would be in the hands of Children's Hospital, I was positive I would heal. Children's was one of the most recognized medical institutions in the country. I believed these doctors would work endlessly to treat my pain and disability. I was confident this place would hold my cure…little did I know that I would quickly find myself navigating through the open seas without a map.

Trying to contact the hospital's renowned pain specialist proved to be an extensive project. It seemed overnight Dad had to become my leading advocate standing up for my health. He had to research the staff to find whom we needed to meet and then he had to continuously call and leave messages. He learned by trial-and-error how to maneuver through the medical system; and after two months of playing cat-and-mouse with voice-mails, secretaries and operators, I finally had an appointment.

Having to wait so long to see a doctor made me anxious. There was so much riding on the outcome of this initial meeting that I became devastated learning the pain specialist I was supposed to see had become unavailable. While some other doctor would review my case, it would not be the same. This doctor was in his fellowship. That meant he had completed his residency but was still studying his specialty. I obviously was unhappy. *How could this even happen? Was he qualified to treat me?*

After almost five months of bi-weekly doctors' appointments, I had become a pro at initial consultations. Realizing these were thorough, agonizing and long visits, I knew exactly what questions would be asked and how to respond. Since I came prepared for the painful arm strokes and hand squeezes, it startled me when The Fellow did not do any of that. Instead, he hurried through the exam almost uninterested. He took minimal notes and rarely engaged in conversation. It was as if my health did not matter to him. I was just some case subject.

Although RSD was his first inclination to my problem, The Fellow did not feel comfortable diagnosing me without performing a nerve conduction test and an intramuscular EMG. While these tests would be uncomfortable, the results would be extremely beneficial to the doctors designing my treatment program. The decision was easy for me. Seeing that this could unlock the secret to my pain and fisted hand meant I had to do it. Temporary discomfort was worth long-term healing, so on the next available opening, Mom and I returned for what would be a horrific experience.

∞

The nerve conduction test used electrical current to show if the conduction of my nerve impulses worked adequately. By placing electrode patches on the surface of my skin, this test entailed electrically stimulating my nerves. As one section of the nerve was stimulated, another electrode placed further along the same nerve pathway, would detect the electrical impulse.

The EMG was slightly different. It determined whether abnormal muscle activity stemmed from a nerve disorder or weakness brought on from reduced use or atrophy. This was the more painful test because of the repeated insertion of a needle into my muscle.

Not even The Fellow's warning prepared me for the agonizing and electrifying misery that was to come. For the next horrific hour, I endured constant stabs, pokes and prods. I squirmed and fidgeted on the table while sweating through my hospital gown. Feeling as though the room were about to cave in on me only made the pounding in my chest more erratic. Although I kept reminding myself that I was here for a reason, I grimaced and wailed each time the electricity passed through my distressed nerves.

Once the torture was finally over, Mom came into the room. The Fellow then explained how we needed to schedule another appointment to receive the results. My temperature rose as my face turned redder and redder. I wanted to hit somebody. Was he kidding? This was not fair—*had I not waited long enough?*

Before either of us could even respond, The Fellow strolled out of the room handing my chart to a nurse who had to reveal the worst part: the pain specialist I had yet to meet was out of town. As soon as he returned, someone would call to schedule a follow-up.

Three weeks of unreturned phone calls and no word from the hospital upset me. By now, the pain had begun to override my life. I no longer slept at night due to the burning in my right arm. Moreover, whenever I did fall asleep, it seemed as if my alarm clock would ring fifteen minutes later. Large crowds frightened me because the tiniest bump exacerbated my hypersensitivity. School attendance became impossible from the pain and lack of sleep taking its toll on my body. If I could make it through one class period a day, I was doing well.

My life had completely changed. While I was no longer part of the story, life somehow continued without me. I had turned into an outsider unable to join in the fun.

After a month of waiting on Children's, Dad lost his patience. Unable to sit back and continue to watch his daughter suffer, he called the hospital and demanded to speak with the chief of staff. It was unacceptable to him that we never received a return call to schedule a follow-up or been notified of our initial cancelled appointment. Three months had passed since Dr. Gloom referred us to this institution, and we were still waiting to meet this mysterious pain specialist. This was deplorable, and the chief of staff owed us an explanation.

The chief of staff arranged an appointment for me on the following day…

While I was happy to be getting answers, this whole experience bothered me. *How many people end up drowning in the great abyss that is the medical field?* If my dad had not persisted or demanded adequate care, how much longer would I have had to wait to receive the help I needed and deserved? This experience taught me one of the hardest yet most significant lessons: as a patient, I could not sit back and observe. If I wanted to get better, I would need to take initiative.

As we met at one of the hospital's private clinics nearby, I sat between my parents on an uncomfortable couch in a cold and sterile room. I was silent. I could feel the tension surround me as four sets of squinting, beaded eyes stared at me from every direction. I shifted my weight from my right side to my left—this was going to be an interesting visit.

Not a group to drag out the suspense, the designated spokesperson for the hospital was cutthroat and frank. "Unfortunately, we cannot offer you any further assistance. We can refer you to places that might be able to help you."

With the results of the nerve conduction test and EMG faring in the normal range but bordering abnormal, the findings were inconclusive. Because there were no concrete conclusions and I was eighteen years old, the team felt it was in my best interest to go elsewhere. They had two suggestions: UCLA Medical Center or Stanford Hospital.

UCLA was located six hours from our home while Stanford was just an hour away.
We chose Stanford.

Harbor Half: The First Three Miles

As I return my attention to the race and feel sea-salt air whip through my hair, the fear of the unknown that used to be only associated with my illness creeps up inside me. I start to lose focus watching the large crowd stampede in front of me. I search for a fluid movement of graceful arm swings, wave-like breathing patterns and light, soft steps. Yet jogging alongside the other runners makes it difficult for me to manage my pace. *Am I going too slowly?*

Having relied heavily on a support team during my entire medical journey, I find myself still needing outside assurance. Luckily, Rick is beside me for support and encouragement. Being my personal cheerleader, he is quick to say, "You are doing fine. All you need to do is block out the noises, the people and the distractions. Many will start strong and peter out. Remember, we are only in the first mile so your only concern should be on your breathing and stride. You are not going to finish last, but you must begin to concentrate on your own progression."

As I listen to his calming words, I realize this journey is about **me** *finding myself.* I must begin to own my inner-strength and acknowledge that I can conquer any dream. My future is in my hands.

With the first mile-marker only steps away, I glance at my stopwatch to check my speed: eleven minutes, forty-two seconds. I am proud of myself. I turn to Rick for praise, but he is already looking at the uphill climb to the top of the Harbor Bridge. I gulp back saliva and look at the steep grade staring me down. There is no time to celebrate baby steps...

"You have got this, babe. Don't stress or worry because you love running uphill. This is nothing compared to what you have been through." I half-smile at him as I wipe sunblock and sweat from my forehead. Then I take a sip of the cold Smart Water in my light blue CamelBak. *He is right:* in comparison to what I have endured, this climb is nothing.

During the past nine years, I had made impressive strides, experienced far worse and beaten more staggering odds than trekking up a measly hill. Just like I refused to be pushed aside and blatantly ignored all those years ago, I refused to let this incline bring me to my knees. *I am a fighter and I will make it to the top.*

Making my way up the rise energizes me. I feel like a true athlete, a strong and capable survivor—a warrior. Seeing that I am the only one who can squash my dreams gives me a much-needed burst of adrenaline to pass three middle-aged women who are now walking up the hill. I easily could have given up during the days of darkness and solitude, but somehow I knew my light was still out there shining bright. All I needed was to reach it: *and now I have.*

Taking larger, powerful strides allows me to reach the summit in about four minutes. I smile wildly at the cameraman before staring exuberantly over the darkened gulf. Even with my moments of struggle, I kept going and made it to the top!

I giddily descend downhill ever so grateful for the blessings in my life as Rick begins to instruct me to relax my leg muscles. This is my chance to conserve energy and allow gravity to do the bulk of the work. I must remember I still have eleven more miles to go, and I will have to face this hill one more time on my way to the finish line.

Soon we exit the causeway and travel along a plain, semi-desolate access road with two gas stations at differing corners. As this is the least scenic portion of the course, I am alone with my thoughts. Thinking about how nothing in my life had panned out quite how I expected causes my heart to race. After so many years of dreaming of being healthy and alive, now that I am there, I feel lost and unsure. *Could I really overcome the darkness and reach happiness? Had I let go of my past?*

I approach mile-marker three mostly discouraged. While I know I should be happy, seeing so many runners ahead of me makes the fear of finishing last more crippling and real. My muscles tense as my past feelings of rejection, unworthiness and shame boil to the surface. I do not want to let anybody down.

When I began training, my goal was just to complete the race—to be able to finish the thirteen miles. Now that did not seem good enough. *Now* I wanted a finishing that would bring me pride as well as satisfaction. I raised the stakes, and inadvertently unleashed my insecurities of not being sufficient.

Sensing my worry, Rick quickly pipes in, "You are doing fine; do you feel ok?" I quickly take a mental scan of my joints, muscles and bones. "I feel fine. I just don't want to be last. I want others to be proud of me, but I fear I am going to let them down. I am so tired of feeling not good enough…"

"Stop those negative thoughts now. Relax and just run. Training was the difficult part: this is supposed to be fun. Don't let stupid feelings and self-deprecating thoughts bring you down. You know what to do so find your zone and coast."

Chapter 4

LPCH

I remember looking at my alarm clock when I heard my parents stirring in their room. In less than fifteen minutes, Dad would be waking up my brother, Dan and me. Yet today Dan was the lucky one: he would go off to school while I would head to Lucile Packard Children's Hospital at Stanford to undergo the implantation of a stellate-ganglion catheter. This was the first time I feared the outcome. I was scared if a complication arose from the procedure, I might never walk again. *Then what would I do?*

My parents and I were all silent the entire seventy-minute drive from our house to Stanford. The only audible sound in the car was coming from Don Imus on the radio. As I looked into the passing cars, I wondered what everyone else would be doing on this particularly beautiful Spring day. I figured they were not about to be confined like me within the four walls of a hospital

My heart beat faster as Dad pulled up to the front entrance of the hospital. *Was I ready for this life-changing moment?* While this was where I was supposed to step out of the car and confidently saunter in to my new home, I had trouble standing. Mom helped me, and together we walked inside. I was a trembling, nervous wreck. *This was not how I envisioned spending the last six weeks of my senior year of high school.*

Lucile Packard Children's Hospital had nice carpets, pleasing paint choices and amazing artwork. If it were not for the small feeble children walking down the halls with masks and IVs, I could have easily mistaken the inside of this beautiful building for an art museum. As we made a quick right to enter the admittance room, padded bold-colored chairs lined two walls. In another corner of the room stood a child-sized table filled with coloring books, Lego toys and picture books.

Life seemed so surreal. I squeezed my pillow and stuffed dog. My stuffed dog had been with me through everything. I had received him when I was hospitalized at three years old for an "unidentified virus." Despite him now being old and grey—and me being eighteen—I still loved him. He somehow calmed me down.

Dad walked in the room and sat on the other side of Mom. I could sense his anxiety and hopelessness. For the past few months, his spirit had diminished to virtually nothing. He had become a shell: continuing to move, act and talk through the autopilot that lives in us all. Mom was the same way. Although she smiled, it was never a true grin, but the scared smirk that always appeared on her face when she was afraid. *What had I done to my family?*

My heart sank into my stomach until I heard my name called. *This was it.* A technician led me to a cubicle in an adjoining room to begin the long and draining admittance process. I told her my name, age, weight, address, insurance information and the reason for the stay. As she left her tiny workspace to gather papers from the printer, I glanced outside to see the sun peer its head over the horizon. The weatherman was correct: it would be a perfectly sunny day.

She returned to her claustrophobic office and handed me my ID bracelet. I was now *Nicole Hemmenway: 3-South inpatient at Lucile Packard Children's Hospital.* With the admittance process finished, my parents and I made our way to the OR to meet the doctor. Dr. Brown was the head anesthesiologist at LCPH whom I met two weeks prior at my initial consultation. He seemed to understand the basic philosophy behind chronic pain, which made me like him.

He did not expect the procedure to last longer than forty minutes. By implanting a small catheter in the stellate ganglion region of my neck, I would not need a typical IV line. This would make the administration of medications much easier on my body. Although the tubes connected to the catheter would need changing every three days to prevent an infection, I would be on a continuous drip of three drugs known to calm and relax muscles while assisting in pain control.

Dr. Brown's thorough explanation impressed me, and I felt I was in the best of hands. He then asked if I had any questions. I blanked. Frozen and tense like a deer caught in the headlights, I was unable to speak. Of course, I had questions; but the question was whether I really wanted answers. I decided to stay quiet. I knew I was ready, and I did not need to work myself up.

Being prepped for surgery was an experience. I had always assumed an OR would be quiet and serene. Therefore, it shocked me to see such combustion and energy behind those sterile doors. People frantically swarmed the room as nurses and techs talked amongst each other to make sure all the necessary supplies were present. It was as if I was at the circus where clowns juggled as acrobats walked the tightrope all at the same time. It was utter mayhem, and I was the focal point.

I remember it began to feel like an out-of-body experience when I discovered I would have to be awake throughout the mini-procedure. It was crucial I be able to communicate with the doctors in order for the catheter's correct placement. This terrified me. Even with a mild sedative and pain relievers administered through a temporary IV line, I did not know how I would handle watching Dr. Brown stick a five-inch needle into my neck. *What would they do if I still felt the pain?*

By the time one of the female nurses tried to start an IV in my left arm I was nauseated and sweating profusely. Try after try, I felt needle after needle puncture my skin without any results. She could not find my vein, and my pain was increasing.

Thankfully, Dr. Brown returned to the room and took over. He tapped the skin around my elbow in order to locate the perfect vein before inserting the needle. The hard part was finished, and the drugs begun to disperse into my blood stream. Now I needed to relax and trust those performing the procedure.

It took mere minutes before the room appeared fuzzy and my sight blurred. Soon I could only make out large objects. *The medicine was working.*

Due to Stanford being a teaching hospital, medical students were encouraged to take part in procedures. While I understood this was hospital protocol, I never thought this would pertain to my case. Therefore, I naturally became uneasy when a cluster of students in pale scrubs surrounded my bedside. As they attentively listened to Dr. Brown's detailed explanation on the proper technique for implanting a stellate ganglion catheter, I begun to panic. My head spun and my skin turned clammy. I fearfully looked around the room and became restless. *Could one of these students accidentally hurt me?*

My monitors signaled. As nurses rushed toward me, Dr. Brown told me to breathe deeply. My heart rate had jumped significantly high, and he needed me to calm down. Yet I was too scared to relax. Lying helplessly on the operating room table, my life flashed before me. I was not ready to let unfamiliar people control my fate. Sweating through my hospital gown, I stared in sheer terror at the bright surgical lights above my head. *I had not signed up for this.*

Dr. Brown ordered the nurses to administer a second dose of muscle relaxants to normalize my breathing and heart rate. The sense of urgency in his voice petrified me and seemed to bother his students who begun to glance nervously amongst each other. When I felt the cold liquid enter my veins, my eyelids immediately drooped. Even though I could still hear the beeping of machines, the scrambling of people and pressure on my windpipes, I was peaceful. No longer worried about a procedural error, the chaotic noises that echoed through the room begun to fade and my world went black.

I woke to Dr. Brown's deep voice. "Nicole, we are getting your parents. You did wonderful."

I was relieved. With the minor surgery behind me, I could now focus on the big picture: getting better. After investing all my hopes and dreams into the Pain Team's course of treatment, I believed this was where I would heal.

∞

I was still unconscious when I reached my new room on 3-South. It was a private room with a window seat and views of the hospital's inner courtyard. Considering the beauty of the rest of the facility, the bareness of the room surprised me. I had a bed, closet and hospital table. There was no phone or television because these were prohibited on 3-South. Placed on the rehabilitation ward, patients like me were supposed to concentrate on recovering and not outside distractions.

As the anesthetics wore off, the pain intensified, and I felt the discomfort of the foreign object lodged near my throat. The heaviness of the tubes pulled on the bandages making my skin itch and sag. Swallowing was difficult due to the quarter-sized catheter protruding slightly out of my neck. All I wanted was to rest the remainder of the day.

Soon the rheumatologist for the Pain Team barged into my hospital room. Dr. Drill was direct and forthright. She took her work seriously and demanded respect. While being extremely knowledgeable in her field, her lack of warmth and charisma unnerved me. Since her bold personality frightened me, I hardly breathed when she checked my vitals and looked at the affected site. Not until she was certain an infection would not form near the catheter site did she smile and tell my parents and me she would be back tomorrow. Then she was gone. She reminded me of Superman—swooping in to help and leaving as soon as she finished. This was just her job, and there was no time to chat and visit.

I looked at Mom and Dad and half-heartedly grinned. *This would be a long day for us all.* As an exhausted-looking nurse hurried into my room to administer my oral medications, the physical therapist arrived to meet me. I briefly remembered meeting Sharon at the previous meeting. She was in her late-thirties with an earthy, eco-friendly style. Sharon was calm and gentle.

Sharon believed my pain was severe, and her only objective was to help me heal. She did not pretend to know more than she did. In fact, she said we were teaching each other. After growing accustomed to doctors acting as if they had all the answers, she was a breath of fresh air. We were a united front with our main goal centered on my health and well-being. I admired her honesty and knew she was a person who would fight for me.

She next explained my typical hospital routine. Each day I would meet with her once in the morning for biofeedback and breath-work and again in the afternoon for body exercises and hand stretches. I also would see an occupational therapist twice a day to work on fine motor skills and learn to perform everyday tasks again like feeding myself and getting dressed. Along with these appointments, I had school and the planned group activities. My assigned psychologist would visit with me one hour a day, and every week my family would partake in family counseling. Lastly, meals were thirty minutes long and eaten in the ward's recreational room.

It was an overload of information. With a pounding head, my still-foggy mind went blank. There was no way I could comprehend all of this, so I just followed Sharon out of the 3-South corridor where we turned right. Twenty-five steps later, we made a left down a long hall and entered the physical and occupational room.

I looked around but saw nothing special or out of the ordinary. It was similar to all the other rehab clinics I had seen. There was a sink, computer, three rectangular tables and an old stationary bike. Blue-padded mats lined the floor next to the mirrored wall, and in the back of the room were shelves filled with games and toys. They had Connect Four, Jenga, puzzles and dolls. While it was a six year olds paradise, I had no idea how any of this stuff would help me. I wanted to ask Sharon many questions but found myself ushered into a smaller room before I had a chance to speak.

This room was cold and bare. With dreary filing cabinets, an examining table and old computer, I easily could have mistaken it as a storage room. As I wondered why I was here, I noticed the small black box hooked to the computer with hanging wires. This was the biofeedback machine.

Sharon told me biofeedback was a helpful tool in reconnecting the mind with the body. By applying electrical sensors over different muscles, this machine could monitor and graph the muscle activity and tension of my right arm and hand. In essence, biofeedback could re-teach my body how to control involuntary and voluntary responses.

I had previously tried biofeedback at another rehabilitation facility and was not impressed. However, it was not as advanced as this machine. Learning I could play games like catching eggs in a basket or racing cars around a track made me a bit more receptive. Moreover, the reason I resisted this treatment in the past was that I was under the impression it would correct the problems *I* created myself.

Yet Sharon's explanation was completely different. She told me I should view biofeedback more as a teaching mechanism: a tool to show me that the disease did not control me. While it might seem as though my muscles and nerves were not working, by combining this technique with breath-work, we could monitor the most miniscule changes taking place inside my body. I had to realize that the power to heal resided within me.

I slowly headed toward the examining table for my first exercise in guided imagery. Fully aware of the catheter protruding out of my neck, I was cautious not to damage the dangling tube. I carefully lay on my back while resting the machine on my left side. Being in such a flat position put more strain on the gauze and I felt the lump in my throat grow. Even with pillows propped under my knees to keep my back aligned, I was miserable.

In a whispered voice, Sharon asked me to focus on my diaphragm breathing. The more I tried to silence my mind, the more thoughts accumulated. I became flustered. I felt as if the pressures of the world rested on my shoulders. *Would the therapy be able to work if I was not in a meditative state?*

I heard Sharon ask me to imagine spraying a color throughout my body. "What color is it?"

Without thinking, I blurted out "fuchsia." Such an automatic response even baffled me. Fuchsia, a vibrant magenta color, came out of left field. I did not even particularly care for that bright hue and yet it was the first color to enter my mind. *Why fuchsia, and what did that mean?*

I felt my abdomen rise and fall in one synchronized manner as I continued to breathe in-and-out. With each breath, I was to see the paint spread further inside my body. Minutes passed and nothing seemed to happen. Thinking I was concentrating too hard, I tried harder to quiet the ongoing noises in my mind. Soon I began to hear the sound of my breath.

With each inhale, I felt as though a wave had reached the shoreline. On the exhale, the water returned to the sea. It was an incredible feeling not to feel alone. With the Universe opening up for me, I could envision the radiant deep pink within my body. It was a warm sensation that pacified my nervousness and apprehensions. I felt alive…until I noticed the dark void in my right shoulder, arm and hand. *What was going on?*

Sharon quickly reassured me I was safe and this was a natural response. She then tried to help me color in the blackness that plagued my right side. Nothing changed. The area stayed dark and disturbed. Frustrated by my inability to succeed, I could not understand what was wrong. *Why could I not do this?*

Yet I had done exactly what Sharon wanted. The purpose of this exercise was to show how my body no longer associated with my right upper limb. Somehow, my brain had temporarily disconnected itself from my right arm. I could not see the fuchsia because my body thought my right arm no longer existed. Therefore, I could not save a limb until my body recognized its actual existence.

An imaginary boulder lifted from my shoulders and freed me from the guilt and shame that seemed to haunt me. Now I had proof that I was not crazy. Nor had I exaggerated my symptoms. This showed that my brain and spinal cord impeded my recovery, and I was not to blame.

Sharon and I made our way back to my hospital room in silence. I now understood the importance of the mind-body-spirit connection in regards to healing. Hope in better, brighter days seemed possible. While I was still very sick, now I knew I would heal. I could once again dream of happiness and normalcy. Sharon had allowed me to believe in miracles. *I was on the road to recovery.*

I was still flabbergasted when we met Mom and Dad in my neutral-toned room. As Sharon explained the biofeedback process to my parents and answered their questions, I felt my face flush. My body temperature continued to rise as the four of us trekked back to the therapy room to meet my occupational therapist.

∞

Beth was personable and bubbly with shoulder-length blonde hair. Her casual conversation style struck a chord in me, and I found myself immediately drawn to her exuding happiness.

Instead of firing off medical questions, she inquired about my favorite movies, music and hobbies. I was shocked. *She actually was interested in getting to know me as a person.* This was the first time in nine months that anyone in a professional capacity had listened to me.

We all sat at one of her rectangular worktables where I learned how every session would begin with stretching to improve my fine motor skills. I would also have to complete a homework assignment each night. The work would mainly consist of writing, coloring or painting. Even though it would be challenging and time consuming, it should be fun. I rolled my eyes and smirked. I was sure an activity such as gluing Popsicle sticks together was fun for a ten year old, but I was eighteen. I was not going to enjoy these tedious tasks.

Beth must have noticed my snide glance because she quickly replied that fun was what we made out of every experience. "I promise we will have a good time. These tasks may seem childish to you, but I am sure they will still make you laugh. Besides, life is too serious. Sometimes we need to revert back to kids and let our inner-child play." She then giggled as she handed me the black-and-white Mead notebook that would become my writing journal.

Beth continued to explain that my homework also included the continual use of my right hand to function. Specific movements would re-strengthen my hand muscles while reconnecting my brain to the right side of my body. Although it made sense that repetitive motions were the best way to reconnect the mind with the body, I was confused. How could I do any of this with zero mobility in my right hand? I was crippled. *Had she forgotten that I could not eat, write or type because my fingers had tightly clenched into a fist?*

I watched her walk to the cupboards above the sink and rummage around. She returned with three different sizes of rubber hose. In the middle of each circular hose was a small hole where she inserted a pen. This made the grip larger so my atrophied hand could hold it. All I had to decide was which grip was the most comfortable.

We started with the medium-sized built-up pen. Prying my fingers out of my palm caused deep burning which slowly subsided once my digits snapped shut around the pen. Beth placed a piece of paper in front of me, and asked me to write my name. I was shaking. I had not held a pen with my right hand in almost a year. My penmanship looked messy as the ink flowed onto the paper. It was illegible. It looked like it had been done by a five year old who just learned how to write.

Looking at my scribbles made me feel defeated. Feeling like a puppy caught chewing on a shoe, I sheepishly lifted my head only to see my parents beaming faces. They were proud of me. To them it was a miracle that I could even hold a pen. I had just overcome what used to be a huge setback. Dad reminded me that I took baby steps before walking.

Baby Steps.

The philosophy of baby steps intrigued me because it was an interesting way to view my current situation. Since I had to retrain my right hand to do everyday tasks, I needed to look at the smallest increments of success as true accomplishments. My recovery was not going to be immediate and that meant celebrating the tiniest of improvements.

I begun to feel slightly better about myself as Beth started to stretch my hand and extend my tightened tendons. Her touch was excruciating. It was as if she had placed my hand in a bucket of dry ice. Continuing to straighten my locked, clenched fingers, I felt fire—deep, piercing fire. Every bone and joint in my right hand and wrist burned. Wanting to escape the pain, I held my breath and counted to ten.

Ten, nine, eight, seven, six, five, four, three, two, one—*When would she be done?*

Perspiration dampened my clothes, and I let out a small moan. *This must be what torture felt like.* As my muscles tensed and constricted, I worried how much longer I could withstand the pain. I wanted to scream out in agony but found myself unable to speak. When she finally released her death grip on my hand, it instantly shriveled back to its fisted position redder and larger than before the manipulation.

Thinking she tore every ligament in my fingers, I kept staring at my clamped hand. I tried shaking my fist to calm the throbbing, but it would not go away. The pain was electrifying, and Beth did not seem to care. Instead, she informed me that my first homework assignment was to eat dinner and breakfast with my new built-up utensils. Then she sent us back to my room to wait for my counselor.

I called the psychologist the Professor because he was an intern three months shy of teaching at a prominent East Coast university. He was quite younger than my other doctors but his fair complexion and pre-mature balding made him appear just as old. I liked him more than I liked The Shrink after my initial consultation. It was there that he assured me our conversations were confidential and his role was to serve as a mediator between the doctors and me. However, I remained reserved and skeptic.

Our first session as psychologist and patient took place in one of the hospital's many outside courtyards. It felt nice to be breathing fresh air and to look up at the blue sky. Although he said he wanted to know more about my life, I sensed an ulterior motive. I felt he did not listen to me as I told him about school and the hardships I faced during my mom's bout with breast cancer. He seemed bored when I explained how struggling with a life-and-death situation changed me as a person. I tried to convey how completely helpless I felt after her diagnosis until I began volunteer work to release my fears and worries. Yet he was not interested in my growth or progress.

Instead, he solely focused on the days my mother was ill. *So how did that make you feel? What were you really thinking when you discovered the severity of your mom's cancer? How are you handling the stress now that she is in remission?*

I felt I had committed a crime and was on trial. He was the prosecutor who would stop at nothing to get a guilty verdict. The world I once knew no longer existed. I glanced at his shiny watch; I still had ten more minutes before I could escape his arrogant, egotistical questioning. I wanted to strangle him. There was no way I could do this every day: this was a joke.

As soon as the session ended, I bolted out of the courtyard irritated. After having to defend my integrity for an hour, I just wanted Mom and Dad to console me. Except they were leaving for the evening…and now I had to act brave and face this nightmare alone.

While I knew they would return tomorrow, I was not ready to say goodbye. I bit my inner lip and gave them each a hug and kiss on the cheek. It was hard not to cry or beg them to stay when they exited my room. Even though I knew I had to stay here in order to get better, I wanted to go home with them. I wanted our family dinners watching Jeopardy where Dad gave an impromptu geography lesson. I wanted Dan to make me laugh and Mom to comfort me. I was tired of always being the one left behind.

As soon as my parents left, the head nurse came to get me for dinner. Being required to eat as a group, I now had to join the rest of the patients on my ward in the meal room. I felt out-of-place taking the last seat at the large rectangular table. Everyone else looked so much smaller than I did. I smiled and acted overly friendly to the petite girl sitting on my right; it was strange how even in a hospital setting I wanted to make a good first impression. When we went around the table introducing ourselves, I discovered shocking news. Not only was I the oldest person by five years, but I was also the only non-anorexic.

I was exhausted when I returned from dinner and decided to go to bed. The day had been a whirlwind of excitement. Despite being physically drained, my mind was running a mile a minute. I could not stop thinking how I had a catheter inserted in my neck that continuously administered drugs to my weakened immune system.

I grieved for my old life and had to remind myself that I would get better. This was just like camp. I had scheduled classes, different group sessions and planned mealtimes…yet instead of healthy bodies running around, there were sick people.

Chapter 5

Hospital Protocol

My first night was rough. I tried my best to block out the sounds and smells of the hospital but it was hard to do. Hearing the beeping of machines, the cries from other rooms and the not-so-soft whispers from the nurses' stations made sleeping a challenge. Then with nurse rotations occurring at two in the morning, I found myself abruptly awoken to a new nurse rummaging in my room to reexamine my stats. I did not know how anybody became accustomed to the constant prodding…

The following morning I woke to a nurse checking my heart rate and blood pressure. After recording my vitals, she handed me a sheet of paper outlining the days' activities. It illustrated where I was supposed to be and what I would be doing throughout the day. This would become my personal itinerary. Then she instructed me on the policies and rules of the wing. I discovered I could not leave the ward unless an adult checked me out at the nurses' station. It did not matter that I was eighteen. If I walked around the hospital, visited the cafeteria or viewed the rooftop gardens, I still needed a suitable adult to accompany me.

While I thought the rules were absurd, I attempted to follow the guidelines set in place. After all, I was in a children's hospital. Taking a deep breath, I put on a clean pair of striped pajamas and made my way to breakfast. I timidly looked around the room—I was the only person not attired in jeans and a cute top. Thinking there had to be a dress code, I begun to apologize for my appearance when a brown-haired girl told me we could wear whatever made us feel comfortable. It did not make sense to me why anyone would dress up. *Did they not know we were in a hospital?*

I ate my oatmeal fully aware of the little, beaded eyes staring in my direction and wincing. Just like an owl carefully watching its prey, the other patients never took one eye off me. Besides the rapid stirring of Ensure, the room was eerily silent. I became frustrated trying to use my built-up spoon. Paranoid by an audience judging my food choices and irritated that my hand shook made me lose my appetite. I did not want to speak to anybody so I kept my head facing down and pushed my bowl aside.

My first group counseling session with my ward directly followed breakfast. I did not want to talk about my so-called problems. The whole premise of coming together to express our fears and personal issues seemed unusual to me. I had never felt comfortable opening up to complete strangers, but now I had no choice.

I strolled through the quiet hospital corridor until our moderator motioned us into an available conference room. Apprehensively looking around the room, I sat down in the first swiveling office-chair. I felt insecure surrounded by such thin bodies. Even though I knew they were all very ill, I felt huge in my pajama bottoms and Dad's over-sized t-shirt. It was obvious I did not fit in…and I did not want to be there.

The ragged woman overseeing this nightmare cleared her throat and reminded us that what we said in this room stayed in this room. Then she asked if anyone wanted to begin. It did not take long before little squeaky voices discussed the most plaguing hospital issue: why was lunchtime five minutes shorter than any other meal? As I could not relate nor understand the significance of this question, I remained silent. I kept one eye on the clock and the other on the person speaking. This served no relevance to my recovery. *Why did I have to be here?*

When it finally ended, we all walked back to 3-South where I met Sharon for physical therapy. From physical therapy, I had a half-hour break before I saw Beth for occupational therapy. Lunch followed and then the girls and I joined Beth for group OT. We mostly prepared foods like chocolate chip cookies that nobody ate except maybe the nurses and me. My most dreaded appointment of the day was next on the agenda.

The Professor had become a broken record whom I now despised. Only interested in my mother's cancer, I found myself either yelling or not speaking. We would be arguing or sitting in complete silence for an hour. Both were excruciatingly painful.

From psychotherapy, I would again rejoin Sharon and Beth for the second time of the day before attending Group Fun. This was a nightly ritual where 3-South patients would meet to play games, participate in crafts or spend time with animals the hospital allowed to visit. I actually enjoyed this time because of the humorous moderator who made sure I laughed. Dinner would promptly follow at six. And somewhere in between all these classes and meetings, my team of doctors would visit to check my progression.

I followed this schedule religiously and tried to respect the program in place. Although I was giving up a lot now, I believed these sacrifices were small if it meant gaining back my life. I had two choices: I would either accept defeat or fight like hell. Wanting to live the life I had always envisioned—going to college, getting married, having a dog, raising a family—left me no option. *I had to fight like hell.* I was unwilling to give up on my dreams for the future. Missing some moments was better than losing all of them. Therefore, I had to press on.

∞

As days turned into weeks, I started missing family and friends. Hospital life was foreign to me. I never realized I would feel so alone and isolated. When it looked like I would not attend my own high school graduation, I became more and more withdrawn. To think I had waited four years for a moment that might not happen crushed me. All I wanted was to be a normal senior.

Three days before my high school graduation I had no idea if I would be at the ceremony. My principal had kindly told my parents she would hold a *smaller* version of the celebration when I was well and invite the entire senior class. I refused. While touched by her sweetness and thoughtfulness, I did not want a sympathy graduation. I wanted to be with my class on our actual graduation day. I had already missed prom and senior cut-day; I could not miss receiving my diploma.

Even though many staff members at the hospital diligently worked to make this dream come true, it did not look good. Concerns over infections and health risks from not being in a sanitary environment arose. Then the health insurance company began to question why I needed to be inpatient if I was physically able to attend such a ceremony. I was facing an uphill battle and believed I was doomed to miss my special day.

Tensions mounted two days before the event. There was still no word from my insurance company. While the hospital caseworker in charge of my situation directly contacted my health insurance every few hours, Dad prepared me for the worse. I remember falling back on the bed and burying my head in my pillow. This was awful. There was no way I could handle all the stress of the hospital, the pain and the thought of not being at the ceremony. *This just was not fair.*

With twenty-four hours before the ceremony, I still was unsure of the outcome. Though I learned there had been some progress, we had yet to receive final word. I could not believe this was really my life. Anxiety took over as each hour passed. I could not eat. Pacing the width of my bedroom, I could not complete my writing assignment for Beth. I was useless.

I was already on the verge of a nervous breakdown when a nurse entered my room and told me to pack my belongings. There was a patient needing twenty-four hour supervision and since my room was directly in front of the nurses' station, I had to switch rooms. Hoping this was some sick joke, I scoffed. Yet she was serious. I really had to move…

"I am not leaving this room. It is mine and I need my peace and quiet."

The nurse just ignored my ranting and said I had twenty minutes to pack. I remember calling Dad in tears and begging for help. He needed to stop them. *There was no way in hell that I was packing my belongings and changing rooms!*

Dad tried to calm me down saying this had always been a possibility and the best thing I could do was cooperate. Then we would figure it out later. I disagreed. I kept on screaming at the nurse. Even refusing to move or get off the bed did not faze her. She quietly put my clothes, cards and toiletries neatly on my rollaway bed. *How could they do this to me?*

Yelling outlandish threats, I suddenly looked up and saw the Professor standing nervously at my door. This might have been the first time he had seen a patient uncensored and out of control. Although he usually disgusted me, I was glad to see him. I thought he would have to help me because that was his job.

I had begun to cry uncontrollably when he asked the nurse to leave and told me hang up the phone. Unable to hold in my pain any longer, I blurted out everything. He listened as I told him I was alone and miserable. I felt like an outsider since no one else on this wing had the same problems as me. I could not live with someone when I had medical homework that required much concentration.

The room stilled as I waited for him to speak. I needed him to understand my health was on the line. There was no way I could cope with this move. While I held my breath hoping he would make things better, I knew I was in trouble the instant he opened his mouth. He did not care about me: he was the doctor's puppeteer. He was always going to be on their side.

Although he felt sorry for me, he could not change the situation. I would have to switch rooms. I went ballistic. He had lied to me, and I knew I would never trust him again. I begun throwing the posters and cards already placed on my hospital bed onto the ground. With the Professor unable to console me, the staff called Dr. Brown.

It bothered me that Dr. Brown only came as a last resort to pacify my nerves. I did not need reassurance that everything would be fine—what I needed was for people to listen to me. I was screaming for help but no one heard me. No one seemed concerned by my major meltdown. All Dr. Brown did was increase my medications. Drugs would not fix this problem; the only way I would be ok was if I had my own room.

I sobbed as the staff wheeled me down the hall to my new room. My life was spinning out of control, and nobody was coming to my rescue. I felt misled, misunderstood and misjudged. Believing the doctors were putting my health in jeopardy, I wanted to leave and never return. I wanted my old life back where I did not have to worry about being uprooted from my room in the middle of the day.

News about my recent antics spread like wildfire through the hospital. Beth even decided to cancel the remainder of my afternoon therapy sessions. Thinking a break from my usual routine would be for the best, she planned to take me on a hospital excursion. The thought of glimpsing my former life depressed me. Yet just like everything else in the hospital, the decision was out of my control. Beth wanted me to breathe fresh air, so therefore I was going to breathe clean air.

As we walked out of the hospital's double-doors and crossed the street to the Stanford Shopping Center, a solid lump formed in the back of my throat. I was scared to be out in the real world again. Feeling as if I had no one to protect me, I ironically longed for the safety and predictability of the hospital. My heart beat faster with each step I took. Here I was standing exposed in my pajamas with an unusual object jetting out of my neck.

However, my insecurities faded once I felt the warmth of the sun penetrate my skin. I then begun to smell the petunias and admired the vibrant colored daffodils. I watched hundreds of busy people go about their day without a care in the world. I was having fun as we shopped at stores like J. Crew, Banana Republic and Ann Taylor. This distraction allowed me to be a teenager.

It was fitting then that as soon as I begun to really laugh and feel normal, it was time to return to the hospital. Wishing this excursion did not need to end, I became quieter and more distraught the closer we got to 3-South. *I absolutely hated it there.*

Thankfully, Dad had already arrived. Although we were still waiting for a decision regarding tomorrow, he wanted to see how I was handling my new room. My roommate was a selective mute who needed dialysis every other day. As a selective mute, she chose whom she would speak to and the rest of us had to communicate through writing. I was furious. The reason I was stuck in this awful place was that I lost mobility and function in my writing hand. How could the staff not see how this arrangement would be detrimental to my recovery?

Dad promised to straighten the matter out next week during the team meeting. Right now, he needed me to be strong…which was hard for me to do.

Sniffling and hiccupping, I glanced up and saw my caseworker standing outside the door. The room spun and I immediately panicked. The caseworker held the answer to my fate. I tried to decipher whether I would be attending my high school graduation based on his body expressions and mannerisms, but he had a poker player face. It was impossible to read him… until he started to grin.

He had just received word that I could leave the hospital premises on a six-hour pass. I was speechless. This meant everything to me. Overwhelmed with emotions I was unable to express, all I could bring myself to say was thank you. My dream had come true; *I was going to graduate with the rest of my class.*

Chapter 6

New Beginnings

Graduation was a pivotal moment in a young person's life, and I could not wait for Dad to arrive at the hospital. I finally felt at peace. For the first time since I became an inpatient, I was joyful, giddy and content. Now I just wanted to get the day started.

Dad entered my room followed by Dr. Brown. To this day, I can recall our conversation about whether I should disconnect the pump to avoid any programmer malfunctions or tube blockage issues. I thought it would be safer not to have long tubes hanging from my neck, but Dad was hesitant. Once Dr. Brown assured us both that it would not affect my health, he administered twice my usual dose and disconnected the pump. Then we were free to leave.

The drive home was comfortably quiet. Since nothing could accurately describe the emotions we both felt, there was no reason for either of us to ruin a profound moment with words. I exuberantly smiled while staring out the window at the other cars. This was what it felt like to live.

Butterflies formed in my stomach when I saw the trees' branches encasing the road of our street. As we pulled into the driveway, Mom rushed to meet me. She gave me a hug as we hurried to my room to put on the white cap and gown. Yet something felt wrong. It was as if I was a stranger in my own home. *This was not where I was supposed to be right now.*

Thinking how this pivotal life moment almost did not happen made my anxiety soar. I had been waiting four years for this day, and now that we were pulling into my school's parking lot, I did not know how to handle the situation. I wanted to absorb every detail, but I was too overwhelmed. My life had significantly changed since the last time I stepped foot on campus.

I was different. My day-to-day concerns no longer included whether so-and-so said hi to me in the hall. I had grown up.

My classmates and I met in the cafeteria before the ceremony. As I stood next to the head dean, she announced my arrival to the rest of my class. With the room erupting in applause, I became embarrassed and self-conscious. *How did everyone know my story?* For my own safety, she then instructed my class not to touch or hug me. The swarm of people who were seconds ago rushing to say hello instantly took three steps back as if I had the plague. Again, I felt like an outsider.

I began to sweat as the throbbing in my hand worsened. Being the center of attention made me uncomfortable. I tried to control the radiating pain, but I felt as if the room was caving in on me. Soon I started seeing black-and-white dots. I knew I needed fresh air, so Meredith took me outside.

It was just too much too soon. After all, less than two hours ago a nurse had been taking my vital signs and helping me get dressed. Breathing deeply like Sharon had taught me seemed to help. My head stopped spinning and my knees no longer felt as though they would buckle. We returned to the room in time to form the procession lines.

I was in shock when I walked into the school auditorium and heard the music. Looking around the large crowd, I spotted my parents, my grandparents and Dan crying. It was great to see Dan because I missed him so much. I felt guilty that I was the cause of his grief. I realized this moment meant just as much to them as me.

The actual ceremony was a blur. I know I heard some amazing speeches and sang a few songs before it was time to receive our diplomas. Even though the assistant principal asked the entire auditorium not to applaud until all diplomas were distributed, my class cheered for me as I walked on stage. I will never forget that moment. Not only did it evoke such strong emotions in me, it served as a testament to my amazing classmates. In my mind, I had not done anything extraordinary. This day was special for all of us—we each had accomplished an important milestone. Therefore, showing me such admiration and love was truly an honor.

As the ceremony ended, the Class of 1999 proceeded to the inner-court for our graduation picture. The day had just begun for the rest of my class with parties to attend, lunches to eat, relatives to visit and then Grad Night. Grad Night was a tradition. It was the most anticipated event of our senior year. That evening my entire class would return to school and celebrate the evening locked in the safe auditorium…while I would be back in my hospital bed missing more fun.

Leaving the school was tough. As my friends were still celebrating, my parents and I were already in the car driving back to the hospital. The ride was silent. None of us knew what to say about that deep pang. I had just graduated and should have been walking on air. Instead, I only felt an aching void. My life was not the same as my peers, and my future was unknown. While I hoped to attend Creighton University in the fall, college might not be a reality for me anymore.

Throughout the seventy-five minute drive, I questioned the ways of the world. It still did not make sense how I went from being a young adult on the verge of spreading her wings to a patient in a hospital dependent on machines and medicine. It was only ten months ago that I had my own aspirations for the future, but now that seemed unrealistic. Where did I belong: with the sick or healthy?

My stomach churned pulling up to LPCH. I knew that once I walked through those doors my life as a civilian no longer existed. My heart sank as the three of us apprehensively entered 3-South. As a nurse reconnected the pump and administered twice the usual amount of medicine, my life of freedom was over. I became a prisoner again. *This could not be real. This could not be my life…*

I cried myself to sleep that night. As grateful as I was to have attended my graduation, it also pained me to know I was not the same person anymore. Returning to the cold, sterile environment of a hospital only hours after such a life-changing event devastated me. I wanted to be with my friends. I wanted to share in this exciting time rather than being stuck painting and discussing my feelings with questionable specialists. *What had happened to me?*

I woke the following morning having to attend our usual weekend group activity. This particular day our moderator wanted to play a game of hopscotch. I was not in the mood for such childish games, so I sat down on a chair and watched. This did not go over well with the moderator who, after verbally scolding me, handed me blue chalk and told me to write on the patio ground.

That was the last straw. *Who did she think she was telling an eighteen year old to write on cement with chalk?* I furiously walked out of the room thinking about how I should have been leaving Grad Night. I should have been laughing with my friends. I should have been happy… but I was not. *Who would be happy confined to a damn psych ward?*

While I had planned to return to my room, I found my new roommate connected to a dialysis machine. Needing to be alone and with nowhere else to go, I fled the ward and aimlessly walked up and down halls and stairs. I could not handle my situation any longer. They treated me like a three year old here. Forcing me to participate in some stupid game of hopscotch was not going to help my hand or stop my pain. These rules were ridiculous.

Minutes later, I heard my name called on the hospital's PA system. I knew I was in for a lecture as soon as I saw the group moderator standing with the nurses from 3-South. Naturally, she was livid and spent five minutes hissing at me for breaking hospital rules. She even threatened to record this incident in my permanent chart while promising to bring this discussion up at next week's Team Meeting.

I lost my composure quickly. Unable to hold my tongue, I fired into her for being uptight and mean. I told her I was glad she wanted to discuss this topic because I thought it was absurd that an eighteen year old had to play hopscotch. Then I stormed off to call my parents. I had had enough of these rules, and I wanted out. If they did not address these issues soon, I was going to leave the hospital. After all, I was an adult, and I had the power to check myself out.

∞

I had attended a Team Meeting every week since I arrived at LPCH. This was where my entire team of doctors came together to discuss my progress with my parents and me. It was like my report card: I learned about my improvements and their concerns. While these meetings usually took place on Thursday afternoons, due to my recent outbursts, Dr. Brown moved the meeting forward to Tuesday.

I just sat on the couch with my head down when I entered the room. There was no way I would be speaking first. Dr. Brown began the meeting on a positive note. I had made some documented improvements over the past few weeks due to my biofeedback work. Beth followed him by discussing how I was writing up to five pages a day and my penmanship was becoming more legible.

That was when the pleasantries ended.

While Dr. Brown summarized my less-than-satisfactory sessions with the Professor, Dad interjected. He had a more important question for Dr. Brown to answer. Knowing he had a son my age, he asked him if he could see his son willingly play a game of hopscotch the day after he graduated from high school.

Dr. Brown did not even hesitate when he blurted out no. The room grew silent. As I lifted my head up, it looked as though a light bulb went off in everyone's minds. With my actions put in perspective, the doctors realized I was not their typical patient. *I was not a child.*

Although I had a moment of happiness, it faded quickly. I was still livid everyone in that room had betrayed me. The entire time I had been at the hospital, the Professor had been giving the "Team" accounts of our conversations. *How was that legal?* I thought there was a strict confidentiality agreement between a psychologist and a patient of legal age. I could not trust anyone. I refused to put up with the lies, deceit and constant scrutiny anymore. I now wanted out.

Mom and Dad looked just as shocked as the Team when I said I wanted to go home. Dr. Brown was quick to say that he could not let me leave the hospital and begin outpatient therapy with the catheter still in place. Too many risks were involved. If I chose to leave, it would be without the stellate ganglion catheter.

Because he felt the medications were helping, he did not recommend that course of action. Their current method of treatment was in place for a reason. It had proven to be the most beneficial for the majority of their patients. While he felt terrible that I felt misled, he reiterated the importance of the team coming together. They had better solutions to help me heal by working as a unit.

Yes, but I was eighteen years old. This made me a legal adult, and therefore, no one had the right to share private information unless I gave consent.

I did not budge on my demands. Something had to change. I could not continue to live like this—constantly feeling miserable, alone and lost. Then it hit me; as much as I wanted to leave, I had nowhere else to go.

If I did not recover soon, I could not start college in the Fall. What would I do then? On the other hand, I also questioned whether the treatments were even working. Was the catheter the reason I tolerated the grueling therapy, or were the techniques Sharon and Beth taught me allowing me to handle the pain on my own? I was stuck.

I finally heard a voice coming from the far right corner of the room. It belonged to Dr. Lake, the outpatient psychologist whom I only saw during these meetings. She felt if I just switched hospital wards, then I would no longer have the mandatory sessions or strict rules that I found tedious, impractical and unnecessary. I slightly perked up until she told me I would most likely share a room with three other people on another ward. Also, it would be mandatory that I visit her daily for counseling.

Hearing the stipulations made me cringe because I valued my privacy and despised psychotherapy. However, the pros still outweighed the cons. I agreed to her terms and two days later found myself resettled in 3-West.

Life became much easier. With no mother hens watching my every move, I felt free. Now I could have visitors and freely walk around the hospital while continuing my grueling sessions with Beth and Sharon. This was what I needed, a sense of independence.

Even though my hand had not regained any natural mobility, I was making positive strides. In occupational therapy, I had finally become skilled at the art of coloring within the lines, and was learning how to finger paint. With Beth's instruction, I also began to stretch my own hand using my body as resistance. She even had me begin typing with the help of a special brace designed just for me.

In physical therapy, I had begun to master many of the biofeedback games while becoming proficient in breath work. Sharon started to share her personal techniques to decrease stress levels and calm the body. She and I also worked on my gait and posture. The progress might have been small, but it was still progress. I had to remember baby steps.

Yet I was not at peace confined to a hospital. While I loved how my friends would call often, it became difficult to hear about the excitement and fun they were having in the *real world*. Life had not stopped because I was gone. It was nearly July and I had been in here since May. I had missed major events in a young person's life: the end of high school, prom, graduation parties. *What if I also missed college?*

While determined to regain mobility in my right arm and hand, I was also plagued with doubts. Holding onto hope became a challenge. As it became more of a challenge for me to believe I would heal, I faced more moments wondering if recovery was even possible.

It was then that I began throwing myself pity-parties. Realizing I needed to grieve in order to heal, I allotted myself five minutes a day to be angry, depressed or scared. During that time, I could scream or curse, pout or cry. I did whatever made me feel better, even if that included throwing pillows across a room. It was my constructive way of handling the frustrations so the disease would not consume me. I could feel the pain and then move forward.

∞

Although I forced myself to stay strong and upbeat, as the days continued to pass, my pity-parties lengthened. It was devastating to think I had been at Stanford for five weeks and was a long way from being better. I was losing my patience. Each day I was still in pain and could not move my hand, my faith in recovering dwindled. *Would I ever get better?*

Thankfully, my moments of questioning life were nearing an end. Waking earlier than usual one morning, I saw I had twenty minutes before the entourage of doctors arrived for morning rounds. I decided to call Meredith. When I went to reach for the phone, my right hand unexpectedly slackened. I could not believe it. I quickly tried to move each finger afraid this might have been a dream. They all twitched. *Oh my goodness, my miracle had arrived.*

I slowly raised and lowered all four of my fingers at the same time. While it was painful because my tendons shortened, I was still moving my hand. I marveled at my own accomplishment. All the pain, stress, disappointment and hard work had been worth it.

My body trembled as I quickly called home. Hearing dad's apprehensive voice only made my heart pound faster. I was sure he thought I was calling to complain. He had no idea that this phone call would be different. *This call would change his life…*

I talked extremely fast when I blurted out the news about my hand. He was shocked and asked me to repeat what I had just said. While I again explained how my hand surprisingly opened when I reached for the phone to call Meredith, I heard a long sigh followed by laughter. With this obstacle almost behind him, his veil of sadness had lifted. It was okay for him to look forward to the future because he now knew his little girl was going to be just fine. Whistling into the phone, he promised Mom and he would arrive soon. Then he hung up.

When Dr. Brown and his flock of fellows entered the room, he automatically grabbed my chart to review my vitals unaware of my huge grin. Like an actress ready to nail the greatest scene of her performing career, I slowly raised my right arm and begun to spread my fingers. The stunned group closed in around me. It was humorous to see such educated men gawk at my feeble, frail hand. Every one of the white coats wanted to ask a question or examine my limb because they all wanted to say they had a significant role in my recovery. Yet I ignored the followers and focused solely on Dr. Brown's genuine smile. This was a big moment for us all, and his sense of relief meant everything to me.

Soon the inquiries begun:

"When did this happen? How did it happen? What was I doing?"

I was the center of attention, answering questions and explaining the events of the morning. The entire time I talked, I stared at Dr. Brown nod his head in disbelief and pure delight. This was such an atypical recovery that he was at a loss for words. Although he had to leave to finish rounds, he scheduled a Team Meeting for later that afternoon and prepared me to expect many visitors and specialists throughout the day.

I stopped him as he made his way to the door. With my hand now opened, I wanted to go home. Seeing no reason to stay cooped up in this hospital, I asked if I could leave tonight with my parents. Dr. Brown turned around and looked me squarely in the eyes. "No, Nicole. I am sorry but we are going to need time to watch you to learn how this happened." I slumped back against my pillow thinking of a rebuttal when it hit me; *he thought my newfound mobility was temporary.*

I was with Beth when my parents finally arrived. Determined to make the most out of my mobility, I was pushing my body to the limit. Even though my tendons seared whenever Beth stretched them, I worked through the agony. I was a fighter. I would hold my breath or divert my eyes to the board games in the back of the room. I moaned or shook my legs when the blistering burn became too intense. It was torture, but I would have done anything in order to heal.

When my parents entered the room, they were both bright and cheery. It was not until they saw my five atrophied fingers extend that they lost their stoic appearance. Looking at my swollen Vienna-sausage-sized digits, Mom smiled as Dad's eyes welled with tears. They were shell-shocked. Neither blinked or took their focus off my hand as I proudly continued the exercise of slowly lifting and lowering each finger individually. The light at the end of the tunnel was getting brighter. *I was finally on the road to recovery.*

While I could not leave the hospital that day, the Team agreed to outpatient therapy after a twenty-four observation period. As long as I did not have any setbacks, I would be able to go home. Therefore, only thirty hours after my mysterious recovery, I was on my own in the real world. That summer was the best time of my life. Despite having to return to Stanford five days a week for aggressive hand therapy, physical therapy and psychotherapy, I had freedom again. I visited with friends, slept in my own bed and drove a car. I was happy just to feel normal.

Chapter 7

Omaha

I had less than six weeks to regain my strength before I left for college. While I knew the Pain Team was not thrilled about my decision to go to Creighton University, I did not care. I had already made up my mind and was not going to defer my first semester. I had to live my life. This was my chance to grow as a person, and I refused to let the anxiety of the unknown control how I lived today. I was ready to begin a new chapter in my life…I was ready to put the past behind me.

The Stanford doctors were hesitant because they did not believe school was the best decision for me right now. They feared my progress might be temporary and the stress of being far away and dealing with classes could lead to a serious flare-up. Yet they understood my desire to attend college, so they devised stipulations.

If I went to Omaha, I had to register with the Center for Students with Disabilities. This was so I could receive extra time for tests and have a note-taker for every class. I also needed to become a patient of the pain clinic at St. Joseph's Hospital, the teaching hospital associated with Creighton. Lastly, it was mandatory I continued physical and occupational therapy three times a week while finding a local psychologist with whom I would regularly visit.

I agreed, and a week later was on my way to Omaha, Nebraska.

The airplane ride from California to Nebraska was awful. Throughout the flight, I felt a pulsating sensation in my right arm and hand. My fingers swelled, and my hand turned splotchy red. I gulped back my fears by taking a handful of Tylenol. Although this should have been a red flag, I brushed off the burning and inflammation by focusing on the adventures ahead me. *I was going to college...*

Creighton University was a beautiful campus with cobblestone pathways, old brick buildings and a large fountain directly in front of the chapel. Since I had spent my entire education in smaller community-based institutions, this school was a perfect match for me. There was a familiarity and warmness I felt when walking around the campus. Even though I was a thousand miles away from my comfort zone, I was at home here. I belonged.

College life was great. I enjoyed the freedom of being on my own and experiencing new situations. I discovered my voice and formed my own opinions. Although Omaha was very different then the San Francisco Bay Area, and many of my social philosophies differed from my newfound friends, they never judged my beliefs. This was a time of exploration and growth for us all. It was the first time any of us were on our own and we were learning life lessons together.

However, life was not all roses and daisies. I started having more and more physical setbacks. At first, I just noticed that the amount of time I could spend in front of the computer was slowly decreasing. Then my symptoms worsened. Soon I found myself unable to focus on assigned readings. I could not write more than three sentences without my fingers tightening and aching. As the swelling and throbbing became more frequent, I had to take pain relievers just to get through the day.

Even physical and occupational therapy did not help. My health was declining. Moreover, it was a challenge to get medical attention due to my age. In the state of Nebraska, nineteen was a legal adult. In California, it was eighteen. Because I was only eighteen years old, I was unable to schedule appointments, sign documented papers or even be able to buy certain kinds of prescribed medication.

My parents had to approve everything via fax or phone. If I had blood work, the doctor would notify my parents with the results. If I had an x-ray, my parents would learn of the findings. If I needed a new medication, my parents would have to sign a waiver agreeing to the prescription. It bothered me because the longer I had to wait, the worse my symptoms became. My age was jeopardizing my health.

In late October, I attended an off-campus retreat. This retreat was for students involved in Freshmen Leadership Program, otherwise known as FLP. This was a program designed for freshmen interested in future leadership roles. Through meetings, prayer services, philanthropies and retreats, I learned how to excel and succeed in life. I met wonderfully talented, idealistic peers who were committed to making a difference just like me.

The retreat was an amazing experience for me. Not only did we bond as a group by participating in trust-building activities like blindfolded hikes in the forest and free falling, I finally opened up about my pain and disability. Sharing my own story dealing with the heartache of chronic pain was freeing. I realized I no longer needed to hold on to the façade: I was ready to be honest with myself.

Even now, it seems ironic to me that the moment I became real with myself, my life fell apart. A group of us had been moving furniture in order to clean the retreat house when I accidentally banged my right hand against one of the wooden tables. Suddenly shooting pains traveled up my arm and down my spine. I tried to shake the pain out of my hand, but the throbbing persisted. The splotchy red and white spots had already begun to appear on the back of my right hand when I boarded the bus. *This was not good.*

The ride home seemed to take forever as I kept a watchful eye on my hand. It was as if I were spectator at a UFC fight; while horrid to watch, I could not turn my head from the image plastered in front of me. By the time we arrived at the school, my right hand had become a pseudo claw. While I could still move my fingers if I concentrated on extending my digits, as soon as I stopped, the disfigured limb would reappear.

I called my parents immediately. While devastated there was not much they could do far away, so they told me to see the physical therapist and pain specialist. Yet nothing the hospital offered seemed to help. The pain continued to intensify as my motor skills declined. Three days later, my hand returned to its fisted position.

In spite of my best efforts to study and focus on my workload, my grades plummeted. I had no choice but to drop two classes. I felt I had let everyone down. It was impossible for me to stay positive when I viewed myself as a failure and a source of disappointment. Luckily, I had formed a strong group of friends who offered advice and lifted my spirits.

With the Thanksgiving holiday less than two weeks away, my friends encouraged me to return home earlier. They felt the distance between my doctors at Stanford and me at Creighton was adding unnecessary stress. My anxiety was only making my pain more intense; time away would help me recover.

I chose to return to California a week before Thanksgiving.

As soon as I arrived home, I immersed myself with doctors' appointments and therapy. I wanted answers and needed them quickly. The Team had set up a new treatment program for the remainder of my stay. Even though no one dared to say to me, "I *told you this was going to happen,*" I knew it was on all of their minds. To them, I had rushed the recovery process so I could attend college. While I knew they were concerned and wanted me to be well again, it was obvious they had all seen this coming.

The Pain Team's plan was threefold. The first order of business was to undergo a stellate ganglion nerve block for pain relief. Then I would begin the strenuous regime of daily physical and occupational therapy. Lastly, I would have to meet with Dr. Lake as she saw fit.

Although their program overwhelmed me and I was not exactly excited about counseling, I did not object. I had to show them I had matured and was ready to do whatever it took to return to good health. Therefore, I stretched my hand as Beth told me and worked on my breathing with Sharon. I even tried talking about my frustrations with Dr. Lake—but my symptoms did not improve. I was still a gimp in chronic pain when I returned to Creighton, and I struggled through the end of the semester.

Home for Christmas, I attended more doctor appointments while spending time with family and visiting high school friends. I worked tirelessly on regaining mobility in my hand during my three-week vacation from cold, snowy Nebraska. Unfortunately, nothing changed. Now it was the New Year, and I had to again return to school worse off and in terrible pain.

I soon found myself falling further and further behind. There was no way I could not keep up with a normal schedule, and unless I took summer classes, I would not graduate with my friends. While I tried to carry on and persevere, a part of me felt defeated. I was not good enough.

With no control over my life, I soon developed panic attacks. My first episode happened in the elevator as I was heading back to my dorm room after class. I just remember suddenly not being able to breathe. My automatic response was to hug my knees so I dropped to the ground while gasping for air. Sounds muffled together forming white noise, and I could not talk. I was terrified, but since embarrassment and humility took priority, I made sure I nodded when a friend asked if I was ok.

When the elevator opened on the eighth floor, a procession of students streamed out to assist me. While two of my peers helped me to my room, another went to find my Resident Advisor for help. My heart thrashed around in my small chest cavity as I sat on the edge of my bed. I continued to rock back-and-forth until objects in my room begun to blur and fade. Tears streamed down my face as my left arm went numb and pins-and-needles plagued my forearm. *Was I dying?*

It was then that my RA entered the room and told everyone else to leave. Grabbing my arms, she handed me a brown paper bag and instructed me to breathe slowly into it. As she wiped the tears and sweat from my face, she asked if I would count to ten. Petrified, I did what she told me. I was sure that I was about to die, so she had to keep reassuring me that I would be fine. This was just an anxiety attack. All I needed to do was calm down. Everything would be all right.

It took about ten minutes before my breathing steadied and I could lower the brown bag to my side. Lying in the fetal position quivering, I began to ask questions. I wanted to know why this occurred and what it meant. I needed to know if something was wrong with me. My RA told me panic attacks were common among college students, but she still wanted me to see my doctor as soon as possible.

It was a Friday evening. In no shape to spend hours sitting in a chaotic Emergency Room, I told her I would go first thing Monday morning.

I did not do much that weekend. After having another "mini-attack" the following evening, I opted to stay close to my dorm room. Despite a quicker recovery, nothing could ease my fears. I was still unnerved. I refused to talk to my friends about my concerns because I was embarrassed and did not want them to think I was crazy. Therefore, I just kept telling myself I was overreacting and this would pass. *This would pass.*

I thought the worst was behind me when I had no problems on Sunday. Believing the episodes had passed, I skipped my doctor's appointment the following day. I felt it was useless to tell anyone about my mishap unless it was serious. My doctors already thought I was mentally ill and I did not need to add fuel to their fire…I sadly learned not going was a big mistake.

Two nights later was my weekly FLP meeting. Within fifteen minutes of sitting on the hard fold-up chair, the room begun to sway. I tried my best to breathe deeply, but the air seemed stuffy and my hands became clammy. Images blurred together as voices echoed. Wiggling in my seat, I continued to choke and cough until I knew I needed air.

Standing up with the help of a friend, I went outside to lie on the cold pavement. I was shaking as I counted to ten praying this nightmare would end. A concerned security guard making his usual rounds offered assistance. I did not want anyone's help; but since I was too weak to stand on my own, he brought me to my feet and escorted me back to my dorm.

As I hung on to him, he spoke about the dangers of me being alone on campus. In his opinion, it was imperative that I contact my doctors. I did not know what to say. Embarrassed that I cancelled yesterday's appointment, all I could do was bashfully thank him for his kindness while promising to contact my doctor immediately.

However, I did not call the next day. I was too afraid that Stanford would demand I return home. Therefore, I put off the inevitable and went about my life to the best of my ability. I was in denial about the progression of my disease. It was easier for me to disregard the issues; I was not ready to face the truth.

∞

My favorite day of the week had always been Thursday. Having so many medical appointments, I had arranged to have one day free from classes a week; that day was Thursday.

After attending morning physical therapy and doing homework in the early afternoon, I decided to go to the gym. This was something I did faithfully when I first arrived at school but stopped once my hand closed. It just became too difficult. The pain increased whenever I worked out, and I was too humiliated to ask my roommate to tie my running shoes. *It was not her job to take care of her disabled roommate.*

For some reason I had a change of heart on that particular day…

I remember I arrived at the school gym and went straight to the stair master. Programming the machine for twenty minutes, I began pumping my legs up and down. The first two minutes went well. I was enjoying my workout and beginning to sweat. Yet my euphoria faded fast. Soon the sounds of people chatting and the pounding of feet on the treadmill turned to a loud, droning noise. I immediately left when I saw black-and-white spots dance around the room.

Stumbling back to my room crying, I thought about how my life was going nowhere. I had finally had enough. With tears streaming down my face, I picked up the phone and dialed Stanford. I had reached a crossroad and needed to reexamine my priorities.

College was a life ambition. It was where I thought I would find myself. Although I based a great deal of my identity and self-worth on being a college graduate, I started to wonder if there was more for me to learn outside of the classroom. Now I had to rethink my values and make a life-altering decision: *do I stay in school barely keeping my head above water or do I return home making my health my number one priority?*

Not wanting to make a drastic, impulsive decision, I sorted through the pros-and-cons. College would always be there, but the chance to heal might not. While I wanted to be in school, I began to see that it was not in my health's best interest. Leaving college would not make me a failure, but it would show my courage and determination to recover.

Right now, I had to fight for my life. Just as I could no longer run from the pain, I could no longer hide from the disease. I could not let my ego squash my chance at future happiness. Unless I confronted my fear and asked for outside help, I was going to drown. I had to stop pretending everything was *fine.*

I could not live the rest of my life like this. It was not acceptable that I no longer enjoyed my own company. I needed a change so I could stop despising who I had become. If I did not want to be in excruciating pain, then I had to return home. I made my decision.

While certain I had made the right choice, I had to wrestle up the nerve to tell my parents. I knew they would support me but I still felt as though I had let them down. I was ashamed that I did not have the inner-strength to see out the year. *I felt like a quitter.* My hand shook as I picked up the phone and began dialing. With one number left to dial, I took a deep breath and knew there was no turning back.

Remarkably, my parents also felt leaving college was in my best interest. They too had reservations with me being at Creighton. Both of them knew I was not receiving adequate care from the staff of doctors in Nebraska, and the added stress of school was increasing my pain. Since I would have my family and the team of doctors at Stanford whom I had grown to trust, I had a greater chance of healing in California.

Even though I knew going home was the right thing to do, I would miss my friends. Saying goodbyes was awful. Part of me wanted to change my mind and see out the rest of the year. Except I knew I could not waste more time. My days living in Nebraska had passed, and it was up to me to move forward.

Chapter 8

Returning Home

Arriving home was depressing. While grateful to be finally receiving proper medical care and attention, I had not thought about what I would do with my time when I was not in therapy. It never crossed my mind that the rest of my high school friends were away at school. Lacking the energy to do normal, everyday activities like grocery shopping made me spend much time alone. Even with family by my side, I was sad. I felt totally pathetic and lost.

Thankfully, I found a saving grace in teaching. As a child, I had attended the neighborhood parochial school where I made lifelong friendships. Once my old elementary school principal learned I had returned from college, she offered me a position as a teacher's assistant. With only five weeks left of school before summer, she wanted me to start right away. The job was my refuge; it was a place free from the drama pertaining to my health.

I had no time to dwell on my own situation when I was around children. My students were unimpressed with my illness, because in their eyes, I was not sick or disabled. I was just their teacher, and all they wanted was my undivided attention. It was that simple.

Teaching gave me a new purpose for living. Not only did I have a reason to get up each morning knowing I would smile and laugh, but I was also happier and more fulfilled. My days teaching in the mornings and traveling to Stanford in the afternoons were hectic, but worth it. It brought balance and a greater meaning to my life. I felt whole again.

∞

The aggressive outpatient regime at Stanford began immediately. I was having two nerve blocks a week while attending occupational and physical therapy four times a week. I visited Dr. Lake once a week and saw a psychiatrist as needed. The program was rigorous. While the hour-and-twenty minute trip to Palo Alto was exhausting, I knew what was at stake. I had to do this so I could return to Creighton for the Fall semester. I was determined to heal.

To help me deal with my recent panic attacks, the psychiatrist prescribed anti-anxiety medicine. Hearing him say I needed a substance to clear my head angered me. I felt ashamed. I prided myself on being strong and I did not want others to see me as the crazy, depressed girl who could not cope with life unless drugged. All that I had left was my dignity, and it seemed that they were taking that away from me too.

The drugs were awful. I spent many nights in the Emergency Room because of serious complications and side effects. I suffered from breathing difficulties, erratic heartbeats, rashes, hallucinations and an impaired gait. These undesirable symptoms made living impossible. One evening I even called the police station adamant that an intruder was going to kill me. Because I hated that uneasy, out-of-body feeling, I visited my psychiatrist weekly to adjust medications.

Meanwhile, Dr. Lake had me complete a questionnaire to determine the gravity of my anxiety. The results showed I had a moderately severe case of obsessive-compulsive disorder. This meant I needed an aggressive treatment program to teach me how to manage my issues with control and order. The first step was letting go of the old routines that were harming my body. I needed to see that my world would not fall apart if I did not brush my teeth three times in a row. These beliefs were only hindering my health, and I had to stop living life feeling inhibited.

The advice I received from Dr. Lake was immeasurable. Using the tools needed to overcome my fears, I began to notice an improvement in my anxiety. Even my panic attacks decreased as I retrained my brain to respond to varying stimuli in an appropriate manner. With her techniques working, we begun tackling my issue with exercising.

Due to my previous experience at Creighton's gym, the thought of exercising in a busy facility overwhelmed me. While I logically understood I was in no physical danger, *knowing* I was protected and *feeling* protected were two completely different concepts. Petrified of having another attack in such a public place caused Dr. Lake to take a systematic approach with me.

First, I had to recognize there was not an underlining threat to working out. I needed consciously to understand I was safe and had nothing to fear. When I was able to accept the above statement as truth, my next task entailed driving to the gym and sitting in the parking lot. Dr. Lake wanted me to stay parked until the alarming, dreadful, anxiety-ridden feelings subsided. This was where I would use the tools I had learned, like focused-breathing, to gain control over my fear. Within five minutes of constantly reminding myself I was not in harm's way, I felt a shift in my thinking and soon became relaxed. *Her program was working.*

Dr. Lake then wanted me to walk around the facility, preferably during "off" hours. I decided to go on a Friday evening as they had a tendency of being *slow* nights in a gym. Driving to the gym around 11:30 that evening, I had to convince myself that I was prepared. I felt slightly better knowing I had decided to take "Don't Panic: Taking Control of Anxiety

Attacks" by Reid Wilson, a book Dr. Lake recommended with me. It focused on overcoming panic attacks, and I thought it might calm me down if I got overwhelmed.

I remember clutching the book as I entered. Although my blood pressure rose when I walked inside the brightly lit building, I just took a deep breath and reassured myself I was fine. *I had done it.* I had taken all the baby steps, and now it was time to exercise.

As another one of Dr. Lake's *baby step* tactics, I avoided the stair stepper altogether. She wanted me to sidestep the piece of equipment that led to the initial fear, so I walked over to the treadmill. Less than twenty people were inside the gym that night, and the majority of them were upstairs weight training. My heart raced as I stepped on the second treadmill in the last row and began to walk. I listened to the music playing over the gym's loudspeakers and concentrated on my breathing. Miraculously I felt perfect. Watching the minutes pass by empowered me—here I was exercising again…and I was not dying. *This was huge.*

I could not wait for my follow-up with Dr. Lake. For the first time in a long time, I was progressing. I had completed a task that once seemed unattainable, and I was proud of myself. I knew if I could beat panic attacks, I could beat any future battle. I was regaining control of my life.

At the same time that I was dealing with my stress and anxiety issues, I was also working with Beth and Sharon. Beth focused on weight-bearing activities, stretching and writing homework assignments, while Sharon concentrated on breath work, biofeedback and core-balancing exercises. With newer studies showing a link between exercise and a decrease in nerve pain, Sharon became interested in getting me active. She hoped by increasing my time on the stationary bike that I would receive pain relief. After all, exercise was the greatest way for the body to release endorphins, our natural morphine.

When I combined the works of these three women, I found myself getting a whole-body approach to healing. Yet even with their support, I was still seeing minimal progress. The more time passed the more conscious I became of the Pain Team's ever-growing skepticism. Although I knew they were sympathetic to my situation, it was obvious their cynicism was mounting. Frustrated, I would schedule appointments with the Pain Team. I wanted to know why I was not improving and what we could do to fix it. Yet they had no answers and instead questioned their original diagnosis.

Months passed and soon it was the beginning of August. Now I faced a new reality—I would not be able to return to Creighton University. Rightfully upset and distraught, I soon detached from those around me. I even started to resent my team of doctors and wondered whether they had my best interest at heart. Undergoing three or more nerve blocks a week without receiving any lasting effect put a strain on the doctor-patient relationship. We finally had reached a standstill. It was time for drastic measures.

In mid-September, Dr. Brown wanted to meet with my parents and me to discuss the next phase. The three of us arrived in Palo Alto on a clear, cool autumn morning ready to face another pointless day of hand stretches, counseling and doctor examinations. By this point, I began to doubt the medical profession. It had been over two years since the initial incident, and I still was not pain-free or able to move my right hand. I just wanted to live a normal life again.

As we entered the now familiar waiting room, I looked around and saw infants, toddlers and little children. While most of them were in wheelchairs without hair and missing limbs, they were still happy. Watching them giggle and play with the train tracks and bright red and green Lego toys stacked in the corner of the room made me realize how fortunate and blessed I was. My life was only on hold, but it was not ending. If they did not let their setbacks stop them from living life than neither could I. However, as I glanced at the parents of the children and then looked toward my parents, I saw the same gloom and despair. *What had I done to Mom and Dad?*

My drifting thoughts abruptly ended when I heard the nurse call my name. The four of us made small talk until we reached my room at the end of the long, narrow corridor. I sat in a chair waiting for Dr. Brown while staring aimlessly at the plain white walls. All I wanted was to be healthy. I could not wait to be able to clap my hands, move my fingers or get through a minute without a throbbing sensation dominating my thoughts. I wanted to scream and yell. *Why could no one help me? What was wrong with me?*

I glanced at the clock; each passing minute seemed to take hours. Finally, I heard the soft echo of a tap on the door, and Dr. Brown strolled in to the institutional-looking room. I was nauseous and petrified to look at him. My head began to swim, and I had trouble hearing. With a blurred vision, my breath became faint, and I gasped for air. This tall, middle-aged man whom I trusted and adored was now the Grim Reaper. He held the key to my happiness in the palm of his hand. Panic took over me. He had the power, and once again, I was the helpless victim.

As he approached the cold steel examining bed, I began to shake uncontrollably. I was tired of hearing the excuses. I did not want to know that my rare condition led prominent doctors to question why my symptoms did not fit any diagnosis. The lump in my throat started to expand. I needed positive news. Although my eyes started to glisten while my face turned pasty, I refused to lose my composure. *I had to keep it together…for my own sake.*

To avoid the tears, I bit down deep into my lower lip. Dr. Brown stood in front of me holding my limp, clammy, discolored hand. His eyes looked as if they were reaching into the back of his brain—most likely trying to recall information he once learned on rare neurological disorders. I studied his face for clues, but he seemed to be puzzled with a stern, despondent gaze. Then his appearance shifted to a more assured, confident demeanor. As his mouth begun to form the words, time just stood still. Here was my moment of truth. These next few sentences would determine my future.

Without further hesitation he bluntly told my parents and me that after months of muddling between diagnoses, he was quite sure I was suffering from complex regional pain syndrome (CRPS). CRPS was the newest name for RSD. *I could not believe it.* After all this time of trial-and-error and flip-flopping between diagnoses, he was validating my pain. My blood pressure significantly dropped, and I begun to see black and yellow spots. This was the first time I did not care if my eyes welled with tears for I now had what I wanted: a diagnosis.

Dr. Brown went on to explain the reason it took so long to identify the CRPS, yet I was not listening. I was so relieved that I did not particularly care. While I had many questions regarding available treatments, my mind was too scattered. All I could do was repeat what he had just said. I was like a parrot, clinging to my master's every word. I found myself repeating everything he would say in order to make sure it was not a dream. *Had he actually said that I had CRPS and there were procedures that might help?*

Dr. Brown did not want to hinder my chance for a full recovery. Despite having used up all the resources at LPCH Stanford, there were options available. He now wanted me to see another pain specialist who dealt with adults and more severe cases. He was a local, world-renowned neurologist who specialized in pain management. With one clinic in San Francisco, he also had another practice twenty minutes from my house. As this doctor had more experience treating CRPS, Dr. Brown felt this specialist could do more for me than his own team at Stanford.

My earlier drab face turned into an immense smile. This was the first time I felt free from the heavy weight upon my shoulders. Things were looking up; my moments of uncertainty and misgiving were over. I had hope and faith that I was going to be all right again. I would overcome this long-fought battle…my time had finally arrived. *I would survive.*

Harbor Half: The Miles Leading up to the Halfway Marker

With a deep pit forming in the middle of my stomach anytime I think about my past, I try to concentrate only on the current moment. Gazing over the calm waters, I look toward the horizon and see the sun peaking out. It is going to be a beautiful day.

As the temperature rises slightly, I begin to sip water from my CamelBak every five minutes and consume Clif Shots, an organic electrolyte-enhancing gel. Listening to the water sloshing in my backpack eases my trepidations. There is a unique rhythm between the water's movement and my feet hitting the heated gravel. Turning off my iPod, I jet down the road in a blissful disposition.

Recognizing that I possess all the tools needed to cross that finish line reassures me that I am going to be all right. However, the feeling of contentment vanishes the second I look ahead and see a blurry image coming closer and closer. *It is a person;* more specifically, it is a runner. I cannot believe the first runner passes me only minutes after I completed four miles. How can I be finished with just four miles when he has already done nine?

My face muscles droop as if I instantly suffered a stroke, and the flushed apple-red color of my cheeks fades. *How is this possible?* Rick brings me back to reality. "Nicole, remember this marathon is a personal competition. It is your own accomplishment, so you must stop looking at this run as a race."

I tell myself that running a half-marathon when Western medicine believed I would be wheelchair-bound or dead was incredible. If my dreams of walking, showering, and dressing myself have all come true, then so would this. I can do this as long as I hold on to faith and believe in myself.

All I can do to stay sane is constantly repeat my mantra to myself: *This is not a race. I did not train to compete against anyone but myself. This is about me proving to the medical world that labels are irrelevant and only hinder people's chances of survival. This run is for hope.* However, I still feel like a slow, pathetic failure.

We exit the causeway for the second time as more and more runners dart by on their way to the finish line. As we enter what is supposed to be the scenic wetland habitat, I look down the long road and find no visible end in sight. Claustrophobic from the looming trees that seem destined to cave in on me, my lungs instantly constrict and the pain intensifies. *This is not good.*

Calm down and continue to breathe. As soon as you relax a little, your body will loosen—you are hurting right now because your muscles are so tight. Just look at the beautiful scenery. So far, you are doing great.

I know I have to pull myself together, but I lack the capacity and willpower to do so. The pain controls me. I look at the wildlife; it is not calming, tranquil, or beautiful. Just like the pain, the trees and shrubs are roadblocks hindering my progress. No matter how hard I try to win, the damn beast always finds a way to hunt me down. I have become a victim once again.

As my back aches, the joints in my ankles burn uncontrollably. Ruthless stabbing jars each passing stride, and I feel a hundred pounds heavier. Every step I take only intensifies the searing anguish besieging my poor heels and toes. *What is wrong with me? Why am I having such a hard time? Why is my body acting like this **today**?*

"Come on, babe. Don't slow down; we are doing well." Clapping his hands, he shouts, "Let's go! Let's go!"

I just want to hit him and tell him to shut the hell up. He doesn't understand: no one understands. How do I go on when the pain is that severe?

I knew the weather had been terribly unstable the past week with a cold front, thunderstorms, and a return to warm temperatures. This meant my nervous system was again out of sorts and in overdrive; running only exacerbated my strained, hypersensitive, burning pain. Up to this point, I had done everything possible to stay healthy and fit. *How could God do this to me on such an important day?*

"Focus, Nicole. If you need to, walk a few steps. Then let's go. You are a mile away from the halfway mark. You can do this. Pull yourself together."

I glance at Rick while rolling my eyes and huffing. Soon I am venting and cursing. I knew two days ago that the treatment wasn't working and my beat frequency was set wrong, but Doc didn't listen to me. I quickly crumble as my feet are completely numb and shooting pains travel through my low back and hips. My breathing becomes erratic and shallow as I limp. I do not know if I can make it to the end. *How would I face everyone if I quit?*

Seeing the fear of failure tattooed across my face, Rick jogs right beside me, carefully pondering his choice of words. I think he knows he has the power to determine my mindset for the remainder of the run.

"You've got this, baby. Just keep putting one foot in front of the other. You are doing so well, but you have to start relaxing so you stay loose. I know the change in weather is affecting your ability, but you are strong. I *know* you will finish these thirteen miles.

"Nothing is different about this run than any others we did during training. All the grueling workouts and long days spent at the gym in order to prepare are finished. I want you to be able to enjoy this because *this* is the fun part. Now if the pain is that bad, let's walk a while. But if you think you can push through, let's keep running. You know you can do this … and I *know* you can do this."

He was right.

As if I released a massive boulder from my back, feeling returns to my feet and I can jog again. Quitting may have been a temporary relief, but I knew it would be permanently detrimental. After all the hell and torture I endured over the years, running was literally a walk in the park. I needed to pull myself together—no more whining, complaining, or making excuses. I wanted this run and I wanted the glory. *I wanted a life free of boundaries.*

Chapter 9

Starting Over

A personal referral from Dr. Brown was the reason Dr. Vine's staff scheduled my initial consultation two weeks later. Although this was a short time to wait to see such an esteemed doctor, it felt like an eternity to me. Given the choice, I would have seen him at that exact moment. The nagging pain was making me crazy. It was with me twenty-four hours a day, seven days a week. I did not have the luxury to waste any more time; my life had been on hold long enough.

I was on edge the morning I was to meet Dr. Vine. Fearing what his opinion would be regarding my health made me nauseated. *I needed him to believe my pain so I could finally get the help I deserved.* I remember thinking my heart was going to beat out of my chest as my parents and I drove in silence to his clinic. This was the day I would finally learn my new treatment program. This was the day I believed I would meet the man who would save my life.

I nervously tapped my left leg as I sat in the back seat of the car and stared at the clear blue sky. Useless thoughts wandered through my mind in an attempt to escape reality. I wondered what Meredith was doing and thought about my friends in Nebraska at the same time. I thought about Dan and hoped my fifth-grade class did well on their math test. I even figured out what I wanted for dinner that evening. Anything to keep my mind distracted from the present moment and what was to come.

My head was spinning when I walked into Dr. Vine's office and sat down. I apprehensively looked around the room and panicked. *Did I look like every other patient?* Sweat fell from my brow and down my cheek as I noticed a room filled with moaning, decrepit people. Each was shaking in pain just like me. My heart ached. Seeing others like myself forced me to realize this was not a bad dream; this really was my life.

As a young blonde nurse called my name, I slowly got out of my chair and followed her down a long, narrow hall. It was like an out-of-body experience when we entered the neutral-toned room. I immediately took my position on the examining table as my parents sat in two folding chairs along the wall. The nurse then took my temperature and blood pressure. She tried to comfort me by saying everything would be fine, but I did not believe her. My life would never be the same again. After jotting a few notes in my chart, she left the three of us alone to wait for the doctor.

A couple minutes passed before I heard a soft knock on the door. The doctor was a relatively tall man with glasses and slightly curly hair. He introduced himself as Dr. Edward Vine. He shook our hands before plopping down on the makeshift desk against the wall. "So, what seems to be the problem?"

As I went over the occurrences of the past two years, I could almost envision the inner workings of his mind. Even though he did not always look in my direction when I spoke, I sensed he was actually listening to me.

I started to squirm as he approached the table to look at my hand. Seeing that I was nervous for him to touch my extremely hypersensitive limb, he quickly assured me that he only wanted to view it. I rested my right fist in the palm of his hand and he carefully studied the disfigurations. Then he had me raise my left hand for comparison. I liked his thoroughness. It made me more confident that he might formulate his own opinion instead of relying on previous doctors' reports.

He continued to speak matter-of-factly when he asked me to dangle my legs off the table. He needed to test my nerves and reflexes. Removing some strange-looking devices from his pocket and placing them next to me, he warned me that this next exam would cause discomfort. He used three various instruments that were each made of metal with different heads to test my sensory perception. One had a broad, blunt tip, while the next had a slim, more defined, piercing tip. The last one had many spiky, jagged points that rotated and moved when rolled along a surface.

He then began rolling each object over both arms to poke my skin. I fidgeted and winced throughout the torturous ordeal. It felt like he was slicing the skin on my right arm with a newly sharpened carving knife. I wanted to yell for him to stop, but I knew I had to be brave. This test was the only way he could properly determine the range of my hypersensitivity and the progression of my disease. Biting down hard on my bottom lip, I focused my attention on my parents while trying to stay calm.

He did not say anything when he finished, but instead picked up the tools and positioned them back into his coat pocket. As he gathered his thoughts, my body froze. I was anxious for answers. I could not keep living a life of uncertainty. His mouth opened and I found myself cringing; I could not handle more bad news.

Surprisingly, not only did he believe that I had CRPS, but he also felt we needed to take an aggressive approach because of the severity of my muscle contractions (dystonia) and muscle weakness (dystrophy). He described his treatment plan as being a whole-body approach, and had confidence that I could heal if I followed his method precisely. This meant I had to consent to weekly meetings with a psychologist and continue physical and occupational therapy with professionals he recommended. His adamancy shocked me. Nevertheless, I wanted this pain to end, so I agreed to his rules.

Dr. Vine wanted to change my medication and try one final nerve block. It was his hope that a slight modification in drugs might lead to a difference in my overall health. He therefore prescribed barbiturates, which were considerably stronger than any medication I had taken in the past. However, time was of the essence. If we did not see desirable results quickly, the next option was a trial run of the spinal cord stimulator.

I thought my head was going to explode from an overload of information. My life had completely changed within minutes. I had been waiting more than two years to hear a doctor say I had a serious problem and it was not in my head. While this diagnosis was scary, it ended all the whispers and gossip. Dr. Vine had validated my pain. I had CRPS, and he was determined to help me. Together we would take all the necessary measures to get better.

∞

Although I dreaded meeting Ellen, my new psychologist, the appointment went better than I expected. From the beginning, I explained my hesitancy to trust anyone in the medical field. After sharing my past incidents of betrayal and ridicule, I was surprised when she then opened up about her own experiences dealing with the medical profession. She too was battling a chronic disorder. Understanding firsthand how difficult it could be to never feel acknowledged and accepted, Ellen could relate to my pain and fear.

Since her role was to help me cope, she did not want our visits to cause me more anxiety; that would be unproductive. Unless she asked for my permission to speak with my doctors, everything would be confidential. While her honesty and forthright nature were commendable, it was hard for me to believe her. I still worried that she would betray me, just as The Shrink and The Professor had.

Ellen was the liaison between Dr. Vine and me. That meant she had to listen to both of us in order to mend miscommunications. While I figured that this had to be a difficult task, she seemed to handle the situations with ease and integrity. She always managed to bridge together our views and philosophies, so all sides were happy with the treatment program.

I had more difficulty adjusting to my new physical therapist than to Ellen. This was because my physical therapist appeared to know little about CRPS. It worried me that instead of giving me a program, she wanted me to tell her what I did at Stanford. I felt seeing her three afternoons a week was a waste of my time and a hazard to my health. It seemed as if I was regressing. I knew I needed to confront Dr. Vine.

I was scared to do this, so I went to Ellen for advice. Although I did not want to shake the foundation of trust with my new doctor, I could not stay quiet and risk my future. Because my health was important to me, Ellen helped me find the courage to stand up for myself. She gave me the confidence I needed to tell Dr. Vine how I thought his particular therapist was hindering my growth and exacerbating my symptoms.

I shook as I waited for him to enter the room. Although Ellen said everything would be fine, I was still unsure. He had made it very clear in our first meeting that he knew what was best and he would only send me to the best. I did not want to step on his toes by questioning his authority. But I also had to do what was right for me. If I did not feel comfortable with my physical therapist, he needed to know why.

My heart stopped as I saw the doorknob turn. I had to be the first to talk, so I took a final breath before blurting out my uneasiness with my therapy. I was sweating through my T-shirt by the time I finished. *What would he say now?*

Shockingly, Dr. Vine listened and agreed with me. He knew he needed someone else and was already in the process of finding a new, reputable therapist. I could not believe it. Not only was I proud of myself, but I was finding my voice. *I was learning how to become proactive in my recovery.*

The next therapist Dr. Vine had me meet was Mitzi. Mitzi had an energy to which I naturally gravitated. She was spunky, successful and extremely smart. I respected her strong will and grew to admire her tenacity. It was refreshing to see that a woman could hold her own in such a male-dominated profession. Impressed with her extensive knowledge of the disease, I felt I had finally found someone I could trust within the medical field.

I started seeing her three days a week, but that was quickly increased to five because of the progression of the disease. Each day, I spent ninety minutes exercising and stretching my hand. Therapy was intense and extremely painful. With my sense of touch severely impaired from hypersensitivity, Mitzi believed desensitization work would be the most helpful. I hated it. Having to place my disfigured hand in a container filled with ordinary items was awful. A hand towel felt like sandpaper. Cotton balls were glass shards, and uncooked rice felt like pebbles. This treatment was excruciating but necessary. If I was going to heal, I needed my body to understand that small Lego pieces were not actually sharp blades.

After two months of numerous appointments with Dr. Vine, Ellen and Mitzi, I still was not progressing or receiving pain relief. Such a slow response to treatments frustrated me because I thought these specialists were going to get me better. I felt defeated; my life would never be what I had hoped and dreamed. When it became obvious that medicine alone would not alleviate the pain, Dr. Vine knew it was time for a more drastic approach.

Revisiting the idea of implanting a spinal cord stimulator (SCS) slightly concerned me. Since I was unaware of the technicalities of SCS, it helped when Dr. Vine described the procedure as a method utilized to control pain through low-intensity electrical impulses. The stimulus would trigger select nerve fibers believed to stop pain messages transferred to the brain. By interrupting these signals to the brain, my body would foolishly believe I was not in pain.

Very thin cables called leads were responsible for delivering the electrical pulses to the nerves along the spinal cord. Dr. Vine would insert these leads in the upper portion of my spine. He would then connect them to a generator (otherwise known as a battery) in my upper right buttock. The generator was in charge of producing the intensity of the electrical current through the leads, which I could easily reprogram or adjust using an external remote control.

Dr. Vine went on to explain how I would have to lie on my stomach and be cognitive throughout the implantation. They would use lidocaine, a local anesthetic, to numb the skin and surrounding tissues. An X-ray machine would be required to ensure proper lead placement. During the procedure, an electrocardiogram (EKG), blood pressure cuff, and a blood-oxygen monitoring device would check my vital signs.

This was a lot of information for me to digest in ten minutes. It was as if I was living in an alternate universe. Was my doctor really talking about spinal surgery?

While my parents and I appreciated his honest and informative account of the procedural steps, we needed more time to process. This was a big deal, and I needed to make the correct decision. Dr. Vine completely understood and sent us home with a movie detailing the SCS.

I watched the tape shortly after my parents dropped me off at the house. The production was cheesy, but it presented the information well enough that I easily made up my mind. Even with the risks involved, I believed the end result outweighed many of the possible consequences. Now I only hoped my parents' worries would lessen after watching the video.

Mom and Dad sat down to watch the tape outlining the procedure after dinner that evening. When it was over, there was complete silence. I knew they were having a difficult time with this decision. I was their only daughter, and they would never want to put my life in jeopardy. Therefore, I did not give them time to think it over; I told them I wanted to do it.

I was a month away from being twenty years old. Since it was my health and future on the line, I felt I needed to make the final decision. I would schedule a trial run of the external SCS to verify its effectiveness. If I deemed the treatment successful, I would have the internal device implanted. If I did not feel the spinal cord stimulator was helpful, it would be easy to remove. I had nothing to lose. *I had to try this therapy.*

It was hard to know if my parents agreed with my decision. I could see the fear in their eyes as they glanced at each other. They were quiet and subdued. They each nodded. Even though they supported me, it was apparent that such a procedure was emotionally killing them. I felt like a bully had just kicked me in the stomach. *I was the reason my parents were hurting.*

Two days later, I called Dr. Vine's office and informed his personal scheduler I was ready to try the external SCS. He enthusiastically told me I had made a wise decision. Then he scheduled the procedure for the following Wednesday. I could not believe it: *I could be pain-free in six days.*

∞

The days passed slowly, and my excitement turned to anxiety. I could not sleep, and I began to eat neurotically. One minute, I was nauseated, and the next second, I wanted a hamburger. I was a total wreck. I wanted so badly for this treatment to work. This had to be my cure.

I remembered being nervous sitting in the waiting area of the outpatient surgery clinic. *Was I really going to allow someone to insert wires along the length of my spine?* When a nurse finally called my name, I had no more time to think about the what-ifs; it was now go time. The nurse was an older woman who was not very pleasant. Scooting me into the pre-operating room, she handed me a hospital gown that I quickly put on so she could connect my IV. Then she abruptly left. Waiting was nerve-wracking. My quality of life depended on the outcome of this procedure, and my hopes were high. I did not want to be let down again.

Twenty minutes later, she returned to escort me to the OR, where I was positioned on my stomach. Lying on the cold table, I felt someone untie my gown. I was exposed and frightened until a kinder nurse covered me with warm blankets. I just closed my eyes and rested my head on the stiff table beneath me. After I was administered medications to pacify my nerves, the room started to fade and my speech slurred. It was like my earlier procedure at Stanford where I could still hear those in the room talk, but I had difficulty comprehending or responding to their questions.

I immediately felt pressure along my back when Dr. Vine began the procedure. Terrified as to what this meant, I tried yelling, but my senses were slow and impaired. I was losing my mind, thinking this might cause paralysis. My heart rate jumped, causing the nurse holding my left hand to remind me that I needed to squeeze if I felt pain. I forcefully gripped her fingers. The whole room stopped. No one spoke except for Dr. Vine, who needed to know what I was feeling.

It was then I learned that pressure was normal but pain was not. The rest of the procedure went off without a hitch. With the help of the X-ray machine and a thin, long needle, he placed the leads along my spine. Now was the time I had to interact with the doctors. In order to determine the proper position of the wire, I had to explain the sensations I felt when he activated the device. *Did I feel a tingling sensation in my right arm and hand? Was the frequency too intense for me? Did I feel the current in other areas of my body?*

I was overwhelmed and had no idea how to answer so many questions. Realizing that my responses determined the success of this therapy only added more stress. I did not know what they considered a positive reaction. Agitated at Dr. Vine for not informing me about this earlier and frustrated at myself for not being more coherent, I found myself shutting down. I could not do this. How could I possibly give feedback on something I did not even understand?

Dr. Vine revised his inquiries and slowly walked me through the questions.

Did I feel a small tingling sensation in my body? Yes.
Was it only in my right arm and hand? Mostly, though I could feel a little stinging down the right side of my back.
Was the frequency or the current too intense? While it was not overly painful, I felt a rush of energy in the arm that made the inside of my hand feel flush and very warm.

He then made some slight alterations before asking me the same questions again. Yet this time my answers were different. Now I only felt tingling in the lower portion of my right arm and the sensation was much more bearable. This was what he wanted to hear, so he took a final set of X-rays to mark the lead placements and then stitched up the incisions. He was done.

My parents and I learned of my restrictions as I lay in a post-operative recovery room. I could not shower or lift anything heavier than five pounds until I saw Dr. Vine tomorrow for a follow-up appointment. Since an ideal trial period lasted between seven and ten days, I had to take antibiotics to ensure there was no infection at the incision site. The nurse handed Mom a packet of information re-explaining my limitations and numbers to call in case of an emergency. Then we were free to go home.

I was sore and tired by the time we finally pulled into our driveway. Dad had to help me into the house as Mom hurried to the store to pick up my prescriptions. I had spent so much time consumed with the actual procedure that I never even thought about the recoup or increased pain—until now. Lying on my aching back, all I thought about was the unrelenting misery. *When would the pain let up?*

The rest of the night was a blur. I remember tossing and turning to get comfortable. The bandages itched and my spine was tender from the implanted wires. My hopes of being healthy and pain-free had not come true. To say I was discouraged would have been the understatement of the year. My life had turned upside down.

While I held on to faith that tomorrow might be better, the soreness and discomfort worsened the following morning. With the pain increasing, I was thankful I had a doctor's appointment. I needed more explanations as to why this was happening to me. What did Dr. Vine consider normal pain after such a procedure? How long would it be before I felt relief in my hand?

Sitting in the plain exam room, my parents and I waited for the doctor. I kept shifting my weight from one side of my tailbone to the other, becoming more stir crazy with each passing minute. When the door opened, I was shocked not to see Dr. Vine. Instead, a woman with a hard metal briefcase half-heartedly smiled. Her name was Lynn Vine, and she would be assisting her husband in today's consult.

Lynn was a certified nurse who once worked for the manufacturing company of the SCS device. Because of her experience with programming the stimulator, she was here to help adjust the beat frequency to better suit my needs.

Shortly thereafter, there was another tap on the door and Dr. Vine entered the room. He grinned at me before examining the bandaged site. I tried to explain the discomfort in my back and tingling in my arm, but he seemed uninterested in my complaints. He told me those sensations were normal and to be expected. I was healing perfectly, so there was no reason to worry.

He turned his attention back to his wife, who had started changing the frequency of the stimulator. She began to ask me questions concerning the intensity of the current and the sensations I experienced. I felt like a deer caught in the headlights. With no idea how to answer, I looked toward my parents for advice, but they seemed just as clueless as I did. I panicked. It was up to me to help her yet I could not. Nobody had told me this would be so hard.

Suddenly I felt less burning in my hand. I had been waiting for the moment when the nerve pain lessened, and now that it was here, I could breathe again. As Lynn disconnected her machine and stepped out of the room, I was at a loss for words. All I could do was focus on the tiny waves of current passing up and down my right arm and hand. My hope for better days returned. I was certain the spinal cord stimulator would be my cure. *I was on the road to recovery.*

With such promising news, my parents decided we needed to celebrate. Any decrease in my pain was a reason to rejoice, so we ordered pizza and rented movies. While a simple, low-key evening was just what I needed, it was not what happened.

I remember I got up to use the bathroom in between movies. As I was walking down the hall, I unexpectedly felt a tug and pull coming from the bandaged area. I froze and screamed for my parents, petrified that moving might cause more damage. Dad reached me first. He looked tense as he noticed the external wire tangled around the guest room's door handle. *Oh God, I just pulled out part of the external SCS.*

With Mom frantic, Dad went straight to the kitchen and immediately paged Dr. Vine. None of us had any idea what this meant or if I could now be in physical danger. Panic took over as the pain quickly increased in my pathetically disfigured fist. I knew I was in trouble.

We all waited next to the phone as Dad kept asking the same question over and over: how did this happen? I had no answer for him. All I knew was that I was walking down the hall when my body pulled backward.

Soon the phone rang and it was the doctor. Dr. Vine was upset this had occurred but reassured us that I would be fine. There was no way I had pulled out the actual leads, because he had firmly attached them to my spinal wall. Instead, I had ripped the cord connecting the leads to the external machine. This meant I would no longer benefit from the procedure.

Unless I began complaining of extreme pain or showed signs of severe side effects like slurring or temporary paralysis, I would be all right. After telling Dad he now wanted me to come see him Monday morning in San Francisco, he said goodbye and left my parents and me speechless. *What would I do until Monday?*

The next two days seemed to pass very slowly. I was upset and frustrated at myself. Just when my pain had finally begun to subside, I somehow ruined it.

Dr. Vine performed a thorough examination of my spine on Monday. I wanted to vomit, waiting for him to speak. Concluding that I had not harmed myself or showed any sign of infection was a relief. This meant I had not damaged the leads or injured my body.

He then cleared his throat. I prepared myself for the worst. I had noticed this was a characteristic of many doctors when they had not-so-good news. Yet he had nothing terrible to tell me. Instead, he was convinced that I had shown enough positive results in my very short trial period to move forward with the implantation.

It was settled: I would undergo the spinal cord stimulator implantation after the first of the year.

Chapter 10

Implantation

The next three weeks hurried by as the Christmas holiday approached. Having friends and family constantly around was like a vacation from my day-to-day life. With doctor appointments and therapy sessions being the focal point of my daily routine, I no longer was a child. I now made important decisions about my life, and these choices determined my future. Therefore, it was nice to pretend to be a young adult again.

As it was on every New Year's Eve, my parents got together with the Quinlan family. The Callaghans, Kelbers, Moriartys, O'Briens and Quinlans were childhood buddies of my dad. It was a unique bond to remain close friends for over four decades, and they supported each other during the good and bad times. Dan and I grew up with these families. They were a part of our extended family; we vacationed with them and celebrated special occasions together. While we usually were always together, New Year's Eve was different. We spent New Year's Eve only with the Quinlan family.

However, this year, I was twenty. I wanted to forgo tradition and stay home with my friends. My parents agreed, so I invited over a few friends from high school. It was an evening filled with laughter and a night when I could forget about my pain. We told old stories, shared new adventures, and danced around the family room, all while eating cookies and pizza and drinking champagne. *I did not realize how much I had missed feeling normal.*

I only had socks on that night, so when I ran from the kitchen toward the family room, I started sliding across the linoleum. Losing my balance on the slippery floor, my left big toe made direct contact with the corner of the wall. Pain abruptly swept through my body. As it became more and more difficult to walk, I told Meredith I thought I broke my toe. She just laughed and said I was fine; it was not as if I hit the wall *that* hard. I tried to act brave for the rest of the night, but the throbbing and swelling became hard to ignore.

By morning, the pain had escalated, and I knew I had done more than bump my foot. It was as if Murphy's Law described me; I had the worst luck. We had all been dancing and running around with socks, but I was the only one who got hurt. I could not believe this had happened to me. Not knowing what to do, and frightened I might be in trouble, I called my parents at the Quinlan's house.

Instead of telling them the truth that I slipped in the kitchen, hitting my foot on the doorframe, I told them I accidentally banged my foot against the wall while trying to dance. I did not know why I lied or how I thought that story sounded better. But I was so scared they would be angry that I thought a spruced-up account would be more believable. I could tell Dad was flustered when he told me to visit the emergency room if my foot was really bothering me. Otherwise, he and Mom would leave the Quinlans' in about an hour to come home. Then he hung up.

Although I wanted to go to the ER, I decided to wait for my parents to return. I received the third degree as Dad drove to the hospital. "How did this happen? What were you doing?" No matter how many times I told him I was trying to dance like the cheerleaders in *Bring it On,* he knew that was not the truth. Why was I lying about something so trivial?

As we reached the parking lot, Dad helped me out of the car. I went into the waiting room, where the woman at the admissions window instructed me to wait for an available room. Sitting on an uncomfortably padded chair, I scanned the room, trying to determine the ailments of the other patients. Knowing that those with severe problems were first to be seen, I was relieved no one was bleeding or curled over in pain. Maybe the wait would not be too long.

It took a half hour before I heard my name called. A hospital orderly whisked me to radiology, where I had a set of X-rays taken of my left foot and toe. Now I had to wait again to see the doctor. Although I tried not to focus on the pain in my toe, I could not help but wonder if the CRPS would spread. I was petrified. I bit down on the inside of my cheeks to hold back the tears. I had to keep believing I would be fine.

The ER doctor returned. I had fractured my big toe. Since there was little to do for a broken toe besides letting it heal on its own, he gave me a hospital boot that had a stiff sole to ease discomfort when walking or standing. I was discouraged. Although relieved to know what was wrong and why I hurt so badly, I wanted the doctor to ease the pain and reduce the swelling. I needed him to tell me I would be all right and this would not affect my CRPS, but he did not. Instead, he just told me to rest.

The upcoming procedure was less than a week away, and I was overwhelmed. Thinking that the CRPS might spread to my lower limb devastated me. Even with the extra pain relievers Dr. Vine prescribed and his reassurance that I would be okay, I could not shake my fears. I could barely handle my life now; how could I possibly cope if it intensified?

Two days before the implantation of the spinal cord stimulator, Dr. Vine's scheduler called me. Chris wanted to remind me of last-minute details and prep me on the upcoming procedure. The more he spoke, the more I became hesitant. It terrified me to think paralysis was possible if something went wrong. Chris repeatedly told me that Dr. Vine was one of the leading experts in spinal cord stimulation. Naturally there were risks involved, but he emphasized how Dr.

Vine had never made a significant error and the procedure sounded worse than it was. I had nothing to worry about. Everything would go smoothly.

The night before, I tossed and turned. Unable to sleep, I kept looking at the clock, counting down the hours and minutes. All I wanted was to be pain-free with full mobility of my hand, but I could not let go of the what-ifs. *What if something went wrong? What if the procedure failed? What if I was unable the walk the rest of my life?* Tears fell down my cheeks. I was scared and completely alone.

Not thinking about the time difference from Minnesota to California, I quickly picked up the phone and called Meredith. She did not answer. I figured she was asleep, so I left her a detailed message with specific instructions. If any problems arose tomorrow, I wanted her to be the one to tell Dylan, Emily, Kristin, Meghan and Nadine. As I hung up the phone, I automatically redialed her number and left a more upbeat message. My intention was not to worry her but to let her know that I accepted whatever the outcome might be. This had always been my decision. Now was not the time to second-guess or question. I believed I would be pain-free, and I knew the spinal cord stimulator would work.

$$\infty$$

January 12, 2001 was the big day.

I sat quietly in the back seat of the car as my parents and I headed to California Pacific Medical Center in San Francisco. While I held on tightly to my stuffed dog, Dad listened to sports radio. The ride was eerie; it reminded me of the drive to Stanford nearly twenty months ago.

We arrived at the hospital and found a parking spot close to the admissions entrance. Mom smiled and said we were pure of heart. I grinned because this was her favorite expression. I did not really know what it meant to be pure of heart, but I hoped it was a sign of good to come.

Still recovering from my fractured toe, I hobbled inside to check in. A hospital administrator then led the three of us to the elevator, and we exited on the second floor. Here I changed into a gown and was told to wait. Waiting was all I did these days: wait for a doctor, wait for test results, wait for answers. I was sick of constantly waiting.

It seemed like hours had passed before a man in light blue scrubs came to take me to pre-op. I tensed up as he pushed my hospital bed down the corridor and approached the restricted area. I knew this was where I would have to say my goodbyes to my parents, and I did not know what to say.

I wanted them to know that they were amazing, and I wished I could have taken away their fears by telling them I would be fine. Yet I knew I could not. As words were trivial in this moment, I just put on a brave face. I remember smiling and whispering *I love you* before being whisked behind the gray doors.

The orderly then took me to a long, narrow room filled with other beds and patients. This was the holding spot where all patients stayed until their doctors were ready. Curtains hung on both sides of the beds, giving a false sense of privacy. While I might not be able to see those lying next to me, I could definitely hear them. I listened to confidential discussions with doctors and knew of their procedures. I heard some crying, while others moaned or hacked. It was disconcerting to me that I was sharing such an extremely personal experience with complete strangers.

I began to acclimate to my new environment when Dr. Cob entered the room to start my IV line. Dr. Cob was Dr. Vine's fellow. I really liked him. He was younger than Dr. Vine and was very personable. While I hoped he would not leave me in this unfamiliar room, he disappeared as soon as the line was properly connected and the saline solution administered. I almost immediately became antsy. Each time I heard footsteps, I thought Dr. Vine was on his way. Then my anticipation would turn to disappointment when another attending passed my makeshift room to visit someone else.

At last, Dr. Vine came to see me. He asked the usual questions about how I was feeling and if I was ready. While I wanted to tell him I was terrified and freaking out, I calmly answered that I was doing all right except for the bothersome pain in my toe. It was in this moment that I realized how little I trusted or confided in anyone. For some reason, I refused to let others see my fear. *Why did I feel I needed to hide behind strong façade?*

Dr. Vine seemed unfazed by my foot and continued explaining what would happen once I was in the OR. Then he left the room to prepare, and I was alone again, dreading what was to come. When he was ready for me, a different hospital orderly pushed my bed into the cold operating room. My stomach churned as I looked around anxiously; the room even smelled sterile. Three unfamiliar faces helped me onto the steel table and positioned me on my stomach.

I struggled to get comfortable. After a nurse brought me warm blankets for my legs and fixed the blood-pressure cuff on my arm, I met the assisting anesthesiologist. His job was to have me comfortably sedated throughout the procedure. Soon, the medication into my IV made me feel warm and fuzzy.

I became more relaxed and amorous as the drugs continued to flow into my bloodstream. It was an odd, euphoric sensation where I lost the ability to decipher thoughts before speaking. Instead, I just uttered every little detail that crossed my mind. I started to express my great gratitude and affection for those in the room. I loved them all and thought it was silly that I was ever apprehensive about this procedure.

As I carried on with my adoring comments, Dr. Vine indicated he was ready to begin the implantation process. I remember he scolded me for moving my feet and wiggling my toes. After hearing him hushing me and ordering me not to move, I drifted in and out of consciousness. I was lost in an altered universe—that is, until a sharp jolt of pain brought me to my senses.

I soon squirmed on the table, screaming, "I feel it, I feel it!" A nurse squeezed my hand, telling me to remain still. She then spoke to another person in the room to get the assisting anesthesiologist, who had momentarily stepped out. My heart rate spiked as I tried to piece together what was happening. *What did she mean? "Find him?" Where had he gone?*

We were all uptight, waiting for the anesthesiologist to return. Dr. Vine and his fellows stood by the table, telling me I would be all right. I did not believe them—they were the ones who originally told me I had nothing to worry about. The pain was intense, and hearing Dr. Vine forbid me to move—as movement could lead to permanent nerve damage—angered me. I was quickly losing my patience. Finally, the assisting anesthesiologist administered more medication. Once back in my happy, carefree land, Dr. Vine and his crew continued with the procedure. My world went black once again and remained that way until I heard a muffled voice telling me it was over.

I kept staring at the round clock positioned above the nurses' station in the post-operative recovery room. There were three other beds in this large sanitized area, but I was the only patient. The odd sanitized smell, the monotonous sound of machines echoing and beeping, and the metallic taste in my mouth made me restless. I felt uneasy looking at the empty cots next to me. I wondered how much longer I would lie here before someone checked on me. *Where was everyone?* I was about to call out for a nurse when Dr. Vine returned from speaking with my parents. The procedure had been a success.

Although I would be able to go home that afternoon, the hospital needed to monitor my vitals for the next few hours. This was a precautionary measure to make sure I did not have any abnormal symptoms. As a hospital orderly wheeled me out of post-op and back to the second floor, I was reunited with my anxious parents. I was so happy to see their faces—and relieved I could still move my lower limbs. But the sedatives and general anesthetic made me lethargic and dizzy. Not feeling quite like myself made me quiet. Right now, I just wanted peace and quiet.

I was not in the room very long when I heard a knock on the door. A petite young woman peered into the room and introduced herself as a representative from the stimulator's manufacturing company. It was her job to show me how to properly use and care for the device. As she educated me about the machine, I learned how to turn the SCS on and off, change the intensity, and alter the frequency.

However, as she began to explain the more in-depth information, I became overwhelmed. I could not grasp how I could set off store alarms or why I could have trouble in airports and flying. It did not make sense how the sensations changed from sitting to standing or why the company did not recommend using it while driving. I also did not know why she stressed the importance of having a MedicAlert bracelet.

I glanced over at my parents. While I was unable to focus, they seemed to be listening attentively and even engaging in the conversation. Hearing them ask questions on how to register within the SCS database and where to obtain a MedicAlert bracelet was a relief; I did not need to worry, because Mom and Dad would take care of me. Once the representative answered all my parents' questions, she quietly stepped out of the room. I took a deep breath; the three of us were alone again, waiting for Dr. Vine.

Having fasted for more than twenty hours caused my stomach to gurgle. I was hungry and wanted food, but the nurse was apprehensive. She advised me to start with liquids. She only wanted to make sure I could handle sips of juice without getting sick. I had never been a fan of apple juice, so it surprised me how good it tasted. It was cold and sweet, and I just wanted more and more. In fact, I no longer asked for food—all I wanted now was apple juice.

I was already on my fourth glass when Dr. Vine visited. Since it was late in the afternoon and he did not want us to hit commuter traffic, he quickly went over the rules and instructions for the upcoming weekend. He had prescribed antibiotics and painkillers to reduce inflammation and avoid problematic infections. Again, I could not shower until after my follow-up three days later. This was to protect the bandages and stitches along my back from getting wet. If at any time we noticed pus or fluid leaking from the bandages, we had to contact him right away.

While Dr. Vine wanted me to relax as much as possible, he told me I could exercise by walking at a slow pace. I had to remember my back would ache because of the procedure, and I was not able to bend or lift. It was also common for my right upper buttocks to swell over the next couple of weeks from the generator. Although I should be fine, he continued to stress the importance of contacting him if the pain became unbearable or excruciating.

His answers were short and precise. I wanted to know how long the sharp pains from the procedure would last. I needed him to explain again how to use the remote control to change the intensity of spinal cord stimulator's frequency. I would have appreciated suggestions on how to sit or get comfortable. Yet before I had a chance to gather any of my thoughts, Dr. Vine was gone. It would now be up to my parents and me to make it through the next few days.

I was on my own.

∞

Being in my own bed two hours later was comforting yet strange. It felt surreal to think that hours earlier I was lying on an operating table, undergoing a spinal procedure. Every muscle, ligament and vertebra in my back ached. I started to toss and turn, unable to find a position that eased the overpowering pain and discomfort. I was miserable and knew I could not lie in bed much longer before I began to scream. I decided to move to the family room.

I tried sitting in our overstuffed reading chair, but that bothered me too. In an attempt to remove some of the strain from my back, Mom propped some pillows behind me for better support. She then placed other pillows on the foot ottoman while sticking small throw pillows on each side of me for further protection. I could hardly move because of the amount of padding, but I felt much better. The cushions somehow released the tension forming near and around my backside, and that was a huge relief.

I discovered almost immediately that I could not stay in the same position for a long period because my muscles would stiffen and atrophy. Realizing that movement eased the tightening pains, I decided to walk to our mailbox. That short of a distance did not seem to bother me, so I asked my parents to come with me to the end of the street and back home. After completing these brief walks a handful of times without lethargy or additional pain, I felt confident venturing a little farther and longer each time.

Soon I was able to walk three to five times a day for a half hour. Walking was my refuge from my day-to-day problems. I believed my body was creating the endorphins needed to ease my chronic pain and speed up my recovery. While trying to reconnect my brain to my ever-changing body, I listened to healing, inspirational music. These strolls were my only time to meditate and dream of a happier pain-free life.

It was difficult to focus on the slight improvements in my pain levels when the constant buzzing bothered me so much. I was frustrated with my progress. Although I had seen Dr. Vine every week since the operation, I wanted reassurance that the tender scar tissue, strained back muscles and swollen patch on my lower right side were still normal symptoms. To state it simply, I wanted answers as to why the pain was overriding my life.

Dr. Vine's office was running behind schedule during my next visit. Seeing that I was visibly upset and in an extreme amount of pain, the technician said I could meet with Dr. Cob instead. I did not care who I saw. At this point, I just needed to speak with someone who had a medical degree and who could explain what was happening to me.

Moments later, Dr. Cob walked into the room. He had a wide grin and cheerfully asked me how I was doing. I tried to seem positive, so I smiled back and told him I was great. I had no idea why I always said those same words. *I would have no reason to be here if I were really doing great.*

Ignoring my overly enthusiastic remark, he began inspecting my scars while feeling along my spine. When he finished he assured me I was still recovering nicely. I knew this was great news, but it did not change my misery or the fact that I could not handle the ever-present tingling sensation. He suggested I lower the beat intensity while mentioning how small stretches, like those done in yoga, could loosen scar tissue and relieve muscle tightness.

My ears perked. *Would yoga help?*

I wanted Mitzi's opinion before rushing off to the next available class. Since we had started working together, physical therapy had become my favorite part of the day. This was not because I liked enduring intense agony but because I enjoyed the company. I had met many other chronic pain patients, and began to form close relationships. In fact, my dearest confidante was Ann, a lovely person who was my parents' age. The two of us were inseparable. We laughed, cried, and shared our true feelings with each other. I could confide in her; she understood me. Ann was my "chicken soup" for the pain.

If physical therapy was like my second home, Mitzi was like my second mother. She was my lifeline. Not only did she help me sort out future treatment options, she also supported whatever decision I chose. I respected her and wanted her advice on this important matter.

Just from her initial expression, I could sense her hesitancy. While yoga was a great form of exercise and a perfect tool for meditation, she recommended I speak with the instructor first to verify credentials. I needed to work with a person who was well trained and knowledgeable, so there were proper modifications made to each movement. She knew this form of stretching could ease chronic pain. Therefore, her only reservation was the risk that I might injure myself if I followed an improper technique. It was imperative that I did not take the class if I was not completely satisfied or impressed with the teacher's answers. With my health resting in the balance, I would be better off leaving and finding an instructor who could appropriately assist me.

I was grateful for her suggestions, and once therapy finished, I headed straight to the gym. I arrived early so I had time to meet the teacher and tell her about my condition. She had never heard of CRPS or a spinal cord stimulator. But she listened as I explained the excruciating pain, the immobilized fist, and the battery located in my lower back that was connected to leads running alongside my spine. It was reassuring when she asked follow-up questions regarding the placement of the battery and the atrophy in my hand. I knew then that she would help.

She told me she would modify poses for me, but I had to stop immediately if I felt any unnecessary pains or discomfort. Then she positioned my mat in the front corner where she would be better able to watch me. I became a bit nervous as the room crowded with avid yogis. I knew absolutely nothing about yoga. Had I lost my mind? What made me think this was such a good idea? I took a deep breath and sat on my mat until the teacher turned on the meditation tape.

I glanced around the room as I followed her precise instructions. I was completely out of my element. The majority of the class already knew the poses, so they led themselves through the guided practice. Trying to do as many of the positions as possible, I did not even care that she altered my poses in comparison to the rest of the class. I was just proud of myself for stepping out of my comfort zone and even attempting to lay my right hand on the mat to balance my body.

The stretches were so intense that when I held a position, I could feel my legs and arms quiver beneath me. As I started each stretch, my back would burn. However, the more I breathed into the pose, the more I felt my muscles loosen. This was what I had wanted to happen. I might be weak, but I was not frail and I was not an invalid. Yoga had made me feel alive. *I had found relief in an alternative therapy.*

I told my parents about my experience with yoga that evening over dinner. Just by the manner in which they both placed their forks on their plates, I knew that they were not pleased. It was hard to ignore their deep emotional pain. I knew Mom and Dad were always worried about me, and looking at them only made me sadder. I never wanted to hurt my family, and yet every day, I was the reason their hearts ached. It was obvious they were skeptical of yoga. But they had no grounds to object. If Dr. Cob and Mitzi both said it was fine, they had to approve.

Mom decided to accompany me to the weekend class. We arrived at the gym early so I could speak to the instructor about CRPS, but she was running late. It should have been a huge red flag when I sensed she was distracted and stressed as I explained my situation. Instead of listening to my intuition, I let my ego get in the way, telling myself that I already knew the modifications.

The class began the same way, with downward-facing dog, warrior, and cobra poses. However, midway through the session, the instructor switched to poses that were unfamiliar to me. Immediately I heard a shallow *pop* and my pain increased. My body burned terribly. I sat down on the mat, flushed. Thinking I just needed a minute to breathe, I continued with the poses, but the sharp throbbing instantly returned. I did my best to fight through the agony, but it was useless. The pain would not subside.

The enormity of this setback overwhelmed me. I was frustrated and questioned whether my life would ever turn around. By now, the pain and disability controlled my every move. I felt like I was living a lie because I was not nearly as strong as everyone believed. I felt dead inside.

Recognizing that these were self-deprecating thoughts, I knew I needed to stay positive and not jump to conclusions. It was possible that I might have pushed myself a little too far and needed some time to recover. Yet the next day, I still was not feeling any better. The pain now seemed to heighten whenever I activated the spinal cord stimulator. I was devastated.

While I tried to dismiss the elevation in my discomfort when the device was on, I soon could not deny what was happening: the SCS was making me worse. Having to acknowledge that this treatment had failed crushed me. I was in absolute shock and could not understand how it had just stopped working. *Where did it all go wrong?*

This unusual response to the spinal cord stimulator also mystified Dr. Vine. He thoroughly checked my spine and carefully felt each vertebra to determine whether a lead had shifted or moved. There was slightly more inflammation around the battery site and near the three scars, but that would have only caused more sensitivity in those areas. Nothing seemed to be out of place. In fact, my back appeared to be healing very well. He was perplexed.

Not wanting to make a rash decision, Dr. Vine wanted to see if the swelling would decrease in a few days. Maybe time would help the SCS work again. However, in the end, the spinal cord stimulator just stopped operating properly. As much as I wanted this therapy to be my answer, I was no longer willing to deal with the regular manipulations to the stimulator's frequency. It was hard enough to cope with my daily pain, let alone handle the provoked suffering from the doctors constantly tampering with the SCS. This was not the right treatment for me, and I wanted the device removed. *I had had enough.*

Chapter 11

Desperation

It was difficult not to be disillusioned after the failed attempt with the spinal cord stimulator. I tried to keep my spirits up as Dr. Vine figured out the next course of treatment, but the pain kept escalating. With the oral medicines not working, I had difficulty sleeping and fell further into despair. I was desperate for relief. Seeing me become more miserable with each passing hour, Dr. Vine knew he had to act quickly. He scheduled an implantation of an epidural catheter for the following day. Time was of the essence.

The epidural catheter was a fine plastic tube positioned in the epidural space of the spine. Left in place for up to two weeks, the catheter continuously administered anesthetics and narcotics into my system. The hope was for these drugs to bring me much-needed pain relief. However, because of my recent spinal cord stimulator implantation, this procedure would be two-fold. In order to implant the catheter properly, Dr. Vine would first have to remove the leads from the stimulator.

On our way into the city to return to California Pacific Medical Center, my parents and I followed our now typical routine. I was in the back seat, stoically holding my stuffed dog, Mom rode on the passenger side, and Dad drove while listening to sports radio. It was pathetic that after two and a half years, nothing seemed to change on these drives. I looked out the window at the dreary March day, and my mind shifted to my brother.

Dan had been a rock throughout this entire ordeal. Not once had he made me feel guilty for disrupting his life. Although he held no animosity toward me, I felt like I destroyed his childhood. I was the reason he hurt. I caused his pain and worry; I was my family's problem. Tears silently fell down my face as I vowed to make it up to all of them. Someday, I promised myself, my parents and brother would be happy again. *Someday I would make them proud.*

As I walked through the hospital doors, the sterile smell alarmingly comforted me. The whole concept of hospital protocol was now just a part of my typical life. I knew where to go, what offices to visit, and what information I needed to provide. I understood I had to extend my left arm in order to receive my ID bracelet, and knew which floor specialized in what field. The hospital environment had merged into part of my daily existence; it was routine and standard.

After going through admittance, I went to pre-op to get ready for the upcoming procedure. Strangely, I was not even nervous. Since I had grown accustomed to such practices, I was numb to the shock value. Nearly twenty minutes passed before Dr. Vine visited to go over the proceedings. This was when my left hand became clammy as my heart sputtered.

I always got uneasy right before operations. It was not that I was afraid of needles, but I feared having to be awake and semi-conscious. Listening to the surgeons, nurses and clinicians bothered me. It was eerie to know exactly what was happening every second.

Luckily, the unnerving feeling would subside as soon I received the medications. Then I would become dopey and light-headed. Reverting to my childhood days, I would see myself riding my bike around the driveway, playing outside on the grass, and chasing butterflies. I would forget about reality and revel in the past, where I was still naïve with *big* dreams for my future. I would remember the feeling of being whole, healthy and complete.

The procedure itself involved very few steps. Once Dr. Vine administered a local anesthetic, he took a small needle and located the epidural space. Threading the catheter through the needle, he subsequently anesthetized another area. Inserting a similar needle, he tunneled the catheter under my skin in order to provide stability. Dr. Vine further secured the catheter with stitches and a sterile dressing. After that, he began to administer the drugs.

I woke in the recovery room to a hospital tech preparing to move me to the pulmonary care unit (PCU). The medications I received during the procedure still had not worn off; I was woozy as we made our way out of the surgical ward. My parents were waiting in their normal spot, right outside the OR doors. They simultaneously smiled, grateful their little girl was returned to them safely. Dad told me Dr. Vine spoke to them and was optimistic that this treatment would control my pain. I then heard Mom say that they loved me and that I was a trooper.

Although I appreciated the encouragement, I saw through their masks. They could not protect me from the agony I would endure. As much as they would have liked to shield me from the risks associated with the catheter, they were helpless in the situation. When everything was said and done, I had to face the pain, shame and unknowns alone. This was my journey to overcome, and I had to rise to the challenge.

I switched beds, and the staff reconnected me to machines in the PCU. As nurses monitored my heart, liver, and kidney function, my parents stayed as close to me as humanly possible.

The pulmonary care unit was the intensive care unit for heart patients; it was impossible for Mom and Dad to deny the severity of my condition. Looking at their somber expressions saddened me. My health was destroying my family. I wished I could make their emotional pain disappear. *I would have done anything to see them laugh.*

Soon the room became blurry as I began to drift in and out of consciousness. With the multitude of medications impairing my senses, I lived each day in a drugged-out stupor. I drooled, slept, and absently watched television as I continued to drink a vast amount of apple juice. Mom and Dad took turns visiting me while Dr. Vine came each night to review my chart. I had nurses, interns and staff members entering and exiting my room on an hourly basis.

While the constant barrage of company tired me, having such a precise schedule gave me stability. I liked knowing breakfast would arrive at 7:00, doctors would visit at 4:00, and nurses' shifts would change every twelve hours. In a world with so many variables, having some order and direction calmed me. It gave me a false sense of control.

There were some minor changes in my pain levels. Areas that once burned now felt completely numb. I could rub my forearm and feel nothing. Although these sensations were strange, it was positive news. The only problem was that I had yet to detect any signs of loosening in the clenched hand. I still had not regained the movement in my right limb crucial to my recovery.

I was frustrated and depressed. How many times would I put my hope into a treatment that did not seem to help me? Even though I knew the importance of staying optimistic, I could not help but wonder if I was destined to suffer for my entire life. Nothing had gone as planned so far. My world was in shambles, and I could not seem to escape the wreckage.

Things turned from bad to worse when my health insurance company no longer saw the need for me to be an inpatient. They felt this particular therapy was futile after seven days without enough significant changes. I wanted to vomit when I learned I needed to leave the hospital. In my mind, the treatments were working; numb was much better than agonizing torture. I could not understand why I had to stop a treatment when I had not suffered any adverse reactions to the medications.

Dr. Vine felt the same way. Since the incision site looked good and was infection-free, he believed we should leave the catheter intact and continue therapy from home. However, this meant my insurance company would need to approve a home health nurse. It took more than a day of back-and-forth phone calls and paperwork submissions before my health insurance company agreed to twice-weekly home visits. This meant I did not need to give up a possible cure just because mobility had not returned.

This was a big moment for me. Although I had already trusted Dr. Vine, watching him fight for me re-affirmed his commitment to my health. I now knew he would always act with my best interest at heart. For too long, I had dealt with doctors who questioned my pain and discarded my disease. Yet that was the past. Dr. Vine was different; he wanted me *better*.

∞

I was glad to be home. Not wanting to hinder my chance to heal, I followed the strict rules Dr. Vine set forth. I did not exercise or sweat. I took sponge baths instead of showers, and remembered not to hold, lift or reach. Physical therapy also began immediately. Having the added assistance of the medicine allowed me to push myself farther. I made sure to finish my desensitization work, and I let Mitzi stretch my hand for as long as she wanted. This was an opportunity for me to gain strides. I was determined to get better.

In the end, it did not matter. Three days of intense therapy and stretching could not save the epidural catheter. After noticing a slight rash near the incision site during a bandage change, the risk of infection proved to be too large a threat. Dr. Vine had to remove the device.

I remember leaving his office in tears. Nothing ever went right for me, and because I felt compelled to keep up my strong façade, I was living a lie. This pain had tested my core values and beliefs. While I still believed everything happened for a reason, I could not stop wondering why it had to be so hard. How could I continue to keep hope and faith alive?

Life went from bad to downright awful in the midst of my pity party. Without any warning, my entire right side fell limp. I could not walk or raise my right arm. Both limbs hung flimsily at my side. I tried to talk, but my facial muscles were impaired and my speech slower. I had no idea what was happening to me.

Mom called Dr. Vine. Concerned that I might have suffered a stroke, he instructed us to go to the hospital immediately. My heart pounded faster and faster as Mom drove. I was only twenty years old. Who suffers a stroke at such a young age? Sweat dripped down my temples, and my eyes burned from holding back tears. I was petrified. While all I wanted to do was scream and cry, I remained silent. I had to stay strong and act positive. I needed Mom to see that everything would be fine. I would find a way to get through this too.

This was the first time I did not wait to see an ER doctor. Instead, nurses immediately rushed to my side to check my vitals. No one spoke *to* me; rather, they spoke *over* me. As one person wanted to know my blood pressure, another yelled for my temperature. Multiple sets of hands placed electrodes on my chest, while someone told me to breathe. Having so many people frantically working on me frightened me. I just stared at the bright lights while thinking I could die.

Luckily, I was in stable condition, so the hospital ran a CAT scan and an MRI. The tests were long and draining, as I had to lay still for an extended amount of time. All I thought about were the upcoming results; I just wanted to know if I had a stroke.

Learning that I had to wait overnight for answers outraged me. I could feel my blood pressure rise as I became more irritated and flustered. As I only received blank looks and vague responses, it felt like my nightmare would never end. It was as if I was asking the FBI about a private case—no one would tell me anything.

After another hour connected to monitors, the doctor deemed me fine to go home. I was shocked, since I still had trouble walking. How could they send me home without first ruling out a stroke? I limped out of the hospital holding on to Mom for support. My body shook as the tears started falling. Why did it have to be so hard?

I looked up as we exited the radiology department to see Dr. Sands. Dr. Sands happened to be the head radiologist at the hospital, and his son had gone to elementary school with me. After speaking to Mom, he ordered the results, and within minutes had the report: I had not suffered a stroke.

It seemed that a small amount of the medicine had leaked from the catheter during its removal. This was simply an adverse reaction that should subside without any permanent damage in a couple of days. Although he advised me to take it easy and use a cane whenever walking, he felt confident that my gait, speech, and muscle control should improve with time.

I learned a valuable lesson that day. My excruciating pain was also my teacher. Good existed in this world, and each day there was a reason to be happy. Yes, I was very sick and did not have answers or a plausible treatment plan. However, I still had hope. I believed I would heal, and I had my supportive friends and loving family to lean on. While the agony I endured might have been horrific and lonesome, I was never truly alone. *The Universe was always watching out for me.*

∞

The pain in my arm continued to intensify, and soon the disease began to spread. I had already lost complete mobility of my right hand and half of my functional arm use. Now, when I would suffer a flare-up, the pain would travel to my back and the left side of my body. If Dr. Vine could not find a way to contain the pain soon, the disease would ravage my whole body. That had to be avoided at all costs. Desperate times called for desperate measures. Running out of alternatives, my only option was narcotics.

This was not a decision Dr. Vine took lightly. After already spending numerous nights in the ER because of allergic complications from Vicodin, codeine and Valium, morphine derivatives were all that I had left. It came down to this: I needed relief, and opioids alleviated severe pain.

I quickly glanced at Dad—who seemed to be taking the news much harder than I was. He was white and stiff and looked lost and distressed. I could tell he wondered what happened to his baby girl. It made me nauseated to think that while I was relieved to know that options existed, my Dad's entire world had collapsed on top of him.

An outsider might have assumed that Dr. Vine handed Dad a death sentence when he gave him the script for Oramorph. Making one final plea before the doctor walked out of the room,

Dad raised his voice in a desperate manner. "Are you sure this is safe for Nicole to ingest? Is morphine really the only drug that can help her?"

Sensing the despair in my father's voice, Dr. Vine once again assured my dad that I would be fine and that morphine might actually be beneficial to my health. My parents had nothing to fear, because I would be taking the smallest possible dose. He would be watching and monitoring my body's response very carefully, so if anything seemed abnormal, he would stop the drugs. He understood that there was a stigma attached to morphine in society. But this was a suitable drug for chronic pain sufferers, and studies proved it decreased pain levels. This was the correct course of action to lower my pain.

The car ride home was stifling. Neither of us knew what to say, and after watching Dad's reaction in the office, I was too concerned I would say something wrong. I knew that needing such a potent drug was alarming, but I desperately wanted the morphine. I would have tried anything at this point if it might ease the searing pains. Therefore, although I was shocked to find myself using an opioid, I accepted this treatment. But Dad could not; his little girl was not supposed to suffer.

I went straight to the family room to lie on the couch when we arrived home. I could hear my parents talking in hushed voices in the kitchen. They were obviously terrified by the depth of their daughter's disease. However, if there was the slightest chance that morphine could relieve some of my anguish, my parents knew they had to do it. No matter how uncomfortable this treatment plan made them, they wanted me pain-free. I knew they would have found a way to go to the moon and back if there were a promising cure—and that made me feel guiltier. I was ashamed to be solely responsible for my family's heartache. *I was the virus infecting my family's well-being and future.*

Finding the Oramorph was difficult. My parents called every nearby pharmacy, only to discover no one carried this particular type of morphine. Most places said they could order the prescription, but it would take a few days for the drug to arrive. That meant I would have to live in agonizing pain even longer, and to me, that was unacceptable. Without any luck, Mom then dialed the last drug store Dr. Vine recommended, and the owner answered.

He informed Mom that while he did not have any in stock, he would be able to overnight the medication to his store. He then checked some of the hospital pharmacies to locate a small portion of the prescription that could hold me over until his supply arrived the following afternoon. This was what I needed to hear. It was just another sign proving to me that there was a Higher Power guiding me on this path, and its light could fill my darkness.

My heart raced the first time I swallowed morphine. In the past, the only times I had heard this drug mentioned was in reference to a terminally ill person. The realization that I was taking this type of medication at twenty years old startled me. I could no longer lie to myself: I had to be very sick for a doctor to prescribe morphine.

As my body absorbed the tablet, I started to relax from my head down to my toes. My mind seemed hazy, and I could not focus. Then my eyes drooped while my body temperature rose.

Soon the throbbing and burning declined in my upper-right extremity. I could not believe it: *I actually felt better.*

A temporary break from my excruciating suffering was what I had been waiting for. I was still in pain, but the level of anguish dropped three considerable points: from a staggering nine to a strong six. Yet little did I know that I was walking down a slippery slope. From that day forward, my true journey through the medical system had begun. I would stop at nothing to regain my life.

∞

It did not take long before one morphine derivative was not enough. Soon Dr. Vine had to increase my medication and prescribe a second drug known as morphine sulfate immediate release (MSIR). I wanted so badly for the pain to end that I did not care that I had to deal with migraines, constipation, nausea, loss of appetite, night sweats and extreme sugar cravings. I just wanted to feel that numb sensation, yet even the strong painkillers could not kill my pain.

Over the course of the next year, I found myself hospitalized two other times for sleep deprivation and pain control. Dr. Vine would have to heavily medicate me in the PCU in a last-ditch effort to ease the ever-growing pain. Nurses would again attach me to heart monitors and pulse-rate devices, while Dr. Vine ordered a morphine patient-controlled analgesia (PCA) pump. My life was falling apart.

While I received my typical amount of oral medicine every day, I also could self-administer an additional 10 mg of liquid morphine every ten minutes. Using the PCA in conjunction with the Oramorph and MSIR worried the nursing staff. It was their opinion that the doctors were overmedicating me. In fact, I was consuming more opioids than a 300-pound man dying of cancer would have.

Many nurses were livid with my doctors. They viewed my current treatment as medically unethical and detrimental to my overall health. Some only verbally expressed their fears to work on me, while others actually refused to give me my medication. Although the nurses had my best interest at heart, I saw their actions differently; *I was pissed.* I felt they were denying me the chance to live. I needed these drugs to make it through the day, and they did not understand that.

Thinking the nurses had it in for me caused me to question those assisting in my care. Fears that a staff member unfamiliar with CRPS or not used to dealing with a patient in excruciating chronic pain would hurt me inspired my parents to bring a one-inch binder to the hospital that contained general information on my disease. After too many emergency room visits where doctors brought in medical texts to show me the two paragraphs that pertained to my disorder, we knew it was our job to educate and teach. *I had to protect myself.*

While the majority of my stays are cloudy in memory because of the medications, I still have vivid images of certain moments. I remember screaming out in sheer agony while my parents tried to hush me. I could still see Dad's eyes brimming with tears and Dan fidgeting around the room, trying to think of things to say. I know Mom spent nights with me to make sure I received the proper medications. I recall Dylan carrying on normal conversations as I drooled or screamed, and Kathie always bringing me my favorite chocolate milkshake. I remember Meredith visiting whenever she was home from college, to sit at the side of my bed, and Meghan sending beautiful bouquets of flowers.

Other memories include the cold apple juice that I drank by the gallon and my aimless walks up and down the halls. I know I received a beautiful cross from Kathy and Jim, and remember insisting on wearing diapers to bed. I still can feel Peggy and Kathy putting my hair in a tight bun so it would not touch my shoulders. My own hair sometimes caused me to shriek from the excruciating pain. I know the Callaghan, Kelber, Quinlan, Moriarty, and O'Brien families took turns visiting so Mom and Dad had a break. I even remember Dad trying to jump out the window and Mom hopping around in a bunny costume from my many hallucinations. Yet what I recall the most was the pain, sorrow and guilt on everybody's faces. *I was hurting everyone I loved.*

I was clueless when it came to the extent of my problems and the progression of my disease. Because I wanted relief from my daily torment so badly, hospital visits did not bother me. However, this was only a temporary solution. After seven to fourteen days as an inpatient, I would go home until the next time I reached that point of desperation. It was a vicious cycle. The hospital never *fixed* the problem but only hid the underlying issue.

I would continue taking my oral medications at a higher dose whenever I left the hospital. Even though the Oramorph and MSIR lessened some of the pain, it mainly deadened my ability to respond to it. It jumbled my thoughts and made it more difficult for me to react to stimuli. Hearing also became a problem. With a now-constant droning noise ringing in my eardrums, I learned to read lips and nod my head. My 20/20 vision became impaired, and I needed bifocal glasses. Soon I depended on more drugs just to counteract the side effects.

The minimal decline in my pain level did not change the fact that I was still miserable. My inflamed fist burned, and my tightened joints ached. While I had no choice but to stretch and desensitize the hand, physical therapy only aggravated my condition. I tried to push through the agony, but I continued to regress. I could not escape the torment. I had reached my breaking point, and Dr. Vine needed to help me. It was his job to get me better.

∞

Thankfully, Dr. Vine had recently learned of a new study published in the Netherlands that called for an intraspinal drug infusion using Bacolfen. He would implant an intrathecal catheter in my lower spine that would continuously infuse the drug into my system. However, he did not want to implant a pump without first deeming the treatment successful. That was why he followed typical protocol for the Bacolfen trial by implanting an intrathecal catheter for continuous infusion while using an automated IV device.

Because the placement of the catheter held a risk of neurological injury, I would be conscious throughout the procedure. He would also use a fluoroscope X-ray to record images on the operating room's monitor. After locating the L2-3 space in the intrathecal region of my spine, Dr. Vine would mark and anesthetize the skin with lidocaine and bupivacaine. Then he would slowly advance the catheter with the guidance of the fluoroscopic device to the desired location. To minimize the risk of its migration or dislodgement, he would anchor it using a wire-reinforced spinal catheter that secured to the tough connective tissues in the surrounding area.

My mind was spinning; this was a lot of information to comprehend. He would have to hospitalize me for observation during the duration of the trial. While the intraspinal catheter had been proven risky, it could lead to astonishing results. Moreover, there was a higher probability I would regain mobility from this procedure, since it focused on reduced spasticity over reduced pain.

I knew I had to do it, even though the small case study concerned me. After three years of pain and disability holding me back from living, it was time to take a chance. Therefore, I was back in a hospital gown one week later lying on the cold surgical table at California Pacific Medical Center.

Yet nothing changed. Dr. Vine reiterated the fact that I might not *feel* any different, because it was not supposed to lower my pain. He was watching for mini-muscle spasms or a relaxed look to the clenched hand. I just needed to be patient. Although the study had shown slight improvements in a relatively quick manner, my response time could be longer. I could not lose hope in the thirty-sixth hour. I still had five days left in the trial.

Those were the longest days I have ever spent in a hospital. I was on a normal hospital ward because I did not need the constant care and attention provided on the PCU. Unless there was an emergency, I only saw a nurse during shift changes. I was bored from limited channels on the television and headaches that made reading impossible. Seeing no changes in my pain or my spasm only angered me. *When would I get better?*

Either Dr. Vine or his attending fellow visited me each day to document my progress. I was like a broken record asking the same question day in and day out. How long would it take before the treatment began to work? Their response would also always be the same: "We just do not know."

I was living in hell. All I did was sit and stare at my hand, pleading for it to open, flinch, twitch or tremble. Yet nothing ever happened. Dr. Vine confirmed my worst fears after five days of no improvements: the procedure did not work, and I would need to leave the hospital.

The news of hearing that another treatment had failed devastated me. By this point, I was so sick of being ill. I had grown tired of having to stay positive and downplay my misery. I could not stand the guilt I felt for hurting my loved ones. I just wanted to be in college and date guys and go to parties. I wanted to laugh—really, really laugh.

I wanted to be normal.

∞

Soon it was August 28, 2001, which marked my third year of dealing with doctors and pain. Two weeks had passed since I had left the hospital, and I was meeting with Dr. Vine to discuss the removal of the intrathecal catheter. With Dad coming along to learn when the procedure would take place, I was hopeful for some good news. *Maybe he had heard of some new procedure, drug, or alternative therapy that might help me.* I was looking for anything that could keep my dream of being pain-free and physically independent alive.

However, my intentions for this office visit did not coincide with Dr. Vine's. He spoke candidly about the extent of my condition. While I already knew there was not a cure for me, I believed remission was still possible. Dr. Vine no longer did. Since the disease kept progressing, even with the procedures and prescribed medications, the likelihood that I would regain mobility or pain relief was bleak. He was not giving up on my health, but it was time for me to accept my disability.

As he could do little for me right now, he only wanted me to visit him once a month for prescription refills. He expected me to continue my sessions with Ellen while attending physical and occupational therapy with Mitzi. I stopped listening when Dr. Vine began talking about the catheter removal.

Had he really told me to learn to deal with the pain and make the most out of the life I could still lead? Did he really say that I would never get better, and that the pain would not go away?

Trembling, I bit my inner lip so I would not cry. There was no way I would ever accept such a prognosis. I was too young to accept defeat. Scientists were discovering new medical advances each day. I *would* beat this—I just had to hold on to hope.

I fought back the tears as I walked out of his office. My mind wandered while Dad drove. How could I deal with this for the rest of my life? I could not even care for myself. My parents had to cook for me, tie my shoes, drive me, and even sometimes dress and bathe me. Who would ever love me?

When I finally looked out the front window, I was surprised to see that Dad had exited the freeway five miles before our house. "Honey, you are going to heal. I do not want that conversation to sway your spirits or your beliefs. Your mom and I are so proud of you. You are going to lead a normal, happy, pain-free life."

He finished talking right as we pulled into a Volkswagen dealership. "Haven't you always wanted a Jetta?" A huge smile appeared across my face as tears rolled down my cheeks. "I know you are not driving now, but you will again. This car is the proof that your mom and I *know* you will heal."

I was stunned. Words could not describe how I felt, and I feared that speaking would only take away from the significance of the moment. This car symbolized a new beginning for me: a life not controlled by pain or disease. If my parents could still see light in the depths of darkness, so could I. I was not going to let any doctor rob me of my dreams. I was going to win this battle—and this car would remind me of that.

Chapter 12

Botched Surgery

We scheduled the removal of the intrathecal catheter at an outpatient clinic near our home. By this point, it felt normal to be awake for a surgery. There was no reason to be anxious, because I already knew the protocol. I had to fill out paperwork before heading to the pre-operating room. Then I had to change into a gown so a nurse could start my IV. After that, I would have to wait by myself until the staff was ready in the OR. The process was simple.

I remember lying face down on the steel operating table, only to peer up and see a room bustling with energy. While I did not recognize anyone besides the nurse who connected my IV, each person seemed to have a specific job to attend to while waiting for Dr. Vine. The commotion made me nervous. I did not like to see my procedural team stirring around in what looked like a disorganized manner. I wanted them to look calm and ready. *I wanted them prepared.*

Dr. Vine entered the room as soon as I received the pain relievers and slight sedatives. He reassured me that while there were risks because of the close proximity to the intrathecal region of my spine, he had taken all the necessary precautions to ensure a safe operation. He went on to explain how he would also perform a spinal tap after removing the catheter. The spinal tap, or lumbar puncture (LP), removed fluid from my spinal canal for diagnostic purposes. He needed my cerebrospinal fluid to make sure I did not have any inflammatory disease of the central nervous system like Meningitis, Multiple Sclerosis or Parkinson's disease.

He kept talking as he sterilized my backside with a cold antiseptic. I felt a sting from him injecting the local anesthetic. Soon, noises and sounds began to muffle together as the medicine took effect. Despite having felt cold minutes earlier, I now had a fuzzy feeling. My pursed mouth relaxed into a smile, and I let out a sigh of relief. I thought of fields of daisies and sunflowers while drifting off to la-la land. I imagined faint laughter and the sun warming my back. I was happy in this medicated euphoria.

Suddenly, a sharp wave of pain swept over my body. I screamed. *What was that?* I felt my flesh burn from Dr. Vine cauterizing my blood vessels. I then felt him slice through my skin with a blade as hands tore and peeled my bodily tissues. This torment was actually real. In disbelief, I lifted my head and swung my arms, hoping he would stop. While shrieking for mercy, I kicked my legs up and down. They were hurting me!

Dr. Vine was the next to shout and bark orders. If I ever wanted off that table, I had to stop moving. It was imperative that I lie still to avoid serious nerve damage. My heart palpitated, hearing his forceful voice, and by the time two other nurses rushed into the OR, I was drenched in sweat. The pain was excruciating. As they replaced the damp blankets with warm, clean ones, I heard Dr. Vine instruct three other people to hold my body down. Immediately I felt pressure on each leg and between my shoulder blades. Why were they anchoring me to the table?

Dr. Vine again promised not to touch me until the nurses had administered me more medications. However, he needed me to quit fighting his staff, because they were keeping me safe. I knew I should have listened to him, but I was in shock. I began gasping for breath and moaning as an unfamiliar nurse held my left hand and patted my head. She tried her best to calm me, but it was too late. Soon, every conversation in the OR merged into one confusing paragraph.

Why can you not stop? I am in pain. We cannot stop now, Nicole, because we are in the intrathecal space. It hurts too much! We are almost done. You need to be strong and lie still. Give her *more* medicine. But she has already exceeded the allotted amount for her age and weight, Dr. Vine. Give her some more! Nicole, this is it. You cannot have any more anesthetic, so if this does not work, we are going to have to transport you to the hospital in order to finish the procedure. We do not want to do that. I almost removed the catheter, and then I just need to do the spinal tap. Do you think you can handle it?

I tried to pick up my head to see what was happening, but someone held it firmly in place. It felt as if I had been lying on that awful table for hours, and Dr. Vine still was not done. The room spun as I began to sweat profusely. I panicked when I heard the buzzing, vibrating sounds. *What was he doing?* A rush of shooting pains shot through my body as Dr. Vine's drill made contact with my skin. I cried out that I still felt it. I began wailing that I still felt the pain! *Please, God, help me.*

Dr. Vine was furious. "Nicole, you need to calm down and stop moving. We are almost done. Maybe ten more minutes." Inconsolable sobs flowed from me. I again tried to break free from the hands that clamped me down to the table. The wretched smell of burning skin reminded me of pork chops cooking on the stove. The drilling made me think the doctor had secured a nail into my spine. The slicing of skin felt like the worst paper cut imaginable. As the staple gun pinched my flesh together, I shouted at them to stop…only my pleading went unanswered. *Why was this happening? Why had the medicine not worked?*

Then there was nothing. The nightmare ended, and I watched Dr. Vine silently exit the operating room. Tears continued to fall down my face, even after the physical hell was over. I could not stop shaking or sweating. The post-op buzzed with frantic nurses monitoring my heart and blood pressure. Everyone appeared on edge, waiting for my stats to stabilize. I kept asking how this could have happened, but no one spoke. My life had turned into a horror film.

Hearing voices say I was in medical shock terrified me. I had no idea what that meant, but figured it could not be good. Unable to form words, I stared at the bright lights, listened to the beeping monitors, and waited for my teeth to stop chattering. I was scared and wanted my parents. I wanted Dad to make it better, like he did when I was a frightened child. I wanted Mom to hug me and rock me to sleep, as she did when I had a bad dream. However, I knew this time they would not be able to help me. My parents would never be able to erase these haunting memories from my mind.

Finally, Dad entered the post-op and sat by my bed. Just seeing him there made me cry. His eyes brimmed with tears and his voice quivered as he told me everything would be okay. He then brushed my sweaty hair away from my cheek and smiled. I wished I had the energy to grin, but instead I shivered and sniffled. Even though he was trying to stay strong for me, he could not hide his heartache over being unable to save his little girl. I turned my head away from him. All I wanted now was to go home. I just needed this day to end.

I did not speak during the short drive home. As I gazed out the passenger window, my heart beat faster. It was difficult not to feel upset or uneasy after what had happened. *How could the medicine not work?* My head began to throb and I shuddered. This day would permanently scar me. It was impossible to think life could return to normal now. Biting my lip to keep the tears at bay, I realized that my life was no longer in my hands. I had been through too much, and I would never be the same.

We arrived home to Mom and Dan preparing the dinner I requested earlier that morning: pork chops with grilled onions and brown rice. The smell hit me like a ton of bricks. My legs shook as I walked into the family room. My sight instantly blurred, and all I saw were black-and-white dots. Remembering how helpless I was lying on the operating table, smelling my burnt skin made my stomach churn. I gagged. I could not eat supper that evening. Instead, I cried myself to sleep, wondering how I would ever be able to move on.

The next afternoon, my health took an even more drastic turn for the worse. Less than twenty-four hours after the botched procedure, I developed the post-lumbar puncture headache otherwise known as a spinal migraine. I had never experienced such instantaneous agony. I literally was talking with Dan one minute, only to feel as if my head would split open the next second.

The piercing pains left me paralyzed. I remember lying in the fetal position on my parents' bed, thinking that a jackhammer was stuck in my brain. Sounds and lights made the migraine worse. Moaning in desperation, I felt as if an ice pick was plucking through my ears while someone slashed the top of my skull. I could not escape the hell. I clung to my stuffed dog as I cried and quivered in the dark. No one had told me it would be this bad.

My parents were at a complete loss. Although Dr. Vine warned them that this could happen within forty-eight hours of the spinal tap, neither of them had any inclination that it would be this brutal. They had tried to make me comfortable by darkening the room, putting fans near my head, and bringing me my favorite blanket. Kathie had come over with Red Bulls while Mom put a cool washcloth on my forehead. Yet I was still miserable, and the weight of the wet towel increased my pain. Running out of options, Dad finally called Dr. Vine.

He needed advice on how to handle the situation if this migraine lasted days or required a blood patch. There must be some type of medication to bring me some relief. However, Dr. Vine only had discouraging news. Nothing but time would ease my pain. We just had to wait it out. His only suggestions were to lie flat and drink plenty of fluids. Headaches typically worsened in an upright position, and caffeine sometimes reduced the discomfort. Then he hung up, leaving my parents once again scrambling to pick up the pieces of my broken life.

I remember Dad lying next to me on the bed after learning that there was not a quick fix for my torture. He just held my hand as tears continued to stream down my hot face. As I stared into his dull eyes, I begged and pleaded with him to make it stop. Except I knew he was helpless. He would have done anything to make the agony cease, but he could only squeeze my hand and tell me I was brave. I did not understand why everyone thought I was so courageous. I did not feel that way; I felt weak and frail.

"Daddy, make it stop. Please help me. I cannot do this any longer."

I fell apart as the pain became more and more intense. Thrusting my knees into my abdomen, I swayed from side to side while sobbing uncontrollably. I kept insisting to Dad that I was not strong enough to handle the agony. Then I began to question God. What did He see in me that made him certain I could overcome the hell and torture?

Dad stayed with me the entire nine hours the horrific spinal migraine lasted. He listened to me verbally question whether I had the strength and power to continue this battle. He held my hand tighter at the pinnacle of my misery. His presence helped me survive. It was from this experience I realized how lucky I was to have my parents. I knew I would be with them by my side.

While I should have been relieved this nightmare was over and that the cerebrospinal fluid came back negative for all diseases, it took weeks for my life to return to normal. Just hearing a hammer or drill caused me to tense and shake, remembering the nightmare on the surgical table. The crackling, popping sound of oil poured into a hot skillet made my hairs stand on end as I recalled Dr. Vine singeing my blood vessels. I cringed while watching people casually staple papers, because it reminded me of how the doctors fastened my skin together. But it was the smell of sizzling pork chops that was the most horrible reminder of the flesh-burning incident. I was an emotional wreck who could not escape the mental and emotional suffering, and yet, I knew it was time to move forward.

I understood that living in the past would not get me better. I was too young to lose hope, and it was important for me to stay optimistic and keep a positive outlook. I only had two options: either I believed my miracle would come, or I despised life and lived miserably. While I might have lost control of my body, I refused to continue to let the disease control my thoughts. Therefore, I chose happiness and health over misery and illness. But trusting I would heal became a harder challenge once the disease began to spread to my left side.

∞

It was mid-October when my left hand mysteriously closed into a fist. All I remember was going to bed with mobility and waking up unable to move my left hand. I immediately saw Dr. Vine's first hypothesis was that I strained my brachial plexus, an arrangement of nerve fibers running from the spine and neck that proceeded into the arm. It was responsible for the sensory, motor, and autonomic fibers of the arm. Since needles did not seem to bother me, he decided to administer a brachial plexus nerve block that afternoon in his office.

He sterilized the area around my collarbone before injecting the local anesthetic to numb the skin around the procedural site. Then he pushed on my neck until he found the exact placement and began administering the medication. I sat perfectly still, hoping I would feel relief. The pain in my left arm was still present, and my left hand was still immobile. Nothing changed. It had not worked. The brachial plexus had not worked.

Dr. Vine was stupefied, while I was just depressed. Having lost mobility in both hands turned me into a basket case. I could not eat, dress, bathe, or use the bathroom on my own. My attitude on life turned jagged. I refused to leave my bedroom unless I was going to a doctor's appointment. I did not talk unless I needed to answer a question. I only consumed pureed soups, smoothies, or milkshakes, because Mom had to wipe my bottom. With my dignity taken from me, there was no way I could stay hopeful. This was the first time I truly felt despondent and depressed.

I quickly understood that I did not have the luxury of waiting. Time mattered when dealing with CRPS, and I wanted a second specialist's opinion. Dr. Oz was a graduate of the John Hopkins Medical School, which he so proudly referred to as the *Oz* of all medical programs. He was arrogant, cocky, and ego-driven, but Mitzi believed he was one of the best orthopedic surgeons in the area. She told me when something was wrong you should go directly to the best. I agreed.

I was desperate, walking into his office for my initial consult. With Dr. Vine having no other suggestions, the fear of losing both my arms if Dr. Oz could not help me increased. My parents seemed just as terrified and anxious as I did. We all knew my future was riding on the outcome of this appointment.

I became increasingly uptight each minute we had to wait in the exam room. My skin turned clammy, while my stomach grumbled. The temperature in the room seemed to rise twenty degrees as drops of sweat formed around my temples. We were all aware that Dr. Oz was our only hope.

My nerves did not let up until Dr. Oz appeared. He seemed quite cordial as he introduced himself to us and began asking questions. I liked how he asked if he could touch my hands for an examination, instead of just grabbing at them. He immediately ordered X-rays, scans, and a nerve-conduction velocity test. His proactive approach impressed me, and he seemed genuinely concerned with my health. I began to believe Dr. Oz would do everything in his power to see me better.

During my follow-up visit, Dr. Oz told me the test results showed nothing physically wrong; and that meant the CRPS was indeed spreading. Hearing that sentence devastated me. I felt a knot grow in the middle of my stomach. If no one could fix my right hand in three years, what did that mean for my left hand? *How would I live my life?* I looked at my parents' exhausted, pale faces. I did not want to live like this. I could not go on hurting my loved ones.

I was about to get off the table when he proceeded to tell us about his brother and him. They were both going bald. While his brother was having a rough time accepting the loss of his hair, Dr. Oz was dealing with this same loss in a proper and healthy manner. "This is what you need to do too. You need to stop living in denial and accept reality. You have CRPS, and it is not going to get better. You must deal with it. Make the best out of the life you are still able to live."

Was this really happening? Had this man actually said I needed to deal with it just like he needed to deal with premature balding?

I was shocked and appalled that anyone could compare a life-altering disease to the loss of hair. Thinking he must be joking, I glared at him, only to realize he was serious. My arms began to burn. He really thought that my pain was similar to his hair loss. I again looked at Mom and Dad. Their mouths hung open as they stood rigid. I wanted to hit him or pull out the remaining hair he had left. Instead, I decided to ask him two questions in my most authoritative voice while holding my arms close to his smug face.

"So are you telling me that if I were your daughter, you would do nothing? Would you just accept this as part of my life and deal with it?"

Dr. Oz quickly shut the door and began fidgeting in his coat pocket. His eyes widened, as I assumed he was rethinking what he was trying to imply. I liked seeing him in the hot seat. He immediately became apologetic as he attempted to sidestep his previous remarks. But it was too late; he had already offended me.

While I knew he did not mean to minimize my health or intentionally hurt me, he needed to know that he overlooked the magnitude of my condition. I was sure losing his hair had been a huge challenge and barrier for him to overcome, but it was not comparable to the pain I endured on a regular basis. His life was not hanging in the balance—mine was.

I remember storming out of his office in disbelief and rage. Even his measly attempt to contact his mentors at John Hopkins for possible treatment ideas could not take away my anger. Besides being pissed at Dr. Oz, I was also petrified. Everyone believed the deck was stacked against me. The only positive thing about the situation was that it gave me ammunition. Now more than ever I had drive and motivation to prove the medical field wrong. I was not going to let his words or Dr. Vine's or any other healthcare professional's take away my hope. I would press on and fight this disease. I would show the world I could live a pain-free life again. I would beat this damn disorder.

Harbor Half: Six and a Half Miles to Go

I cross the halfway mark thinking about how my life had once been a three-ring circus. With contradicting emotions overwhelming me, I am unsure what to do. I feel joyful yet depressed, knowing I am a long way from done. I feel more optimistic but also pessimistic that my body may not be able to run any farther. I want to feel proud but instead feel more like a petrified schoolgirl.

Looking at my watch, I see we are doing well. I know as long as I stay positive, we will finish in my targeted goal time. Taking another mental account of what hurts, aches, and burns, I think of Shelley's advice: *"When the pain becomes intense, follow the Hawaiian Ho'oponopono theory, and lovingly forgive yourself."*

Always holding myself to such high standards, I knew I was my own worst critic. Therefore, thinking of forgiving myself for being in pain seemed impossible to do. However, I was desperate and willing to try anything to regain mental clarity and physical wellness.

I began to let go and release my "perceived" weaknesses by chanting, "I love you ankles, I am sorry I am hurting you. I love you, hips, and I apologize for the stress and pain."

Incredibly, I feel a shift as my swollen ankles, aching legs, jarring back, and shattering hips surrender to my affirmations. *Oh my goodness, it is working. Thank you, thank you, thank you, Universe.*

Passing mile marker seven boosts my morale, for I have completed more than I have to finish. Because I feel so strong, I am able to push myself harder while keeping the agonizing CRPS symptoms of numbness, tingling, and burning at bay. I even pick up my tempo and embrace the pain and emotions of the past nine years. I am a fighter, and this marathon is showing me just how far I can soar. Nothing is going to get me down or stand in my way. Now I choose health, love, and happiness.

However, my upbeat nature does not last long. The not-so-scenic wetlands make me feel like I am suffocating in a maze of shrubs and trees. I want to scream and hyperventilate. *When will these two miles be over so I can breathe again?*

I begin to run and then walk, run and then walk. Each time I stop, I beat myself up more. With a crushed spirit, it seems I need a pep talk from Rick every other minute. *When did I become so weak-minded?*

"You have got it, babe. The training was the hard part—this should be cake. Just keep it up and remember that *this* is what it is all about."

Although running a bit slower, my stride begins to become more consistent with the music carrying me along the never-ending road. I concentrate on only moving forward so I can escape this doom-and-gloom forest. I deny the debilitating thoughts' power to control me. Toxic and poisonous, they are just fear programs and self-worth complexes.

Making my way out of the wetland preserve is a relief. Now that I have a visual of my last five miles, I see that all that stands between my dreams and me is the long stretch of the causeway, the detour on the access road, and the Harbor Bridge. I check my watch and realize I will be done in less than an hour. As long as I keep moving, *I am fifty-eight minutes from my destiny.*

Chapter 13

Looking Outside the Box

Since I refused to be a cripple forever, I had to find other resources. As my parents and I were fed up with the medical community that had no other options for me, our dear friend Cathy, who happened to be a nurse practitioner, suggested we look elsewhere. It was time to look outside the box. With her support, I started to explore different complementary treatments used in Eastern Medicine. Eastern Medicine's view of illnesses as dis-ease trapped in the body helped me realize that the first step to wellness was healing my inner self. Not until I became mentally, emotionally, and spiritually fit could I regain my physical health.

I first began to research the power of crystals with my physical therapist Mitzi. As she played an integral role in my quest for answers, Mitzi opened me up to a new way of thinking. She had me reading books on metaphysical healing and self-help. It was important to her that I stay positive. Not once did she discourage me from hoping for a miracle, because she knew I held the power to heal myself.

Mitzi believed in the healing power of crystals. She explained to me that for thousands of years, Eastern Medicine had used crystals to heal and protect. Stones could magnetically attract or repel unwanted energy by subtly transmitting and receiving energies. This meant that each type of crystal vibrated at a different frequency in order to promote its own distinct properties of peace and harmony. I was fascinated that a crystal could actually affect one's health, and I wanted to see for myself if they could take away my pain.

I remember feeling overwhelmed as I walked into the store filled with beautiful crystals. My head immediately spun from the strong incense, and I started to see white flecks. The droning noise in my ears made it impossible for me to understand what people were saying. I started to sweat and my mouth became salty. I thought I was going to pass out.

Wobbly and light-headed, I found myself leaning against the counter, where the store owner told Mom I needed water and air. As she brought a hand-held fan near my face, Mom handed me a water bottle that I gripped using my forearms. I took a sip but did not feel much better. My eyes brimmed with tears as the woman behind the counter reassured me that I would be okay. The crystals were over-stimulating my nervous system. I just needed to continue breathing.

A few minutes passed before my hearing returned and images were not fuzzy. I looked around the room in shock. Surrounding me were thousands of crystals in varying shapes, sizes, and colors. While I did not want to get too close to these obviously powerful stones, I could not help but want to touch a pink crystal. I learned it was a rose quartz. Rose quartz released unexpressed emotions and internalized pain while teaching about self-love and acceptance. As the owner placed the smooth, cool stone on top of my left fist, she explained how this crystal aided in the circulatory system. I immediately grinned, amazed by her remark. This was just what I needed, because CRPS cut off circulation to limbs.

A light purple amethyst caught my attention next. I discovered that amethyst relieved physical and emotional pain by calming the nervous system. Amethyst also helped with insomnia. It was strange how I suddenly felt comfort from both these crystals. They were exactly what my body needed to continue this journey. Since I believed I would not be able to leave that store without them, the hippie store owner shared the magic of crystals with me: these precious stones chose their owners. For some reason, that specific rose quartz and amethyst felt I needed them to heal. My mouth dropped open as I stood in disbelief. *Here was another sign from the Universe that I was not alone.*

I felt like I had a second chance at life as Mom and I got back into the car. All I did was stare out the passenger window with restored hope in recovery. Recognizing that crystals held the innate power to heal allowed me to keep believing in my miracle. I truly felt alive and could not wait to tell Mitzi about my experience tomorrow. I now understood what she meant when she said that each of us shared a greater connection to the planet than just existing.

I was ready to go home and lie down, but we stopped at one last store. Morphine had made me crave sugar. While I hardly had an appetite, I ate sweets by the pound. With me constantly consuming licorice, Hot Tamales, suckers and Sour Patch Kids, Mom visited our local candy store weekly to stock up on my craved objects. As the holidays were approaching, the smell of cinnamon and freshly brewed hot apple cider wafted through the store. Seeing the ornaments and Christmas trees made me sad. I had always loved this time of year, but having no mobility in either hand took away my celebratory mood.

As we walked to the back corner to find the candy, I noticed a dark green pendant. I could not help staring at the rich green hues that seemed to swirl together. I wanted to know what type of stone it was, so I asked the man gathering our candy. He picked it up before telling me it was labradorite. Labradorite was a protective stone known for accessing spiritual purpose. As I felt called to that gem, I watched the man slip it into our bag of candy. He said to think of it as an early Christmas present. I was speechless. *A higher power was definitely watching over me.*

∞

Now open to discovering a new way to view my recovery, Mitzi introduced me to Shelley, a certified spiritual response therapist. Spiritual Response Therapy (SRT) clears the subconscious mind and empowers one to break the cycles of disharmony. By removing negative programs that hold us back from living, SRT frees the soul to experience health, abundance, and happiness. In essence, SRT was just another form of counseling. It was another way to look deep into our lives, in order to let go of the negative, disabling beliefs that restrain us from moving forward.

I was a bit skeptical about seeing an "energy-clearing specialist." However, I trusted that Mitzi would not lead me in the wrong direction. I remember the breeze blowing the leaves off the fall trees as I waited on a bench outside her office. Even though the air was crisp, I felt queasy and hot. Meeting with a psychic or intuitively aware person was completely out of my comfort zone, and yet it somehow felt like the right thing to do. I felt I was exactly where I needed to be.

Shelley had long, dark hair and soulful blue eyes that could captivate an entire room. All I could focus on was her natural beauty when she introduced herself to me. Not only was she in stunningly great physical shape, but she seemed spiritually centered too. I liked how she smiled and laughed as she led me into her small office. The room was serene and calm. The neutral paint tones with the bright angel and dragonfly paintings made the walls pop. She had candles lit in various places, and crystals adorned the table and bookshelf.

I sat down at the small wooden table against the left wall, anxious for the session to start. Shelley quickly began by saying a prayer that cleared both of our energies. She used a pendulum as her divining tool and had two books stacked next to her on the table. While I might have questioned pendulums as voodoo practices in the past, this time it felt normal. A sense of peace came over me, knowing there was a much greater reason for me being here. Mitzi was correct: Shelley was going to be the perfect teacher for me.

Shelley soon became my confidante. I learned from her that I had blocked myself from my inner healer out of fear. Never one to preach, she advised me solely out of love. We worked together to let go of the past contracts I had unintentionally made with myself that limited my power. It was amazing how releasing a negative charge gave me permission to let go of grief and misery. She helped me see that my job was to become empowered and not to give up. I had to find self-love and compassion in order to set my soul free.

Shelley also taught me that I needed to start living and loving life. She had me read *The Four Agreements* by Don Miguel Ruiz. These four profound steps empowered me to spread my wings and fly. I no longer took the pessimistic, condescending remarks of doctors personally. Knowing my life's happiness relied solely on me allowed me to stop assuming that every specialist questioned my pain. I learned how important it was to use my words wisely. This book showed me that every word was a verbal commitment and even joking about my condition could disrupt my body's ability to heal. While I could not see the future, I had to put my best foot forward. I was a peaceful warrior who would reclaim her life.

It was as if a bright light bulb turned on inside my head. I saw I held the power to get better. *I was still in charge.*

Realizing that I could heal myself made me hungrier for more therapies that were "complementary." Shelley wanted me to explore the use of feng shui, which dealt with the belief that we influenced and changed our Universe by establishing positive chi (energy) in our space. In essence, the way I felt and acted had a lot to do with the energy field I was submitting to the world.

Therefore, I could essentially change my chi by rearranging small things to create a new environment filled with health and happiness. It was amazing how much calmer and stronger I felt just from de-cluttering my bookcase and hanging a crystal above my bedroom door. Such easy modifications made me feel alert and alive again.

With still no movement in my left hand, Shelley and Mitzi had me look at the healing benefits in color therapy. Color therapy affected the electromagnetic field that surrounded us all. The vibrational charge of colors could either push us closer to harmony or pull us further to distress. Although it was difficult to grasp how a color could affect my health, I wanted to know if different shades could possibly change my mood and bodily functions. Any non-invasive therapy was worth a try, in my opinion.

I learned from Shelley that my personal healing color was blue. Blue symbolized serenity, faith, and willpower. It was also a calming color, which made me feel safe. Since I had to believe in this therapy in order for it to have a chance at working, I wore it, thinking the life force would soon heal me. I imagined the color's cooling attributes lessening the burning sensation in my arms. Blue gave me strength to hope that tomorrow held my miracle.

Although these therapies had begun to heal my mental, emotional, and spiritual states, both hands remained clenched and I still had raging, out-of-control pain. I was terrified that the CRPS would continue to spread throughout my body, leaving me completely bedridden. Thankfully, our dear family friend Cathy offered us another option.

Cathy was a nurse practitioner who wanted me to see a colleague of hers named Maureen. Maureen was not only a nurse but also a certified practitioner of Guided Imagery who performed Healing Touch. Healing touch referred to any type of energy healing, such as prayer, meditation, or energy transfer. It worked through resonance. This meant that the energy of another would vibrate in union with mine to allow my body the chance to heal itself. It was hard for me to grasp this concept, and I was a bit nervous because I did not know what to expect. However, I knew I needed relief. If Cathy believed in Maureen, then I did too.

It was the first week of November when my parents and I traveled the fifty-five miles to visit Maureen. The ride was painfully silent. It was as if an invisible fourth person named Misery was also in the car. Ever since this nightmare began, I had become despondent. I quickly built a wall around me that even my parents could not break down. I just did not want to speak when my life was crumbling apart. It was emotionally easier on me to remain quiet, because I had nothing positive to say.

My heart palpitated as we pulled into the parking lot. All I could do was take a deep breath and pray that she had answers. Dad opened the car door and unfastened my seatbelt. This was it. There was no turning back.

Maureen was beautiful. She had dark black hair and milky white skin that reminded me of Snow White. I remember sitting down in a chair when she spoke to my parents and me about her own personal story of overcoming a blood disorder. Hearing her discuss her own recovery with such passion and wisdom gave me hope for my future. It was as if her warmth and kindness put me at ease. Instantly, I felt safe in her company. *It was time for me to let go and let God.*

Maureen began the session with an aura-imaging scan. She told me that surrounding each of us is a strong vibrating energy field known as an aura. The energy within and outside a person's physical state, called the etheric field, influenced the aura. Maureen had a unique way to show me my aura. As she gently opened my left hand to place it on a sensor connected to her laptop, I looked into a camera. Soon my face appeared on her computer screen, surrounded by a myriad of colors. Chills went down my spine as I saw purples, blues, and whites. I looked at my parents, whose faces were mesmerized by the screen.

Presented in front of me was a printout of my aura. The graphs showing the imbalances between my right and left side disturbed me. It seemed that I favored my left side by a margin of two to one. However, Maureen expected that, because of my recent hand closure. She said that it made sense because of how hard I was trying to regain mobility in my left hand. Moreover, the disease disconnected my brain from my right side; having any energy in that area was a good sign. It might look bad to me, but this was encouraging to her.

I then saw the pie chart displaying the difference in energy between my body, mind and spirit. The largest chunk of the pie went to my body, followed by my mind, and then spirit. Knowing my spiritual side only made up a sliver of the chart also upset me. Ever since my meeting with Shelley, I had been working on a spiritual practice and being "one" with the Universe.

Maureen again assured me that this would change after our session. She also believed that due to my pain, I needed to be living in my body. It would be nearly impossible not to. I had to remember that this was just my starting point. It was a visual for her and me to see which areas needed the most attention and healing.

The colors surrounding my face baffled me. Was there a reason the aquamarine was above my head? Why did it look as if my throat was white? Is it normal that the differing shades of purple encased the blue and white and filled the sides of my head?

Maureen said these colors showed that I was an old soul. I really did not understand what that meant, but both Shelley and Mitzi had told me the same thing. An old soul was a New Age term referring to one's personal intuition and insight that is beyond one's years. Old souls sense universal change and seek to live out their soul purpose. They are searchers and healers who live between the physical and spiritual realms.

Having white near my throat explained how my sixth sense guided me, rather than logic. I had the power to communicate and lead through faith. White expressed inner peace and healing abilities. She said it symbolized cosmic wisdom. Maureen went on to explain the aquamarine above my head showed that I was in a period of transition and change. Being empathetic in nature meant that I wanted to be helping others. But she needed me to understand that I had to help myself first. I had to recover in order to be able to make a difference in others' lives.

The last color she spoke about was the violet around my chest. Violet was a magical and charismatic color. People with violet in their aura tended to have psychic abilities. Since it was surrounding my heart, I had the gift of inspiring others to believe anything was possible. I needed to hear that; I needed affirmation that having hope for a miracle was all right.

Now that I had a better idea what was occurring in and around me, Maureen led me to the meditative room and asked my parents to return in about forty minutes. While nervous to be alone, I was thankful that they would not hear me talk about the pain and guilt. I still wanted them to think I was fine. I just needed them to believe I was strong and could handle everything thrown my way, even if it was a lie. I might have lost my dignity, but I refused to lose my character.

The room was slightly dark, and I heard soothing music playing softly in the background. Maureen helped me onto the massage table, where she asked me to lie down and relax. She was going to first check the alignment of my chakras, the seven main energy centers that existed within and outside the physical body at the etheric level. They were located along the spine up to the top of my head.

Each chakra had a physical and emotional relationship to the health of my body and thoughts. She told me that the most common reason for an inadequate flow of energy in one of these seven areas was because of emotions and attitudes. This was why it was so important for me to be aware of my inner feelings. If I could not release my emotional pain, my energy would stay unbalanced, making disease inevitable.

Even though auras and chakras were foreign subjects to me, her explanation did make sense. All I wanted was for this to work. I was tired of saying I was *healing* but never actually healed. Maureen began clearing and aligning my chakras using a stone pendulum and her own hands. I tried to quiet my mind, but random thoughts ran rampant in my brain. I thought about Dan in school and wondered what shows were on television that night. I felt like a hamburger, as I also remembered I needed to call Dylan. I dreamed of clapping, laughing, and returning to Creighton. *Would life ever return to normal?*

Suddenly I felt strange warmth near my belly button that moved up to my throat. I looked up and saw Maureen moving her hands in a circular direction above my body. When I heard a repeated clicking sound, I became alarmed. Maureen did not even give me the chance to speak, as she quickly reassured me that noise was normal when two energies come together. I rested my head back down on the pillow as she took a seat in the chair near my head. It was finally time to begin.

She lowered the music and began with a short meditation. Her voice was soothing as she relaxed every muscle, starting at my head and working down to my toes. As she calmly asked me to let the energy flow out of my toes and fingers, I began to feel the discordant, frazzled energy leaving my body. Maureen had lulled me into a meditative rest. *It was working.*

Next was the visualization part of the session. Visualization therapy dealt with the belief that before one could accomplish anything, one must first imagine. Studies had shown that imagery drastically changed the chemicals in the nervous system. In fact, the same amount of brain stimulation occurred when participating in an activity or envisioning the activity. Therefore, I realized that in order for me to obtain overall health, I needed to start visualizing myself healed. It was just that simple.

This was difficult for me to do, since I had trouble retaining a mental image of the pain inside my body. Maureen tried to explain there was no right or wrong answer. I had to remember that it was not my job to judge whether a certain image was suitable. If I envisioned my pain as a hammer in my right elbow, then that was what my body wanted me to see. I needed to stop thinking and start feeling, because my spiritual guides would not lead me in the wrong direction.

I became more confident and descriptive in my answer each time she asked me to visualize the pain. I even started having "a-ha moments" as I made connections between my pain and my emotional state. It became quite clear that my chronic pain was a gift to teach me powerful lessons about life, love, and happiness. This disease enabled me to grow as a person and view the world from a different perspective. I saw beauty in the littlest things and believed that good resided within all of us. Through these guided imagery sessions, I uncovered self-love and self-respect. *I found my authentic self.*

Yet picturing where I was holding the disease within the body was only half the battle. As she then asked me to release the hurt from my physical body, I resisted. I could not listen to my gut response of beating the hammer out of my elbow by breaking my bones. My stomach churned as I felt myself at war with my own High Self. Afraid of causing more pain and damage, Maureen had to reassure me that visualization did not need to make sense. It just worked, and it would not hurt me.

Letting go of reason was a struggle for me. After unwillingly losing so much of myself to the disease, I was in desperate need of controlling some part of my life, even if it was only my thoughts. I soon discovered, though, that by recalling an image of a problem and letting it go, the pain would dissipate. Once I stopped hiding behind shame and self-doubt, I could start to reject the labels that identified me as mentally ill or disabled. I could then create new healthy ones that portrayed my perseverance and heart. It was true—the power to heal resided within me.

$$\infty$$

Despite my visits with Maureen and Shelley bringing me hope, I still was without either hand. I was frustrated that the disease was spreading and nothing was working. I was drowning, and I needed someone to throw me a lifeline. Just as I began to believe I had fully lost my way, Bob entered my life.

Bob was a chemical engineer from Texas who worked for a wellness company called Nikken. I learned about him three days after I saw Maureen. Anne was a parent at the elementary school where I was teaching who happened to be a distributor for the same company. She was persistent in her belief that Bob could help me. While I willingly gave her my number, I never imagined Bob would call me three hours later, saying he would like to meet me.

I remember I was sobbing in bed when the phone rang that afternoon. By then, it had been three weeks without the use of either hand, and I was completely depressed. I was tired of feeling worthless and disgusting. I was sick of being a burden on everyone I loved. It was a daily challenge just to keep going when I felt handicapped and crippled. My life was out of control.

Mom answered the phone. Hearing a man she did not know ramble on about resonant energy and magnetic water made her hang up. She did not have time for a stupid telemarketer. Her daughter was in excruciating agony, and all she wanted was to take the pain away.

Bob did not give up. Knowing we were under a great deal of stress, he waited and called back a few hours later. While Mom was skeptical of this mysterious caller, she decided to listen as he explained how he received our number and what he did. Bob told her he worked for Nikken, a company that sold magnetic, far-infrared, and ionized health products to support and maintain health. Since he was coming to Northern California the next afternoon for a conference, he offered to meet us at a nearby hotel. After working with numerous chronic pain patients in the past, he felt confident that he could relieve my pain.

The next day, I found myself sitting in a hotel lobby, awaiting my destiny. It was a leap of faith for my parents to accept a stranger's request to meet their daughter. It also showed just how desperate we all were.

Bob was a tall, brawny man who had extremely high energy. He was loud and boisterous but extremely intelligent. It was obvious that he genuinely wanted to help me, by the questions he asked about my disease and its progression. As he completely validated my pain, he told my parents this was serious. There was no way I was lying about the magnitude of my symptoms. He knew the agony I endured was real and he would do everything in his power to bring me relief. While I felt drained in his presence, I was hopeful he would make me better.

Bob then spoke about Nikken's ionized water. I learned that nearly 70 percent of a person's body weight is water. Water was a necessity of life. Yet as it kept us alive, more and more tap water had shown contaminants of heavy metals, chemicals and sediment. These unwanted substances promoted disorders in the body, which was especially not good for my body. He explained how Nikken's PiMag water technology removed such impurities by using three filtering stages: a stainless steel screen and carbon filter, porous coral sand chips filter, and a silk screen. It also transformed ordinary tap water into pi water, or specially charged ion water. He called it "living water," since it added nutrients the body needed, such as calcium, and magnetized the water.

Bob never slowed down. Instead of allowing us a chance to ask questions, he was already discussing far-infrared products. Far-infrared technology worked through reflection, insulation, and breathability. Ceramic-reflective fibers reacting to my own body temperature absorbed and transformed that energy to either cool or warm my body. These fibers were hypoallergenic and soothing to even the most sensitive of skin. He was certain the Kenko Dream Comforter and the Kenko Travel Comforter would calm my over-stimulated nerves.

Even as I tried to pay attention to him, I felt awkward. In a middle of a sentence, he would suddenly stop talking for a second and breathe deeply. His eyes would close for an instant and then he would look back at me. With each exhale, his body would shake. It looked like he was possessed. I understood I was in trouble and needed to keep an open mind, but this unnerved me.

I guess my raised brows tipped Bob off to my being uncomfortable, because he explained what he was doing. Besides his work with Nikken, he was in the process of becoming a certified Reiki instructor. Reiki was a Japanese technique that used energy transfer to promote healing and balance. There were two ways he could bring me relief. Bob could either place his hands above my body or mentally picture my body while breathing life-force energy into me.

I relaxed as I repeatedly told myself to let go and let God. It was not a coincidence that Bob entered my life. He was here for a reason, and I had to trust. Right now, this was my only chance at recovery. I needed to keep the faith; I had to see what would transpire.

He began to turn his palms toward my body and then quickly flip his palm away. This was his way of transmitting and removing energy from me. He continued to do this near each of my chakras, which made me want to laugh. Seeing a grown man so intently flipping his hands and breathing loudly was funny to me. Yet I knew I needed to stay serious, so I bit the inside of my lip while avoiding any eye contact with Dad.

Soon I felt overwhelming warmth, and the throbbing besieging my left hand began to decline. My face instantly lit up like a Christmas tree. Something was working. Something Bob was doing was making me feel better. I looked around at Anne standing in the corner, beaming. Then I glanced at my parents, who sat with perplexed faces. I had to smile, seeing such a contrast in emotions. This whole experience was surreal. I could not grasp how his energy could change my pain. *Had it just vanished? How could he make it disappear?*

Bob continued his clearing for another ten minutes before he put down his hands and grinned. I was hot and sticky, and my mouth felt parched. He told me that was a normal response after Reiki. It was my body's way of telling me I needed to hydrate and rest. Everyone seemed anxious for me to speak, but I did not know what to say. While the pain had decreased and I felt circulation in my left hand, the temporary relief was already gone.

Bob told me not to get discouraged. Since I had a positive response and felt some change, I was on my way to healing. He then turned toward my parents and stared at Dad. Bob felt my dad had the power to help me feel better. By following a few simple techniques of shifting his palm to and from me while focusing on love, Dad could lower my pain. I was shocked. Why did my dad have that gift and my mom did not? It was as if Bob could read my mind, because he soon explained that Mom had the innate power to comfort while Dad could easily connect with me.

He looked at Anne and asked if she had extra Kenko comforters for me to use over the weekend. He also checked to see if she had any Nikken water bottles that included the PiMag technology. Luckily, she did. We now needed to wait and see what would happen. Although Bob would be leaving Northern California tomorrow, he would be back in a few weeks. Until then, he would stay in contact via e-mail and cell phone. Then I watched him leave the lobby as I stared in disbelief. I knew he would have a lasting impact on my life.

I was overly exhausted from my session with Bob by the time we got home. All I wanted to do was curl up on the family room couch and watch movies. I remember being amazed when I wrapped myself within the Kenko Travel Comforter; this was the first fabric not to aggravate my pain levels.

For forty-eight hours, I did nothing but rest and drink Nikken water. I was gentle with myself and allowed myself to feel everything. If I thought something was funny, I laughed. If I was frustrated, I cried. The bitterness and hostility that had been inside me over the past three weeks dissipated. I was finally free to be me again, and on day three, I noticed the sensitivity in my left hand decreased and my hand began to twitch. This was the greatest sign. *I now knew I would recover.* The Universe had again guided me in the right direction.

Now that I had found my voice, I was unwilling to sit quietly and allow others to decide my fate. I understood chronic pain was a universal health crisis that knew no boundaries and affected everyone equally—the poor and the rich, the young and the old, male or female. With one in four people living in chronic pain, no race, class, or age seemed spared from its debilitating hold. I did not want my suffering to be in vain. Determined patients could bring about change; it was time for me to get involved.

I was fortunate that Dr. Vine recognized my enthusiasm and connected me with Mary Pat, the executive director of the National Pain Foundation (NPF). As a non-profit organization, the NPF advanced functional recovery of people in pain through credible information and education. Their goal was to encourage and teach those in pain to take a more active approach in their own treatment plan.

I immediately contacted her via e-mail and explained my hopes for recovery. I shared my dreams of starting national chronic pain awareness walks, and my goal of becoming an advocate for those who felt ignored by the healthcare system. Validating a person's suffering was important to me. After all, I knew firsthand the emotional distress caused from being mocked and ridiculed by skeptical doctors.

My correspondences with Mary Pat changed my life profoundly. I now had a sense of direction and purpose. I saw that I could use my pain and disability for a higher good. This was the first time I could look past my personal feelings of helplessness, and direct my energy on changing the system. I had found a way to turn the darkness into a bright light. I would not be a victim anymore; I was a fighting survivor.

As Mary Pat appreciated my conviction and genuine commitment to the cause, she asked if I would be willing to speak at the National Pain Awareness Campaign's inaugural conference. This nationwide program was a joint venture between the National Pain Foundation and the American Academy of Pain Medicine. It was the start of a new movement to raise awareness of pain issues and treatment options.

I was honored. Here was an incredible opportunity to inform a group of physicians and pharmaceutical reps from a patient's perspective. It was not often that a person in pain had such a platform to speak freely about the dramatic under-treatment of pain. Working with the NPF was just another tool to help me see beyond my ailment and toward my future.

Combining the therapies of Western and Eastern medicine allowed me to regain control of my life. I no longer allowed my pain or disability to define me as a person. My pain was a part of me that I dealt with on a daily basis, but it was not all of me. As I became more proactive in my own healing, I learned which treatments fit my lifestyle and my body. These new techniques were an outlet for me to release the pain and gain confidence. Though criticized by some who saw these therapies as voodoo, *I knew* what I had to do to get better, and I did it. With this newfound outlook, I decided to make the ultimate decision.

I was going to have the spinal cord battery removed.

Chapter 14

Taking Initiative

I did not care if yoga affected the stimulator's ability to perform. I never wanted to have another implantation. Since the battery's implantation, I had complained about hypersensitivity, inflammation, muscle tightness, and general discomfort in my lower back and upper buttock. There was just no way I was going through that ordeal again. I was willing to try anything once, but I had no desire to re-attempt an unsuccessful, risky procedure, especially when I did not believe a second time would change the initial outcome.

It was therapeutic for me to discuss my worries and concerns with Mitzi. Mitzi had this innate ability to be positive. Believing I knew what was right for my body, she would always encourage me to follow my instincts. She said I was my own best doctor. As long as I took the leap of faith and made this journey my own, I would be on the road to recovery.

With her guidance and support, I found the courage to insist that Dr. Vine remove the battery. I knew his opinion differed from mine, but this was something I wanted. The time had come for me to try other treatments without feeling the constant soreness, tenderness, and irritation caused by the battery.

Although I started becoming more proactive in my treatments, this was only the second time I was taking a stand and going directly against the wishes and opinions of Dr. Vine. While I did not want to hurt him or disregard his medical expertise, I had to stay true to who I was as a person. I could not proceed with another spinal cord stimulator because I no longer wanted a foreign object inside my body. It served no purpose—it was time to have it removed.

Much to my surprise, Dr. Vine agreed, and he scheduled the procedure for early March 2002.

Four days before the removal, I suffered another flare-up. The pain had become atrocious, and I could not rest my right arm on anything. As it stood straight in the air, it became impossible for me to sleep. Mom and Dad rented movie after movie from the local video store to try to keep me occupied, but I cried though the nights while clinging to my new Nikken blanket. With nothing helping ease my pain, Dr. Vine quickly realized I was in need of a medical intervention. He could not afford to have this exacerbation affect the upcoming procedure, so he admitted me to California Pacific Medical Center.

Life in the Pulmonary Care Unit left me incapacitated. Being in a semi-comatose state connected to various monitors and a morphine PCA pump, I could not comprehend the world surrounding me. All I did was drool, cry, drink apple juice, and wet the bed. It was a good day if I recognized my parents or held a lucid conversation. The hospital took away my dignity and pride. Here, only the shell of who I used to be existed.

It did not take long before my group of healers became involved. When the pain had not subsided after a few days, Mitzi and Cathy offered to perform healing touch in my hospital room. Seeing how critical the mind-body-spirit connection was to my recovery puzzle, Mom and Dad were optimistic that my health would improve by combining both Western and Eastern medicine.

I remember Mitzi visited mid-afternoon, because her strawberry blonde hair reflected the sun peering in through the window. As she slowly placed six clear quartz crystals around my body, I began to feel calm. Then she used her pendulum to balance my chakras. Soon the pain lessened. Color returned to my pasty cheeks, and my stomach did not feel queasy. It was a miracle; Mitzi had helped me feel better.

Cathy came the following morning before the surgery. She believed healing touch would strengthen my body, enabling me to recover faster. I saw her use her pendulum as she began the meditative practice. Even though I knew this had to look strange to a passerby, I was beyond the point of caring. I needed relief, and for some reason alternative treatments worked. To me, believing in the mystery and magic of the Universe was not witchcraft, it was smart. I was using every tool I could find to overcome this pain.

Almost immediately after Cathy began Healing Touch, images became secondary, as my primary focus was on myself. I imagined small windmills turning clockwise at the seven main energy centers in my body. I saw red, orange, yellow, green, indigo, and blue surrounding me. My body seemed warm, and I felt opened to the spiritual realm. My worries and fears disappeared—I was "one" with Spirit. I knew I would be fine during the procedure if I could just stay in this peaceful state.

Cathy was still in my hospital room with my parents when the hospital orderly came to take me to the OR. I smiled back at Mom and Dad as the man whisked me down the corridor. I wanted them to see that I was relaxed and centered. I wanted them to know I would be okay.

Nothing scared me anymore. I was ready to have this battery removed. Here was my chance to live a better life.

I still remember nurses positioning me on my stomach under the gleaming lamps. My body shivered as the cold, steel operating table made contact with my bare skin. This would be the first time Dr. Vine would fully sedate me for a procedure. As I felt the cool medicine flow through my veins, I waited for the sedatives and anesthetics to take effect. Soon the room went black, and the bubbling noises silenced. My next recollection was awakening in the post-operating room an hour later.

I took a mental note of my body. Besides my head aching and back being sore, I felt fine. I associated my minimal discomfort with the healing touch I did hours ago. I did not know whether the unexplainable force helping me was God, Universe, or Spirit. And I did not care. To me, they were *all* **one**, and we were *all* **connected**. The only thing that mattered was that a greater source was guiding me.

Dr. Vine appeared at my bedside and told me in a reassuring voice that the procedure had gone surprisingly well. I tried to sit up to thank him, but my head felt heavy, so I lay back down. While I had to return to the PCU for observation, he was confident that I should recover quickly. Dr. Vine would release me from the hospital that afternoon if my vitals continued to stabilize and no complications arose over the next few hours.

I was glad to see Mom and Dad waiting outside the OR doors. It was something I had grown accustomed to over the years, and it made me smile. My parents were my safety net. They held me up when I was down and gave me strength when I was weak. It bothered me that I could not do the same for them. I wished I could ease their pain, but that was impossible. The sadness in their eyes would not disappear until I healed. Therefore, my only job was to get better so they could be happy. The greatest gift I could ever give them was my health, and I vowed to see that happen.

Nurses were already waiting in my PCU room to help me back into bed. I groggily watched two of them reconnect my heart monitors and administer another dose of morphine through my drip. Then I drifted to sleep. I woke a half hour later to Dad reading the *San Francisco Chronicle* and Mom staring at me. Despite some tenderness around the surgical site, I really felt fine. There was no additional pain, and I even had a slight appetite. This was the easiest procedure to date.

I was on cloud nine when Dr. Vine discharged me. That evening, I slept through the whole night and woke feeling like a new person. Relieved to have finally made the right choice, I returned to my perky, upbeat self. I was happy again and life looked brighter. I believed I would be all right now that the battery was gone.

∞

I remember Dad and I were watching college basketball in the family room when Mom asked if I took my afternoon dose of medicine. Her question startled me. I had no recollection of the last time I took it, but figured it had to have been while I was still in the hospital. That was more than thirty-six hours ago.

Going nearly two days without drugs shocked me. It made me think why I even needed them. I had never wanted to be dependent on a substance as potent and habit-forming as morphine. Since I always told myself I would stop taking it when the right opportunity presented itself, I now faced a predicament. Did I really need my morphine crutch anymore?

While it was exciting to think about possibly ending Oramorph, I was mainly confused and overwhelmed. This was such a crucial decision. I first went to my parents for advice, but they were hesitant to offer an opinion. Stopping cold turkey was a big deal. They told me they were not medical experts and did not want me to do something that might be detrimental. Although I understood their position, I was disappointed because I needed someone to weigh the pros and cons with me.

Thankfully, I had Bob. Even though Bob lived in Texas, he wanted to be in California after my surgery to help with my recovery. Time mattered when dealing with CRPS, and he understood the significance. He and I both knew the sooner my body could heal from the invasive surgery, the lesser chance I had of the disease spreading. It was strange how a man I had only met once before now seemed to be an integral part of my life. He had become a godsend to me.

Bob was blunt with his answer. He quickly stated that if he were in my position, he would stop taking morphine. End of story. People continued narcotics because of fear of the agonizing withdrawal. However, I seemed to be managing the pain and lack of medication quite well. It was his opinion that this was the perfect time to quit, since my body was not craving the drug. I was close to forty-eight hours without opioids. Maybe I would be lucky and not face the serious withdrawal symptoms accompanying a decrease in morphine.

His position made a lot of sense. *Why would I turn back now?* I looked at my parents sitting on the couch across from me when he stopped talking. Their faces were expressionless. I knew it was up to me to make the final decision. With so much riding on this outcome, I took a sip of the hot minestrone soup resting in my lap. My heart raced as I sensed that all eyes were on me. Then it hit me: the pain felt the same with or without the drugs. Therefore, there was no need to take such a strong pill if it did not drastically decrease my symptoms.

I was finished with morphine.

I took a deep breath before sharing my revelation with my parents and Bob. Although Mom and Dad's faces stayed inexpressive, I noticed their stiffened posture. This made me sad, because I knew they were worried. Neither of them wanted me to suffer. I stirred my soup before glancing at Bob. He, on the other hand, appeared giddy with excitement. He was convinced that without a battery lodged in my back or narcotics in my system, my body would be able to overcome this terrible disease.

However, I regretted my decision four hours later when I was jolted awake by screaming pains. The agony was instantaneous. With my insides burning, I limped to the bathroom, bent over at a ninety-degree angle. I remember I sat on the toilet, sobbing while I held my head in my hands. Soon I heard a tap on the door, and Dad came in to find me rocking back and forth on the linoleum floor. The stabbing pains in my abdomen were too intense for me to walk. As Dad carried me back to bed, I knew my nightmare had returned with vengeance.

That following morning was a whirlwind. While Bob tried to balance my chakras and cleanse my aura, each time he breathed or shifted his hands in my direction, I would wince in pain. Reiki was not going to work. The withdrawal had begun.

Mom called Dr. Vine's office. As his staff told us to come immediately to the city for a visit, I remember clutching my stomach while leaning my body against the hallway wall. I tried to shuffle my feet, but it hurt too much to move. Even though my teeth chattered from being cold, I was sweating profusely through my favorite Victoria's Secret red flannel pajamas. It felt as if a war was being fought inside my body. The only thing I could focus on was the stabbing, searing, puncturing pains. *I must be dying.*

Seeing Dad walking toward me made me moan. I did not want him to touch me. The idea of him squeezing my aching body in order to carry me to the car sent razor-sharp zings down my spine. He tried to calm my sobs by saying everything would be okay, but his eyes told a different story. His dazed look told me he was petrified too. None of us knew what was happening to me.

It was then that Dad had the brilliant idea of getting the office computer chair. He figured that pushing me to the garage would be the easiest and fastest way to get me to the car. I cried sitting in the wooden chair with my legs held up so Dad could wheel me down the hall to the family room. My world was over if I could not stop this excruciating pain.

The drive to San Francisco seemed to last an eternity. Tears fell down my cheeks as I squeezed my stomach and grasped my stuffed dog. I felt like someone poisoned me with cyanide, since every inch of my skin throbbed and my intestines raged in fire. We were all silent in the car as we listened to sports radio. Today was the second day of the NCAA tournament, and my Creighton Bluejays were playing the Florida Gators. It angered me that I was stuck in this damn car when my team was on television. I wished I could have been at school with my friends, watching this game. *God, how I wished life turned out differently.*

We arrived in front of Dr. Vine's office building as my Bluejays were down by seven, nearing halftime. Knowing Dr. Vine's office was on the fourth floor of the building made me panic. How would I make it from the car to his clinic? Dad told me I would be fine as long as I leaned on him. He would have Mom hold the heavy metal door open for us so I could quickly sit on the bench in front of the elevator. I nodded my head and exhaled. *I could do this; just think baby steps.*

I felt the wind whip my frail body when Dad opened my car door. I grimaced while struggling to stand on my own two feet. Dad was there with support and a firm hand. I slowly took one tiny step after another. I thought I was going to fall to my knees by the time I reached the bench. Sweat poured from my temples and I could not stop shaking. *What was wrong with me?*

It took me about ten minutes to make it to Dr. Vine's office. I plopped, hunched over, into the first chair and turned my head to the right to see the bright pieces of artwork. While I usually loved looking at the bold colors, today it made my head pound. I glanced up and saw Chris, the scheduler whom I had a crush on, behind the desk. I was embarrassed because I had not showered in more than a week. Knowing I must have looked and smelled awful, I wondered if this day could get any worse.

As Chris helped Dad bring me to an exam room, I kept my head pointed down to the floor. No one was ever going to love me. Who would want to be with someone who could not shower, shave, or tie her own shoes? I felt disposable and worried what would happen to me if my parents could not care for me anymore. I hated feeling this ashamed and worthless.

I remember lying on the exam table in the fetal position as we waited for Dr. Vine. I feared his wrath. This may have been the dumbest decision I had ever made. *What made me think I could just stop taking 270 mg of morphine?* Sweat dripped down my neck as I began to convulse. My body was shrieking in pain, and nothing would calm it down. I just hoped Dr. Vine had a miracle pill that would end the agony.

Unfortunately, Dr. Vine told me I was out of luck. The reason I had originally felt better was because of the sedatives, anesthetics, and pain relievers used during the actual procedure. As they wore off, the pain returned; and because I had not taken my prescribed medicine for two days, I was now in the midst of opioid withdrawal. If I did not want to rely on morphine to ease the pain, I had no other option but to suffer.

Dr. Vine warned me the pain would continue to elevate and my symptoms would worsen. This could last a few days or possibly weeks, as the length of time varied per person. He left the decision up to me; what did I want to do?

He spoke eloquently and nonchalantly, as if what was happening to me was not a big deal. *Did he not see that I was dying on his table? Why did this not bother him?*

I looked at my parents. They looked awful. Life just kept getting shittier by the minute. Weeping and cringing from the sheer intensity of pain, I asked Dr. Vine if other drugs could alleviate these symptoms. Hearing him say no caught me off guard. Now I had to figure out if this was what I really wanted. Could I handle this pain for an unknown, extended amount of time?

I tried to disappear by closing my eyes tightly. However, nothing happened. I was still in this stifling office with Dr. Vine and one of his fellows hovering over me. I wanted to scream obscenities and curse the gods that believed I could handle this suffering. Instead, I was silent. All my energy had to stay focused on surviving the next minute. My body was fighting to live.

Dr. Vine spoke next about the possibility of me not responding to the re-administered morphine. It was plausible that my body would reject the drug now that the withdrawal had begun. This made my decision very simple. If Dr. Vine could not guarantee the pain would go away, there was no point in reverting to Oramorph and MSIR again. I knew I had to tough this out.

Dr. Vine just nodded his head and told us to keep him posted if anything significant happened over the weekend. Otherwise, he wanted to see me Tuesday morning. Then he left the room and I looked at Mom and Dad. We were now alone to deal with this nightmare. I was terrified. How was I going to make it through the next couple of days?

Getting back to the car was a daunting task in itself. I was too weak to stand on my own, so I had to lean my full body weight on Dad. Being dragged down the hall toward the elevator made the pain unbearable. Sniffling while gasping for air, I begged the Higher Powers to make my misery stop. I did not have the strength to carry such a burden, and the thought of succumbing terrified me. I was not ready to let go, yet I was not sure I had the will to survive.

I was exhausted by the time we reached the car. The burning in my abdomen caused me to lie in the fetal position in the back seat. As I brought my knees close to my stomach, I felt my damp tank top touch my perspiring skin. I was miserable. Each step on the brake or turn onto a new street made my pain rise and nausea increase. I choked back salty saliva as I screamed to my parents. This was too much for me to handle.

Mom told me everything would be okay as Dad turned the radio up so I could hear the sports announcer. Creighton and Florida were neck and neck nearing the end of the second half. I half-heartedly listened to the screeching shoes of the basketball players and the whistling of the referees. While I knew I would have been excited under normal circumstances, right now my mind could not escape the torture I was enduring.

Because it was Friday, traffic was terrible in San Francisco. I felt trapped and confined, barely inching along the busy streets. The thought of being stuck in an uncomfortable car for an extended amount of time troubled me. Terror set in when I realized I would not make the long drive home. I started whimpering, which led to loud sobs.

Not knowing what to do, Dad called Cathy on his cell phone. She told us to come to her house so she could do a Healing Touch session. While Cathy hoped that balancing my chakras would bring me some relief, she knew spending time at her house was better than being stuck on congested freeways. I did not care what we did, as long as someone could take away my pain. I needed help.

It seemed to take thirty minutes for us to maneuver the six blocks to the Kelber house. By the time we reached their street, I truly thought my intestines would implode. It was strange how much this agony rattled me. I always believed I knew what severe pain felt like, yet here I was, completely blindsided by torturous pain. This was hell.

Arriving at Cathy's house, I gripped the door handle to sit up, when I noticed the steep steps to her front door. Tears fell down my cheeks as snot ran from my nose. *How was I ever going to make it into their house?* I did not understand why everything had to be so difficult. I was certain that I would not be able to make it to the top of the stairs; Dad had to reassure me that I would be fine. All I needed to do was trust him and Mom.

Dad continued to remind me that Cathy would make me feel better. I wanted to scream out that he did not understand the pain I was enduring. But I knew complaining would not heal me. Right now, I needed to have faith. I had to hold myself together in order to get through these next horrific minutes. My only job was finding the strength to climb those stairs.

I gulped back fear as I slowly lowered one leg onto the cement. Dad was in front of me, so I grabbed onto his shoulder with my one working hand as Mom clutched my right elbow. The pain was stifling. Every hobble sent shooting pains up and down my entire body. When I thought I was going to fall to the ground, my parents changed positions. Now I would grab hold of Dad's neck while he lifted me up each step. Meanwhile, Mom stood behind me to help pick up my debilitated body.

Feeling them squeeze me enraged the withdrawal feelings, and I could not help but cry out for mercy. I wanted this to end. *When would I gain back a life? How would I deal with this forever?* I looked up and saw Cathy waiting at the top with a chair. I just had three more steps to go. Holding my breath, I closed my eyes and prayed. I was almost there. I was almost to Cathy, and she would take away my suffering.

I held my abdomen as soon as I sat down. It had only been twelve hours since the symptoms had begun, and I had already reached my breaking point. This was the worst torment I had ever experienced. As much as I hated feeling like a failure or being vulnerable in front of others, I became an emotional wreck. *How could I stay optimistic when everything was so far out of my reach?*

When Cathy suddenly told me I needed to lie on her dining room table, I believed I was going to have a conniption. I had just sat down, and now she wanted me to move again to the high wooden table. My body was tired, and walking seemed impossible. I felt my blood pressure rise as I began to shake. I had lost control over everything, and I just wanted to curl up in a ball and disappear.

Thinking I might vomit, Cathy and Dad helped me to my feet and led me toward the bathroom. I stooped over the toilet, wondering what had become of me. I used to be lively and healthy. It did not make sense that life could shift so quickly. While I had always wanted my "old life" back, now I would have settled for "my life" before withdrawal. How did this happen to me?

Unable to throw up, we moved back to the dining room, where Dad, Mom, and Cathy lifted me onto the table. Cathy had placed blankets and pillows down to make it softer, but it did not matter. Nothing could ease my agony. As I moaned and moved into the fetal position, Cathy asked my parents to leave for an hour. She wanted the house entirely quiet so I would be comfortable. Mom looked at me and smiled her usual "I-am-scared-to-death-but-want-to-make-you-feel-better" grin. Dad just nodded his head, but I could see the tears forming in his eyes. Then they were gone, and it was just Cathy and me…and my incredible pain.

The first thing Cathy did was turn down the lights and cover me with more blankets. She lit a few candles that were on her china cabinet before asking me to lie flat. This was hard for me to do because of the pain in my stomach, but she insisted. Cathy kept promising that I would feel better shortly. She only needed me to trust her. Although I did not want to move, I believed in her healing capabilities and slowly lowered my legs until I was in a straight line.

Cathy began by rubbing her hands together for a few minutes. She then moved her pendulum over my chakras, to see which needed balancing. I immediately felt the energetic pull as she cleared my solar plexus. Warmth and calmness seemed to encapsulate my abdomen as her crystal diving rod spun and spun above my belly button. My nausea eased, and I found myself breathing deeply. Soon the chill that I had felt all day seemed to fade away as my temperature regulated.

I have no recollection of the rest of the session. I most likely fell asleep, because my next memory is driving over the Bay Bridge. Even though the raging pain had not subsided, Cathy had subdued the intensity. The severe angst was temporarily gone, which was a relief. My attention drifted to the radio again, as I was shocked to discover my Bluejays were still playing the Gators.

Mom and Dad periodically asked me how I was feeling throughout the car ride. It hurt too much to think or talk, so I would mumble or whisper that I was okay. All I really wanted was silence so I could listen to the second overtime for Creighton basketball. There was less than a minute to go in this exciting game of up two points and then down one. I just hoped my team would win. While I wished I could have watched it on television, it was fun to hear the announcers shriek as the seconds dwindled. The game went down to the wire, but in the end, Creighton pulled out victorious. Final score: 83 to 82.

Within minutes of arriving home, the paralyzing, unrelenting torment returned. I just remember lying in my parents' bed when the pain hit me like a tidal wave. *My nightmare was far from over.*

As I cried and begged for salvation, my family began taking shifts staying by my bedside. Even Dan helped out after school and volleyball practice. For some reason, Dan made me feel better. All he had to do was sit on the corner of the bed and I would perk up. Most of the time, we would watch television, but I do remember constantly asking him to make me laugh or hold my left hand. His presence was evidence that I was not alone…and I think I just needed to know that people remembered me.

Nighttime was the worst. It seemed as if the hell I faced throughout the day intensified to indescribable torture each evening. As every inch of my agonized body raged in pain, sleep became impossible. Minutes felt like hours, and hours felt like days. All I did was sob uncontrollably. I wanted to rip open my chest and tear out my soul, just to escape the misery; I would have done anything to end my hell.

While Mom and Dad rotated nights staying up with me, they both had very different approaches. Mom focused entirely on spirituality. On the evenings she was with me, she would softly brush the hair away from my face and whisper in my ear. She asked me to view this horrific pain as a possible gift. Maybe I could offer my pain up for someone else in order to alleviate the depths of their suffering. I remember thinking that giving up my pain for another person was an interesting concept. If I had to live through this ordeal, there was no need for others I love to have to endure misery as well. It was amazing how Mom's idea brought peace to my spirit. Even though the pain did not cease, I had found meaning in the agony.

The nights Dad stayed with me were much different. We usually watched ESPN highlights of the NCAA tournament, MTV's new show called *The Osbournes,* and then movies. My favorites were *Father of the Bride, Bring it On,* and *Romy and Michelle's High School Reunion.* I remember moaning while tossing and turning in bed. It was as if a duel was happening within my abdomen, and the jouster was slashing through my stomach lining. Dad would give me his hand so I could bite the fleshy area between his thumb and pointer finger. Although I would clamp down so firmly that I would leave visible teeth marks, nothing could take my attention off the stirring, mind-blowing pain.

With my internal organs feeling as though they were on fire, the burning heat made it impossible for me to eat or drink. Whatever entered my mouth would automatically come back up within minutes. Then I would vomit bodily fluids until I started to dry heave. My poor throat was raw and swollen. I even began to worry that I might soon throw up blood. I could not handle all of this…and yet I knew I could not escape. I was stuck in hell.

As the withdrawal continued to intensify, smells made me dry heave. Nothing could be prepped or cooked in our kitchen, so my parents and Dan ordered take-out or ate cereal. Because I could not be alone, Mom and Dad took turns sitting in the hallway, eating pasta from the local Italian restaurant. Just watching them made my heart sad. How could this be happening to our family?

With my weight dropping significantly over the past few weeks, I was weaker than usual. In fact, I had become a frail shell. Unable to put any pressure on the bones, ligaments, and joints in my legs meant I could not walk. Again, I depended on the computer chair to wheel me from my parents' bed to their bathroom. Life was out of my hands.

While the dark days lingered, I received a welcoming care package. Nikken headquarters had requested my presence at their annual convention in Missouri. Having learned of my remarkable story, Nikken invited me to speak to the five-thousand-person crowd about my experience using the far-infrared products. I was flabbergasted as Dad read the note three times to me. I could not believe someone thought my life was that meaningful. This was such a privilege, but seeing that I could not even get out of bed, I did not know if my health would permit such a trip.

While the news was thrilling, nothing made me truly happy anymore. I felt numb to emotions. Since all I experienced was pain and suffering, it was becoming harder for me to register good times. The guilt and shame I internalized for ruining my family weighed on my conscience every day. I felt worthless and insecure most of the time. *When would it be my turn to spread my wings and fly?*

I was lucky Dad would not stand for my pity party. He was assertive and forceful when he told me I was not a burden. I had a gift, and so many people looked to me for inspiration and guidance. He wanted me to tell him how many people I knew who had been asked to speak to five thousand people. Although I might not be doing what typical twenty-one-year-olds do, I was making a difference. This self-deprecating talk had to stop.

All I did was smile, and told Dad I loved him. I then reminded myself everything happens for a reason. There had to be a greater purpose to all this pain. *I just had to hold on to hope.*

The withdrawal persisted for another few days before the tide turned. In total, I lived through six full days of misery and despair. It took me three days just to manage to limp three feet to the bathroom. Then it was another three days before I attempted to leave my parents' bedroom and walk by myself. My first steps down the hallway were frightening and freeing. Because I was so weak, I had to grab doorknobs as I slowly took baby steps. Yet I finally felt alive. I was out of bed and off narcotics. *This was my independence.*

Chapter 15

St. Louis

My health stabilized over the next few weeks, and I was able to attend Nikken's main convention in St. Louis. Having the company ask me to speak in front of the five thousand guests symbolized hope. For too long, I had seen myself as a failure. I felt extremely guilty for putting such a financial burden on my parents, and it broke my heart that my illness changed Dan's life. My brother never had a normal childhood. Instead, he lived a life in the shadows, as my needs always outshined his.

This was why Nikken's invitation to come to St. Louis and share my story meant so much to me. I saw this as an opportunity to heal and grow. My confidence in the grassroots effort kept me optimistic that doors would open. I naively thought talking about how alternative therapies improved my physical and emotional pain would make a difference in the healthcare system. This convention represented change and better days ahead.

Dr. Vine warned me that traveling was risky. He did not know how my immune system would react to the pressure changes of being in the air after enduring such brutal withdrawal. While hearing him speak about possible problems terrified me, I knew I needed to attend. I felt called to tell my story. Though the fear of suffering another flare-up definitely scared me, my desire to change the world outweighed any of my worries. Dr. Vine understood my conviction and agreed to the trip. His only requirement was for Mom to bring my medications in case of an emergency; so we did.

Just boarding the plane in Oakland with Mom was exhilarating. I was off drugs and beginning a new chapter in my life. Although I had spoken on behalf of the NPF, this was my first talk that required travel…and that was exciting. For the first time in years, I was hopeful that life would turn around.

Unfortunately, the trip turned into a disaster. I remember the turbulent flight left me in extreme pain. My right hand pulsated and throbbed the entire four hours we were on the plane. By the time we landed, I was shaking and fighting back tears. Knowing that I was speaking the following morning did not help my anxiety. *What if the pain worsened and I could not get out of bed?* I tried to remember the techniques Shelley and Maureen taught me, but I was too upset to focus.

My next memory was of the overwhelming convention center filled with thousands of enthusiastic people. I felt my stomach rumble, and the room started to spin. *Was I ready for such a large crowd?* I luckily did not have time to worry about my performance. A Nikken publicist was waiting to bring Mom and me backstage to prepare.

Never had I seen such invigorating chaos. Music techs and lighting specialists were running around, trying to finish last-minute details. There were hair and makeup stylists touching up presenters. I was introduced to the emcee and met the keynote speaker. *This was a big deal.*

Soon someone pulled me away from Mom, and I was standing on the steps behind the stage. I remember the emcee made small talk with me and told me not to stress. He just wanted me to relax and speak from the heart. There was no need to worry, because I would not see anyone past the first two rows. While his advice was helpful, I thought it was much easier for him to say that, considering that his remarks were on the teleprompter. The pressure for this to be perfect weighed heavily on me. *I had to be phenomenal.*

My heart pounded, listening to the man on stage begin to introduce me. I knew any second he would call my name and I would walk out and speak about the impact Nikken products had on my life. I owed a lot to this corporation. It was because of the far-infrared and ionized water that I regained mobility in my left hand. Since Nikken gave me the strength to keep fighting my battle, this was my chance to thank them. I only wanted them to be proud.

Yet, seconds before being called on stage, a Nikken representative dropped an atomic bomb—I could not say the word "pain." Immediately, I freaked out. *How could I share my story without mentioning CRPS or chronic pain?* My mouth became dry, while hundred of thoughts raced through my head. I wondered if I could say agony, hurt, aching, or burning. However, before I had a chance to ask any of these questions, I felt myself pushed on stage. *Crap.*

The glare of the lights made my forehead sweat. I could hear loud applause and then it went silent. All eyes were on me, as a large pit grew in my stomach. My mind went blank before I even reached the podium. With no recollection of what I had practiced to say, I began to panic internally. I just opened my mouth. Luckily, words came; yet it was humiliating to stutter and stumble through what I knew could have been a good speech.

As I exited the stage to pity applause, I kept my head down. I could not even look at Mom, because I felt I let her and Nikken down. This was a total catastrophe. I knew I was better than that, and all I wanted was to get on the next plane. *How could I have done so badly? Did the morphine make me a better public speaker?*

∞

It was a relief to be home. The convention had been exhausting, and I needed time to process what happened. I knew it was just part of my personality to be hard on myself. I was naturally my own worst critic. Therefore, I consciously knew I had not flopped. It was not a perfect speech by any means, but I also had not failed. I shared my story to the best of my ability at that time. Now I had to let it go, so I could focus on my health.

Chapter 16

PCU

My pain had risen drastically since coming home. After days of intolerable searing and stabbing pains, I had to revert to morphine for temporary relief. I was very disappointed in myself. This was just another failure of mine. How had I allowed opioids to become my crutch again?

As the severe throbbing and hypersensitivity amplified, a small gust of wind or a fan circulating the room air would cause my skin to burn. Sleeping was impossible, because I was unable to rest my right arm or hand on any surface. Anytime my arm would drop and touch my bed sheet or pillow, I would instantly awaken in more intense pain. I spent my mornings, afternoons, and nights in bed, unaware of my body's uncontrollable shaking or deafening moans. I remembered passing the time by watching movies and old episodes of *Friends* and *Will and Grace.* After four days of getting less than three hours of sleep, I was in the depths of despair.

Dr. Vine grew concerned and suggested hospitalization. Yet I was reluctant to endure another stint in the hospital. I pleaded for another solution, convinced that there had to be some other drug that would relieve my pain and allow me to sleep. While Dr. Vine agreed to prescribe a combination of medications, he warned me that if this did not work, he would have to re-admit me. My situation was too critical to fool around.

I just nodded my head, relieved to have dodged a bullet. I was sick of the PCU and did not want to go back. As Dr. Vine wrote a script for the pharmacy, he informed me that he would be leaving for Italy the next day for a medical conference. Although he would not be in the country for two weeks, his Fellows would be seeing patients. I did not need to worry about my medical care, because he would be in constant communication with them throughout the duration of his trip. I would be in good hands.

Dr. Vine had scheduled me to return to in two days for a follow-up, but I was back the following afternoon. The medicines had not worked. After yet another sleepless night filled with extreme torture, I became much more receptive to the idea of a hospital stay. I needed to get better soon. Dan's high school graduation was only two weeks away. I wanted to be doing well for him.

∞

As had become customary, I was in a private room on the Pulmonary Care Unit. The nurses monitored me as they administered high doses of opioids through my PCA pump. Though glad to be receiving medicine, I faced another problem: my veins had atrophied from all the previous inserted IV lines. In the past, the nurses always managed to find another vein that would withstand. Not this time; now my veins would burst and close.

The inability to locate a sturdy vein confused the Fellows. They were unsure what course of action to take, and hypothesized that a day of rest might result in finding a more suitable vein. Opting to postpone making a decision for twenty-four hours, the nurses had to constantly watch me and check my IV line for infection or loss of connectivity. Even though continuous prodding inflamed my chronic pain, I would have to be re-poked each time a vein popped.

After exhausting all pliable veins on my left arm, the Fellows agreed I needed a temporary implantation of a peripherally inserted central catheter (PICC line). I learned that a PICC line was a form of intravenous access that prolonged the amount of time I could receive medications, with minimal risk of infection. The procedure entailed inserting a small catheter in the peripheral vein. Doctors would then advance the catheter through larger veins toward the heart until the tip rested in the distal atria of the heart.

At that point, I did not care what the Fellows did, as long as they did it immediately. The past twenty-four hours had been excruciating. My right hand had turned an ashen shade, inflamed to the size of a softball; each finger was the width of a hot dog. I was in unbelievable agony and losing my patience. All I cared about was receiving pain-relieving drugs. For me, time was of the essence.

I remember scolding Dr. Vine's Fellows for their poor treatment as they wheeled me toward the operating room. Dr. Vine had left *specific* orders to perform this procedure as soon as I was hospitalized. I was pissed that they chose to forgo his instructions and jeopardize my health, and I did not care who heard me rant. *How could they allow me to suffer longer than need be?* I did not trust either of them and wanted them both barred from practicing medicine as soon as possible. In my opinion, they were a disgrace and a liability to the pain community.

Thankfully, the OR was ready when I arrived. Nurses quickly administered local anesthetic at the surgical site, as well as oxygen and sedatives. I could feel the heat from the beaming lights penetrating my skin. My pain was off the charts, and I found myself becoming more irritated as time dragged on. *When would they start this damn procedure?* Just when I began to open my mouth to start in on another rampage, my world went dark…and I did not awaken until I heard someone enter my PCU room.

I watched as a nurse stood over my bed to change the medicine bag and inspect the pump for any malfunctions. I knew this was just typical protocol for the PCU. Nurses had to keep a watchful eye on me, due to the heavy medications. The extreme and excessive amounts of medicine may have brought me some much-needed pain relief, but it came at a high price. For starters, my personality and demeanor changed. I would lose my sweet, charismatic nature and would become angry and aggressive or feeble and apologetic. I was just not myself, and it was the consequence of such potent drugs.

Secondly, I would lose my appetite. Besides an eight-ounce container of non-fat milk and a slice of wheat toast that I ate in the mornings, apple juice was the only other thing I consumed throughout the day. My entire nutritional intake came from that sweetly concentrated juice that I seemed to love so much. It was even strange to me that I liked the tangy, artificial, corn-syrup taste. However, I was obsessed with the hospital's apple juice and could drink enough per day.

Besides a loss of appetite, I would lose control over my bladder. With medications wreaking havoc on my nervous system, I was unable to determine when I had to use the restroom. Therefore, I would urinate without warning. This crushed me. *I was a twenty-one-year-old who still needed assistance changing and freshening up.* After days of wetting the bed at night, I could no longer cope with the humiliation and begged the night staff for a diaper. Despite the embarrassment and shame that comes from wearing a diaper, I felt better knowing I would not make a mess.

And like all the times before, I faced severe constipation. With everyone on staff wanting to avoid further complications, a nurse came to my room every other evening to administer an enema. I remember fighting her every night. As I cried, clenched, and squeezed, she would just pat my head. She kept telling me it would be over soon and I was going to be okay. Although she assured me there was nothing to be embarrassed about, enemas destroyed the little self-worth I had left.

As the days progressed, I became less aware of reality and more concerned with imaginary worlds. The concept of time bewildered me. Minutes became hours, and hours turned into days with no defining separation. Lying in a complete fog, I would drift in and out of consciousness. Drool would run alongside my cheek and down my chin as sweat poured from my temples. *I had become lost within my own mind.*

∞

I was convinced that the night nurses wanted to hurt me. Each night they would unplug my pump so I would not have to bother them when I needed to use the bathroom. They said it would be easier on me, so I could make it to the toilet on time; I did not believe them. If the day shift always came to unplug my machine and help me to the restroom, then the night shift should too.

It seemed as if my accidents in bed also annoyed the evening nurses. While the staff did bring me clean linens, they left me alone in my room to change the sheets. Here I was, dizzy, distraught, and in overwhelming agony, and they wanted me to make my own bed. They were mean to me, and I became scared to ask any of them for help.

It bothered me that no one believed I was being tortured after dark. Hearing laughter at the nurses' station as one of the staff members wheeled a clean bed down the hall, saying next time they should just switch out beds, angered and terrified me. *Why were they out to get me? Nurses were supposed to help sick people.* Frightened for my safety, I picked up the phone and called Meredith. I wanted her to come rescue me. When she refused, I took matters into my own hands.

I knew I had to escape. Although I did not have a getaway vehicle, I figured I could call a taxi to take me home once I was out of harm's way. As I slowly sat up in bed, blood rushed from my head, leaving me woozy and unstable. My room was the closest to the nurses' station, and the elevator was directly in front of them. Exiting without anyone noticing would be difficult.

I took a deep breath as I lowered my feet to the ground and then stood up. Stepping forward, I realized I was connected to many different monitors. *It would be impossible to for me to be discreet while hauling all these machines.* I had to think fast, since rounds were in fifteen minutes. The only machine not plugged in was my IV pole containing my morphine bag. I knew I could not survive without these drugs, so I decided to keep the pole with me. As I disconnected the other monitors by pulling off electrodes, alarms began ringing. I could hear the commotion at the nurses' station. *Crap!*

Without much time to think, I crawled to one of the room's corners and ducked behind my pole. I hoped I would just become invisible. The first person to reach my room was one of the traveling nurses. As he stormed in and turned on the light, I came to my senses. There was no way he would not see me. Not wanting to be found hiding in the corner, my gut response was to scream, "BOO!"

He shrieked loudly. Turning in my direction, he found me huddled in a small ball with a slight smirk on my face. As he assisted me back to the bed and reconnected my monitors, he began his interrogation. It was at that moment I could not hold back the tears any longer. Soon I was bawling as I told him I wanted to leave the hospital. I shared how I hated being here alone at night, because he and his friends were awful people. How could they make fun of me and treat me so poorly? What had I done to them to make them not like me?

The traveling nurse was quiet. He just listened to me vent before telling me that everyone did care for me, and no one was intentionally trying to hurt me. He did not deny that they talked to each other about my case, but it was out of a genuine concern over my well-being. I was on a lot of medicine, and that worried many staff members. I needed to understand that the amount of morphine I consumed was the highest many had ever seen. He then paused before telling me he would stay in my room until I fell asleep.

When the day shift arrived a few hours later, I became paranoid. Panicked that the hospital would want me to leave, I stared out my door as the night staff explained my recent incident to the oncoming shift. I did not want them to kick me out of PCU.

I tensed up as the day nurse entered my room. Waiting for my reprimand, I was surprised when she did not mention anything about the previous night. Instead, she only wanted to know why my IV programmer was unplugged. I told her the night staff unplugged it every night so I could use the bathroom on my own. She seemed rattled and started mumbling under her breath as she handed me my oral medications. Then she left the room, and I subsequently self-administered my first dose of liquid morphine for the day.

The rest of the morning was a blur, as reality and delirium intertwined. Lying in a semi-cognitive state, I overheard the caregiver of the patient in the room next door complain to the nurses. She was justifiably livid to learn that her daughter was up all night due to the commotion coming from my room. Knowing that her own child's symptoms had worsened outraged her. I could hear her verbally attack the staff for their inadequate response to the situation. She kept shouting, "I thought this was supposed to be an acclaimed hospital! I believed patients came here to heal in peace and not to be subjected to the obscene squeals of an uncontrollable girl."

I felt terrible as I listened more intently to the argument brewing outside my door. She demanded that changes be made or her family would take matters into their own hands. The nurse soothingly tried to calm her down, explaining how they could move her daughter to the opposite end of the PCU. This way I would not be able to distract her or exacerbate her condition. With the nurse apologizing for last night, I heard the mom insist they move me instead of her daughter. Since I was the one who had caused the problem, I should be the one to suffer the consequence.

However, *I* could not move away from the nurses' station. My condition was considered so severe that someone needed to watch me twenty-four hours a day. That was all it took for the argument that was once brewing outside my door to progress. Soon the mother was threatening my life and the lives of my family members. With her husband being the head of the Mafia, she guaranteed her family would stop at nothing to make sure I paid for what I did to their daughter.

Was she serious? I never meant to hurt anyone. Was I really going to die at the hands of the Mafia?

Terror took over as sirens went off throughout the hospital; nurses had alarmed security. The antics outside my door kept getting louder, and I began to worry when I noticed my door handle turn. My worst fear was becoming reality. Suddenly the irate woman was in my room, standing over my bed. *I was face to face with my attacker.*

She repeatedly slapped my face while trying to wrap her hands around my neck. I remember gasping for breath as she yelled, "I am going to get you. You are going to suffer for what you did, you little bitch!"

Security guards trampled into my room to pull her off me as I pleaded for my life. But it did not matter what I said or how much I apologized. She wanted me dead. With the hospital placed on emergency lockdown, a guard told me the FBI would come to rescue me. I would have to enter the Witness Protection Program in order to protect my family and myself.

The pounding on the door terrified me. I knew I needed to hide my identity so the *bad people* would not find me. I frantically scrubbed down the hospital desk that held my juice, remote control, get-well cards, Kleenex and migraine patches. Afraid of leaving any fingerprints, I piled all those items on my bed and began sticking migraine patches and Kleenex on my face in order to mask my own profile. As the noises became louder outside my room, I began screaming for the nurses to rescue me. I remember hiding under the covers, crying while constantly hitting my call button. *Please save me. I do not want to die.*

Then the door to my room swung open, and I awoke from the hell. A nurse rushed to my side to check my vitals. My heart raced as she then placed an oxygen mask on my face and administered another dose of morphine. Tears fell from my eyes and ran down my cheeks. The nurse continued to reassure me that nobody was out to harm me. Resting cool towels on my forehead and neck, she gently stroked my hair. I was all right. The whole ordeal had been a hallucination from the medications.

Life in the PCU continued in the same fashion for another few days. All I did was lie in a drugged stupor as an IV line protruded out of my neck. My head would bob up and down anytime I closed my eyes. There I would fall into a hazy fog, only to stir when the cool, slippery drool landed on my hand. It was a continual cycle. *I was losing my identity and morphing into "disabled."*

I remember spending hours staring at my hand in complete amazement and utter disgust. Thinking about how a tiny part of my body could wreak such havoc on my entire nervous system disillusioned me. My mangled and disfigured limb repulsed me. With it not even bearing any resemblance to its original beauty anymore, it felt like I no longer had a hand. I was decrepit. *What would become of me if this condition persisted? Who would ever love me or find me worthy?*

I began to devote my energy to regaining mobility of my right hand. Hours would elapse as I willed the claw to move. I would follow Sharon's technique of breathing into the dark void in order to reconnect my right limb with the rest of my body. Waiting for the slightest twitch or tremble made me anxious. Now more than ever, I needed a reason to believe I could still heal. I just prayed every day for my miracle.

Then, one afternoon, I peered at my hand after waking from my latest nap. I was bewildered. Was this another hallucination or had my thumb actually trembled? I opened my eyes wider and stared at my fingers. My thumb was indeed squirming. *Movement had returned to my hand.*

Although giddy with excitement, I was very much aware of what was at stake. I knew I had to stay focused, so I pushed myself to lift my thumb off the other curled fingers. Concentrating that intently made my temples pound. Feeling the impending migraine approaching, I pressed the button on my morphine pump. Instantly I felt the rush of warmth encompass my entire body.

Then I took a deep breath and redirected my attention to my thumb. I visualized my finger reaching toward the heavens. It was miraculous that my thumb actually listened to the neural signals from my brain and pointed up to the sky. Soon my other four contorted fingers started to shake.

I was so absorbed in my breathing and mobility exercises that I had not even realized that Dad and Meredith had arrived for an afternoon visit. It was nice to have company and be able to flaunt my new hand trick. Watching light return to Dad's deadening eyes left me emotional. I was both happy and sad. *This was what he needed to see.* This was proof that keeping his daughter in a highly medicated state had been for the best. The torture and sacrifices were not in vain; the treatments were finally working.

I then settled in for another drug-induced nap, only to wake sometime later to Dad and Meredith sitting in front of me. They both had deer-in-the-headlights gazes. After wiping the drool off my face, I tried to move my fingers again. Much to my astonishment, they were still mobile. I could not believe the leaps and bounds I had made within an afternoon. I was on the road to recovery. *Now I wanted to attend Dan's high school graduation.*

It was three days until Dan received his diploma, and I really wanted to be there. I had recently discovered that the doctors could move the PICC line from my neck and reposition it in my left arm. This would allow me the option of leaving the hospital attached to a portable pump and medicine bag. Knowing I could continue treatments on an outpatient basis gave me the courage to speak with Dr. Vine's Fellows. I did not understand I why needed to be an inpatient if I could do the same treatments at home.

That afternoon, when the three Fellows met with me to discuss my daily progress, I expressed how I wanted to attend my brother's graduation. To do that, I would have to have the PICC line moved as soon as possible. It was a rocky start to an already tense situation. The attending who had refused to follow protocol when I arrived in the hospital was the first to speak. He felt another risky procedure would not be in my best interest. He wanted more time to evaluate my progress before making any sudden decisions.

Was he kidding me?

I was livid and quickly lost my patience. Lacking the ability to restrain my thoughts, words began spewing out of me. As he had already disobeyed Dr. Vine's instructions ten days earlier, I advised him not to continue working in this type of medicine. He was a pain specialist studying under a doctor known for his aggressive treatments and surgical procedures. No patient should be denied a procedure because the surgeon was afraid of surgery.

I could see that my honesty and ruthless candor stunned him. Although he looked flabbergasted at my mean-spirited backlash, he did not argue or rebut my statements. Instead, he only said he would look into the procedure. He would do whatever he could so I could be home with my family for Dan's graduation. However, I had to accept his medical expertise. Since my health was his main concern, he would not promise anything.

He then left the room. I watched him hand my chart over to a nurse before glancing back at me. He looked upset. While I felt some remorse for attacking his worth and credibility as a doctor, I justified my actions—sometimes people needed the brutal truth in order to make the greatest changes.

I hardly slept that evening. The anticipation surrounding my fate unnerved me. Knowing I had two days to undergo the PICC line procedure and leave the hospital was cutting it close. Time was crucial in this matter, and I worried I did not have enough of it. All I wanted was to be home.

The Fellows visited me first thing the next morning. While they reviewed my case and agreed to the new PICC line, there was a slight problem. No operating rooms or radiologists were available until next Monday. My smile faded as I stared at the blank wall. This was terrible news. Then the Fellow I yelled at yesterday cleared his throat. Believing he would gloat or rub salt in my wounds, I prepared for a smack down.

Instead, he politely informed me of one other option: I could opt to have an oncology or radiology nurse perform the procedure from my hospital room. He needed me to know that this would make the PICC adjustment more challenging and extremely painful. I had to understand that the added risks involved could affect whether I would be able to go home this weekend as well.

Possible complications did not matter to me. *I had to take that chance.*

Hours later, a male nurse entered my room and set down a covered metal tray on my bedside table. I remember his first question was whether I was afraid of needles or sharp objects. When I shook my head, he slowly removed the sheet and I began to study the tray's contents. There were iodine swabs, gauze, syringes, needles, and an unknown object I assumed had to be the catheter.

I grimaced at the sight of the large, lengthy needle. I had never seen one so extensive. *Was that going to puncture my skin?* I gulped. While reminding myself that this was for Dan, I also knew the Universe would never hand me more than I could handle. To shake off my remaining fears, I recited one of my favorite prayers:

Angel of God, My guardian dear.
To whom your love, Commits me here.
Ever this day, Be at my side.
To Light and Guard,
Rule and Guide.

The nurse then explained the entire procedure so I would not be afraid or have questions later. Although we chatted and laughed while he swabbed my left arm with iodine, he became silent once he begun tapping and flicking my arm. Now he was in work mode; he was trying to find the perfect vein.

My heart beat faster when I saw him pick up the enormous, ruler-sized needle. I naturally held my breath, watching him carefully insert the sharp tip into my arm. As the catheter slowly crawled up my vein, I could feel pressure and extreme discomfort. It was followed by sharp stinging. This meant the vein had closed. He would have to start the whole process over.

Sweat poured from my temples and down the sides of my face. I took in another deep breath, praying this time would be a success. Yet it was not. Repeating this tedious method over and over again for nearly forty-five minutes was excruciating. I kept biting my inner lip and shuddering every time another vein failed. This was hell.

We were not making any progress. With the nurse uncomfortable continuing much longer, I began to plead. He was my only chance at happiness. I needed this to work so I could be with my family. He just could not give up on me.

Although I could tell he was hesitant to proceed, he agreed to twenty more minutes. Then he was done. I knew we both could not carry on this torment forever, so I held my breath and implored the heavens.

The procedure was agonizing. I thought remaining stiff might make a difference, so I kept my head fixated on the closed door and refused to move. My knees shook as I stoically fought back the tears welling in my eyes. When the pain would increase, I would squeeze my stuffed dog closer to my body. Feeling a needle creep further up my vein alongside the clavicle and pectoral muscle was nauseating to me. *Please, God, help me.*

As the catheter advanced, my pain escalated. Never had I felt such intense jolting, stinging pain so close to my chest cavity. Despite being scared that he might accidentally puncture my heart, I refused to tell him to stop. We were finally making strides.

"I think I got it."

Hearing those words relieved me. As I relaxed my shoulders, tears fell from my eyes. I was deeply grateful to my nurse. I thanked him as he wheeled me into the hall to wait for an elevator. We were on our way to the MRI and Imaging wing of the hospital. Here he would verify the correct position of the PICC with an X-ray.

The room turned fuzzy as I watched him stick the X-ray under the lighted viewing screen. I did not know what to look for, so I kept my eyes glued to him. He was quiet and reflective as he studied the picture. My stomach churned, waiting for him to speak. All I wanted to know was if I would be able to go home. As he opened his mouth, the world stood still.

It was a success; the catheter was resting in the perfect position.

Chapter 17

Home Sweet Home

Due to hospital protocol, I could not leave the premises for another twenty-four hours. This allowed nurses to monitor me and rule out any adverse symptoms or infections. I wanted to object, but I kept my mouth shut. I knew I could not fight policies.

As I sat in the bed, counting down the hours until discharge, I watched my parents deal with the daunting task of contacting our insurance company and the Home Health Care Agency. I never realized all the red tape my parents had to jump through to get me better. Making sure the insurance company approved new therapies was a long, drawn-out process that Dad made look easy. Dad understood the significance of being a caregiver. He learned the names of the people he needed to contact, and he called repeatedly over the next few hours. He literally stopped at nothing to make sure his baby girl received the best care possible…and I owed a lot to him.

Thankfully, my health insurance company permitted home visitations by a registered nurse. Learning the logistics of home health care was overwhelming. A nurse would visit our house every other day during my first week. Then it would change to every three days. These nurses were responsible for changing the medicine bag and tubing. As the medicine would arrive separately and require immediate refrigeration, either Mom or Dad had to be home during delivery.

I was relieved when the hospital administrator came to my room with my release papers. After being confined to the PCU for twelve days, all I wanted was to breathe natural air. I fantasized about dancing in a field of flowers and skipping rocks in a flowing river. I thought about tying a pair of tennis shoes and sitting in a hot tub. How I wished I could have been living out my dreams. When would I be happy again?

The ride home seemed especially long. My left arm ached from the PICC line being positioned directly below my elbow. While I wanted nothing more than to lie in my own bed right now, Mom had arranged a wash and blow-dry for me.

I usually loved getting my hair washed by Kathi. Kathi had been Mom's stylist for as long as I could remember. It was a treat for me to have her delicately scrub my scalp and style my hair. As she talked to me about everyday life, it was the only time where I truly felt like a typical young adult. However, today was not a good day. The pain was stifling, and the only thought on my mind was when I would be better. *How much more heartache would I have to endure?*

The next day went smoothly. The school sat us in the disability section. Although we did not have the best view, we were separated from the massive crowd and covered by an awning. Being in the shade and not having to worry that someone might accidentally bump me was reassuring. I could now relax and try to enjoy myself.

When the graduating class of 2002 finally threw their caps in the air an hour later, I was beaming. I was extremely proud of Dan and his accomplishments. It was a mystery to me where he gathered his strength to persevere. He easily could have rebelled against the cards he had been dealt, and yet he did not. Dan was one of my heroes.

After hugs and a few pictures, Mom and Dad took me home to rest. As Mom helped me undress into my yellow sweats, Dad quickly set up the couch with pillows and blankets. By then, I was exhausted and in a great deal of pain. It was hard for me to walk from one end of the house to the other. I was positive I overdid it. Yet I did not care, because I was able to see my little brother graduate from high school.

The home health nurse got lost finding her way to our home the following day. Frazzled upon arrival, she walked inside and went straight to the kitchen sink. I watched her wash her hands before opening the refrigerator door to take out the bag of medicine. I found her actions odd. She had never met me or been to my house, but she acted as though this was her home.

She finally sat down beside me at the kitchen table and asked me how I was doing. I told her I had left the hospital two days ago but was having problems. I still had not regained my appetite, and I felt extremely tired. It was common for me to lose around ten pounds during a hospital visit. However, I would usually regain the weight within a few days of returning home. Although I had dropped another three pounds since leaving, I was not overly worried. I knew I would eventually gain the weight. It did worry me that I had no energy and currently slept about eighteen hours a day.

The nurse seemed more concerned about my drastic weight loss than my sleeping. With the amount of medication I was ingesting, the nurse told me food was a necessity. I needed sustenance to break down the toxins that flushed the poisonous compounds out of my system. I just nodded my head, because this was not news to me. My parents had been pestering me ever since coming home. I was tired of discussing food. I already understood the need for protein and nutrients. This was not my way of gaining control over my out-of-control life. I loved to eat, but for some reason, the thought of chewing made me nauseated.

As the nurse begun switching tubes and medicine bags, she told me she would continue to monitor my weight and eating habits over the next few days. If nothing significant changed, she would recommend a feeding tube. That way I would not need to consume the food, yet my body would still receive the nourishment needed to stay healthy. Then she grinned at me. I started to feel as though she thought I was not eating on purpose. *Why did no one believe me?*

By now, Mom and I had adopted a bickering relationship. I would not say I was angry at her, but I found myself completely frustrated. She was petrified of the consequences my weight loss had on my declining health. While I attempted to eat ground beef to make her happy, I regurgitated and had to spit it out. It was a rough time for all of us. No one understood how the taste of food could be so intolerable to me.

The nurse's next few visits followed the same pattern, where she weighed and lectured me on the value of proper eating. Soon my weight was down to 109 pounds. I believed the nurse was about to scold me, so I tried to explain why eating was so difficult. Chewing made my gums ache, and every food tasted metallic. It was as if I saw the light bulb turn on in her head. She immediately examined my mouth and discovered little patches of white bumps along my tongue and cheeks. I had developed thrush.

Thrush is a common yeast infection caused by antibiotic usage. This explained my lack of appetite. Certain I would want to eat once the thrush cleared, she prescribed an oral rinse that I needed to swish in my mouth three times a day. The rinse tasted awful. I have memories of crying and gagging on the foul-tasting liquid. I used to plead with my parents not to make me do it. Even though I wanted the sore bumps and metal taste to go away, I despised the rinse and began to lie about doing the treatment.

My weight staggered to 107 pounds two days later. With my health in grave jeopardy, the nurse had no choice but to connect a feeding bag to my PICC line as well. The bag was large and extremely heavy, which made moving around difficult. All afternoon, I worked myself into a tizzy and sobbed. I hated the cold sensation of the liquid draining into my veins.

By the time the weekend nurse arrived on Saturday, my crying episodes were out of control. While she felt she had to disconnect the bag in order to save my sanity, I had to promise her I would begin eating regularly. Otherwise, a different nurse would reconnect me on Monday. Terrified of having that bag reattached, I forced down bird-sized bites of food and tried not to vomit. *There was no way I could live with a feeding bag.*

Later that night, my body started acting unusual. As I walked down the hallway and turned the corner, my right leg completely gave out on me. I was fortunate to be in grabbing reach of a doorknob. Waiting for strength and mobility to return to my limp limb, I began to notice tiny spasms traveling up and down the leg. Then the tremors dissipated, and I regained my balance. I brushed the unsettling feelings aside, thinking this had to be a fluke occurrence.

Yet the next day, it happened again.

∞

I remember I woke early and went to the bathroom to brush my teeth. I was standing over the sink, when suddenly I could not put any pressure on one of my legs. My right leg had gone lifeless again. Not knowing what to do, I leaned my body against the counter and glanced in the mirror. To my horror, I saw my right arm was also trembling. I screamed for my parents, but my vocal cords sounded high-pitched and squeaky, as if I had turned into Minnie Mouse.

My heart beat ferociously as I staggered to my parents' bedroom, dragging my right leg. Their room was mere steps from my bathroom, but I did not know if I would make it. Sweat fell from my temples as I clutched the hall closet doorknob for extra balance. I had no idea what was happening, but I feared the PICC line had moved.

I cried out in a squeal when I opened my parents' door. Taking two more hops, I collapsed face-first on the bed. All four limbs were dead. While I was scared, Mom seemed exasperated and kept raising her voice, asking me what was wrong. I did not know. All I remembered was brushing my teeth when I lost control of my limbs. When I tried to explain this to her, I lacked the ability to form syllables. Mom only heard a shrill giggle erupt from my lips. *What was wrong with me?*

Mom looked horrified as I struggled to control my voice. My wicked crackling laugh sounded like the Joker from Batman. Soon I started to feel sharp pains against my head. *I was violently hitting myself.* I continued ruthlessly beating myself in the chest, face and head without any restraint. Something was terribly wrong.

Mom lunged toward the phone and dialed 911. Her voice trembled as she spoke to the operator about my symptoms. She then called Dad's cell phone. It was typical for him to go in to work on weekend mornings. Because of my many doctors' appointments, he spent most of his weekdays with me. Therefore, Saturdays and Sundays were his best opportunities to finish or begin new projects. Luckily, he was already on his way home and only a block from our house.

I had hardly changed positions since I entered their room. I was still lying on the right side of their bed when Dad arrived. My limbs looked distorted. With the spasms persisting, my body bounced up and down and floundered. I was striking my head and slapping my legs while continuing to laugh in a devilish manner. Mom updated Dad on what had been happening, as he stared at me in fright. I looked like a puppet whose limbs flailed about wildly. This was the first time Dad did not have encouraging words to calm me down. We were all at a complete loss as we waited for the ambulance.

I heard the sirens, followed by quick, thumping footsteps down the hall. My fears were pacified as the two initial paramedics reached the scene. A man checked my vitals as a woman examined my eyes and throat. The baffled look on their faces re-ignited my nerves; it seemed as if they did not know what was happening to me. While I possessed every symptom related to a seizure, I could talk, albeit in mouse-like vocals. Therefore, the only other explanation was overdose from the intravenous PICC line.

Without a clear-cut answer for my condition, they knew I had to get to the hospital as soon as possible. The gurney was already in the hallway, which meant the paramedics only needed to lift me. However, my uncontrollable spasms and convulsions made that impossible. It did not matter that I only weighed 108 pounds; they still could not carefully carry me. I remember the man telling my parents he would be right back before rushing out of the room. He returned minutes later with two other EMTs.

It took three strong men and one woman to raise my tiny frame onto the gurney. They secured me with belts tightened across my chest, abdomen, and knees. Although I tried to fight them, they repeatedly told me this was for my own safety. Then the large team of paramedics wheeled me outside to the ambulance, and we made our way to the nearest hospital.

The entire ambulance ride was surreal. I had two paramedics continuing to work on me en route as Mom sat quietly in the corner. The first order of business was disconnecting my IV bag. It was amazing how quickly my voice steadied after they removed the medicine. Before we even arrived at the hospital, I was forming short sentences and laughing.

As we pulled up to the ER, nurses rushed me to a small room where I heard the paramedics exchange possible diagnoses with the doctors. Two nurses began connecting me to different monitors while re-examining my vital signs. Dad arrived as a saline IV began to flush the harmful toxins from my body. *I could not believe this was happening to me.*

Within minutes, a middle-aged man in scrubs pulled back the curtain and entered. He seemed fairly certain that the lidocaine in my IV bag was the culprit of these sudden seizure-like symptoms. To determine whether this severe reaction was indeed caused by high toxicity levels, the lab would need to run tests on my blood. These tests would take upwards of four hours, so he wanted me to continue with the saline IV treatment in the meantime.

Having some answers relieved me. I knew these specialists would make sure I got better. Yet I was still extremely upset. I felt as though my other doctors misled me. *Why did nobody warn me that this could happen?*

Time crept by slowly in the ER. Mom, Dad, and I just sat in silence and stared. I felt drained when another nurse entered my mock-room to remove the PICC line from my left arm. The sensation of the long, thin tube sliding down my vein nauseated me. While most procedures did not bother me to watch, I had to turn my head away. I could not look as the snake-like tube flowed out of my arm.

Soon I started feeling anxious. It had been an hour since my last spasm, and I just wanted to leave. I felt like the hospital setting was making me worse. The bright lights, ammonia smell, and loud sirens were unnerving to me. My head began throbbing as images blurred. I kept my eyes fixated on the clock on the wall. Another hour had passed, and I was still waiting.

Finally, the curtain opened and I saw the ER doctor standing in front of me. He was here to discharge me. There was no need for us to stay in the hospital if I had not suffered any spasms for more than two hours. Instead, he would call us once the blood work was complete. He then placed me under strict hydrating orders. It was important that I continually drink liquids in order to rid my body of the poisonous toxins. If I experienced unusual symptoms or my parents noticed a relapse, we needed to come back to the ER immediately.

The home phone rang two hours later; it was the doctor. The results indicated that my lidocaine levels were considered "normal." Despite the lab's findings, the doctor still felt his initial diagnosis of a toxic reaction was correct. Taking into account my recent weight loss, he believed my body might not have been equipped to process such high amounts of a drug. He was confident that I would start feeling better by tomorrow, but still recommended we visit Dr. Vine as soon as possible.

Yet when I met with Dr. Vine two days later, he did not seem that interested in what had happened to me over the weekend. He did not even offer to suggest another theory as to why this had occurred. Instead, he increased my morphine intake slightly and hurried out of the room. I was to schedule another appointment for next month.

From this one meeting, I sensed our doctor-patient relationship was nearing an end. It was as though he and I had traveled as far as we could together, and now he had nothing left to offer me.

Chapter 18

My New Reality

While maintaining the limited movements I attained during that last hospital visit, I managed to survive the next few months without any major hiccups. I even attended a weekend trip with five of my dearest high school friends. Spending time at a friend's cabin, we sat by the creek and laughed, enjoying each other's company.

Although it was nice to feel normal and be like everybody else, I could not escape the inevitable. Another summer was nearing an end, and I still was in pain. I was also no closer to returning to school. I realized I would never return to Creighton. In less than ten months, all my friends would be graduating. They would have degrees and be heading into the workforce, once again leaving me behind.

What would become of my life then?

I was really sad. Despite being incredibly grateful that I had partial mobility in my right hand, nothing else seemed to be going right for me. I was still at home, seeing my doctors and attending physical therapy. I had lost patience in my treatment programs. I felt it was based on a more symptomatic approach. Instead of treating the actual problem, we were only searching for remedies to fix the newly discovered side effects.

Where at one time I was pleased to find relief from the medications, I now was wary of the amount and doses I consumed. I could no longer turn a blind eye to the pestering symptoms I encountered from all the drugs. I was taking more than thirteen different pills three to six times a day. While I had medical prescriptions for each of these medications, it seemed unfathomable that I was not overmedicating.

I knew I could not live like this forever. My body could not possibly be equipped to process such extreme amounts of medicine. I was desperate and needed a new plan. *I needed to regain hope.*

∞

With age and experience comes knowledge and understanding. Yet the same was true about wisdom gained through trying and demanding times. Being completely absorbed with my current situation allowed me to disregard many of the warning signs. I understood the need for oral medications. They were extremely helpful and beneficial to millions. However, I also knew that the side effects from one prescription often needed to be treated with another drug.

For years, I had readily participated in the medical field's dance. I willingly played the game of tug-of-war between the medicines needed to ease my pain versus the drugs required to relieve the complications. It was unfathomable how many different drugs I had to take just to make it through a single day. I had become a walking medicine cabinet, and that scared me.

In the beginning, my only complaint was constipation. Concerned that I was only having a bowel movement once a week, Dr. Vine took immediate action. He put me on stool softeners and laxatives, while making me drink fiber and other prescription liquids. I was thankful for his proactive approach, since one drug might ease the discomfort for months, only to become ineffective. The challenge for me was discussing my severe constipation. I felt humiliated and embarrassed. There were moments where I just wanted to throw my arms in the air and cry. I was only in my twenties; how did this happen to me?

Unable to release the ever-increasing toxins also left my stomach in utter distress. With my tight, bulging abdomen extending outward, there were days where I looked pregnant. I could not even stand straight, because of the electrifying pain. When it became normal to see me keeled over, holding my stomach, Dr. Vine again acted. This time he recommended phenergan, an antihistamine used to treat motion sickness, vomiting, and nausea. Yet that alone did not ease my agony. I had also developed GERD, a gastroesophageal reflux disorder.

Otherwise known as acid reflux, this disorder caused me extreme heartburn and indigestion. Food would rise up my throat and then slide back down anytime I ate. All I did was burp foul-tasting acid while wishing I could vomit. With my insides constantly churning, Dr. Vine added other drugs to subdue the unwanted sensations. It was terrible having to take six different pills a few times a day, just to aid my severe constipation and acid reflux.

Dr. Vine prescribed medications to control the inflammation and terrible migraines as well. Retaining large amounts of water and not having bowel movements made my weight fluctuate between five and twelve pounds per day. This was a serious problem because of the added stress on my kidneys. As my kidneys had to work overtime to excrete the toxic liquids, I drank tons of water and cranberry concentrate. Nothing seemed to help flush my system; I now needed diuretics.

I remember how uncomfortable it was to swell. Feeling my skin stretch and pit with the excess fluid was unbearable. I started to feel like the ballooning and shrinking woman. My closet had every size from a zero to an eight, because I never knew what I would be able to wear. While I tried to act as though I was okay with my life, I really was miserable. Living like this was demoralizing. I only kept fighting because I believed in miracles.

I typically had a migraine twice a week. These left me agonizing in a dark room for hours. There were times when Dan and my parents had to tiptoe around the house whispering, because I believed my head would explode. While Dr. Vine gave me strong prescriptions, I also relied on over-the-counter Migraine Ice pads. Mom would keep them in the refrigerator so they would be cool and ready whenever I needed them. I have vivid memories of lying in the fetal position with a Migraine Ice pad stuck to my head and wet washcloths resting on my inner wrists. Then I would lie in bed waiting for the misery to end.

The drugs and disease also affected my hearing. I constantly heard ringing and buzzing in my eardrums. Being unable to decipher what people were saying, I became a pro at reading lips. My once-perfect vision had deteriorated too. Now I needed bifocal glasses to read or drive at night. I was falling apart. As the pain impaired my equilibrium and balance, I also started to lose my short-term memory. I would find myself picking up the phone, only to have no recollection of who I was going to call or why I needed to call them. *The person I used to be was slipping away, and the life I once lived no longer existed.*

I knew something had to change, but I felt stuck. It was difficult to move forward when my sole existence seemed meaningless. I was twenty-one years old and living with my parents. I relied entirely on them to help me through the day. Before Mom left for work, she would fill two thirty-two-ounce bottles with water and leave a sliced apple in the refrigerator. Dad began working half days in the office. He would come home at lunch to take care of me during the afternoons. I felt broken. For four years, the chronic pain had ransacked my body, and it was still not getting any better.

No longer happy with myself, I scheduled more appointments with Shelley and Maureen. It took me a while to see that it was necessary to take a few steps back in order to heal. I knew I needed a break from all the outward stresses and distractions in my life. There was no way I could stay pain-free or healthy if my inner being was unbalanced. Therefore, I made the conscious decision to take off one full year from attempting classes at junior college and teaching.

My body was a vessel, and every part was equally important in obtaining optimum health. I finally had reached that point where I could acknowledge the importance of being spiritually, mentally, and emotionally fit. While I was concerned that doing nothing might add to my feelings of inadequacy, I put trust in the Universe. I had to take a leap of faith that those guiding me on this journey would protect me.

As I kept busy with regular visits to Mitzi, Shelley, and Maureen, I also began attending hypnotherapy sessions and T'ai Chi Chih classes. I had some terrible experiences with hypnotherapy in the past that made me resistant to trying it again. The last thing I needed right now was for someone to tell me my chronic pain was a psychological issue. Yet Shelley was persistent. She really wanted me to see her friend Joyce, because she believed I would finally grasp the importance of this healing therapy. I agreed.

Joyce was an older woman with a docile nature. She had light, short hair and a soothing voice. My earlier trepidation of meeting her immediately vanished once I was in her presence. I felt at ease when she explained that the purpose of hypnosis was to increase brain communication to certain nerves in the body. This would release more neuropeptides and polypeptides, known for aiding in the decrease of pain.

If hypnosis could possibly relieve pain, I was game. My first few visits were interesting. All I did was sleep. It seemed as soon as I sat in the comfortable recliner and Joyce started talking, I would drift off to a happy slumber. While I wished I could make it through a true session, Joyce kept telling me my body must need sleep. I was responding just how my body needed it to. Hearing her tell me each session was a success comforted me. It allowed me to grow at my own pace.

I learned about T'ai Chi from Mitzi. It was in the middle of physical therapy when she began talking about how ancient forms of moving meditations were helpful for chronic pain patients. We already knew yoga was physically too demanding for my body, so she wondered if T'ai Chi would be more beneficial. She wanted me to consider looking at the exercise classes my town offered. That was how I found Denise, my T'ai Chi Chih instructor.

T'ai Chi Chih was a simpler form of T'ai Chi Ch'uan. Based on only nineteen movements and one pose, its purpose was to increase circulation while balancing and developing the body's vital energy. This was known as chi. Slow and gentle movements created a soft continual motion that helped align the body with the mind and soul.

Denise called me before our first class to learn more about how my disease affected my body. She reassured me that practicing T'ai Chi Chih would not jeopardize my health or cause further damage. Recommending that I take it slowly, Denise suggested I only move my upper body and sit in a chair for the first few classes. She wanted to make sure I worked up my endurance. Taking things slowly was starting to become a recurring theme in my life.

As Denise guided me through that first hour, I felt a hot tingling sensation throughout my arms. It was not exactly painful, yet it was not too pleasant either. I learned this was good news. This was a sign that blood was returning to the damaged part of my body and my own energy force was healing my body. T'ai Chi Chih was making a difference. *This was my time to heal... and I was going to make the most of it.*

∞

For some reason, my diet had always been an issue in regards to my health. Feeling it was inhumane to hurt or harm animals, I decided at the age of thirteen never to eat meat again. This meant I was a strictly abiding vegetarian when I was originally injured. Although I loved the vegetarian lifestyle, many of my doctors did not.

They were concerned that I was not receiving substantial amounts of protein. Since my disease reacted negatively to protein deficiency, it was even more important that I consume meat products. I fought my team of doctors for two years because I just did not believe that nuts, tofu, and beans plus rice were insufficient; yet I finally gave in as the pain raged and I feared I would need to leave Creighton.

Meredith was with me the first time I ate meat again. I had been visiting her in Minnesota for spring break, when I told I was going to eat meat and get my belly button pierced. I think my revelation shocked her, because she jokingly said if I ever ate meat, she would get her belly button pierced too. That evening, I ordered a Chinese chicken salad, and the next day we both went to the tattoo parlor for our piercing.

It was not that I had ever wanted to have my belly button pierced, but that I just needed to rebel. Men were controlling every part of my life. I felt I had to do something for me. It was basically by default that I chose a piercing, because I figured a tattoo would be too dangerous and painful. My belly button symbolized who I wanted to be. It showed me that I was just like my peers. *It made me feel like less of an outcast.*

Yet eating meat alone did not change my pain levels. While it seemed as if each specialist had his or her own diet plan for me to follow, in September of 2000, I began my first "medical diet." Dr. Peter D'Adamo's book, *Eat Right 4 Your Type,* discussed the need to eat foods that only supported my blood type. Although it was a controversial book within the medical community, my massage therapist—who happened to be a nutritionist—believed it might reduce the inflammation and pain. I decided to try it.

I knew I had type O blood. Dr. D'Adamo believed this meant I was a hunter and gatherer. Therefore, I should not eat anything containing white or wheat flour, cornstarch, partially hydrogenated oil, coconut, dairy, pork, or foods soaked in vinegar. I could have sweet potatoes, green leafy vegetables, walnuts, rice, and figs. The meats I should strive to eat were buffalo, venison, and lamb. This was obviously hard for me, as I was only eating chicken and ground beef. Not having much luck sticking to this regimented diet, I started looking elsewhere.

Mitzi told me about the yeast free diet. She wanted me to read Dr. Bruce Semon and Lori Kornblum's book, *Feast Without Yeast.* Learning how my body reacted to certain foods while under stress helped me make the necessary dietary changes to control my pain receptors. There were no baked breads, sweets, or alcohol allowed, so I learned to be creative. I would make oatmeal cookies with spelt flour, honey, and applesauce. I located frozen spelt bread that only contained spelt, water, and sea salt. I used brown rice pasta and made my own tomato sauce.

Food became enjoyable again. Knowing that my family and I made nearly everything I ate gave eating a new meaning. It was not mindless but rather spiritual. I was growing—I understood how important the food we put in our mouths was to our actual health.

Soon I developed my own eating style. With all this knowledge of various nutritional programs, I began eating only organic, unprocessed foods that contained no refined sugars or yeast. Committed to this new program of well-being, I began exercising to the best of my ability and started gaining back the weight I lost earlier that summer. With more strength, I also felt more alive. Now I wanted the Universe to send me a sign. *I was still waiting for my miracle.*

∞

During the second weekend in October 2002, my parents had a party to attend. This meant I would be home by myself for the first time in months. While I was happy that they were going out, I was having a rough day. I tried for the most part to stay unusually optimistic, but there were times where I pitied myself, and this night happened to be one of them. This night I was letting the negative feelings get the best of me. I was depressed and I just needed to grieve.

It seemed like everything I wanted in life was out of my reach. I had succumbed to being the "sick one" because I had no identity of my own anymore. Listening to my friends' adventures in college only made my existence more trivial. It was hard not to feel pathetic when I was stuck living vicariously through them. All I wanted was to be the one at the college party who drank too much. I wished I felt the stress of finals…and I most desperately wanted to be the one going on dates and falling in love.

I had seldom dated in the last few years. My last relationship had ended six months prior and was with an older man. While he was kind and extremely considerate of my needs, in the end, my health was too much for him to handle. He could not cope with my ever-changing mood swings or escalating pain. Nor did I want him to. The relationship I had before him was also with someone older, and he too was emotionally unavailable to help me through such difficult times. I think what was devastating to me was how both men had knowledge and experiences dealing with chronic pain. They understood the disease's progression, so hearing them throw that back in my face broke my heart.

I obviously had insecurities about being intimately close to another person. Since my pain would naturally elevate whenever I got near someone, I walked a thin line between feeling alive and feeling pure agony. While I wanted to shy away from any contact, I yearned to be held and loved. However, not having proper use of my limbs made any physical contact difficult. I was incapable of intimacy and unable to please a mate. Feeling as though I was undeserving of love, I gave up on my dreams of marriage and children. I now started to question the purpose of my life without relationships.

Because of my unique life experiences, I knew life was not about stature and money. It was not about prestige or a high-powered job either. The purpose to life was to spread and receive love. Love, health and happiness mattered the most in life—these were the true principles used to measure success and abundance. My spirit ached; would I ever have the chance to experience these ideals? *Would I find love and a soul mate?*

As I became tired of feeling sorry for myself, I knew it was time to pull myself together. Knowing that laughter was always the best medicine for sadness, I turned on the television to reruns of *Saturday Night Live*. Watching the comedians made me thankful for humor. I still could not escape my pain or heartache, but watching the SNL cast do improvisations allowed me to compartmentalize the agony. Even if it was for only one sketch, I was grateful to feel like a normal person for few minutes.

My energy and outlook on life became more optimistic as I laughed at the funny segments. Somehow, I had broken out of the darkness and found my way back to the light. I recognized that while my contribution to this world might seem minimal, I was still a contributing member of society. The most amazing group of people surrounded me with daily encouragement and prayers. It was time for me to begin directing my thoughts on the blessings in my life. I had to stop feeling sorry for myself.

The phone then rang. Thinking it would be my parents, I was shocked to hear my old elementary school principal on the line. She and her husband had gone to a wedding that evening, where they happened to sit next to their old neighbors. As they talked about their children, she discovered that one of their daughters, Sara, had been dealing with a serious nerve and pain disorder called RSD. She too had seen some of the best specialists in the pain field and tried every mainstream procedure and medication. She spent numerous nights in the ER and hospital without finding relief. Then her physical therapist discovered a doctor in South Texas who used the STS treatment. Having nothing to lose, Sara and her mom went to Texas, where she found her miracle.

As she continued to explain the treatment and Sara's condition, I became disoriented. *The sign I had been praying for had finally appeared.*

My principal believed this was my answer. Listening to her old neighbors talk about the pain and torment Sara endured reminded her of my story. She told me to write down their phone number, because she wanted me to call that evening. There was no need to waste any more time. Then she said she would be in touch tomorrow and quickly hung up. Holding the receiver in my hand, I took a deep breath and dialed the number.

I waited in the family room for my parents to get home so I could tell them about my night. But as I shared my intriguing news with them, they seemed reserved and apathetic. Their lack of excitement baffled and miffed me. I did not understand why they did not seem happier to discover that there was another treatment. *Hope still existed.* I finally just went to my bedroom, disgruntled and angry.

∞

As I got out of bed that following morning, I noticed Mom's flushed face as she drank her morning coffee in the kitchen. With the excruciating burning in my hand, I overlooked her jovial demeanor, while searching for my medicine. All I wanted was to take my morning dose so I could lie in bed. It was then that Mom told me her exciting news.

"I just spent the last hour talking to Sara's mom about the doctor who treated her daughter in Texas. Did you know that he invented this machine after he developed RSD?"

While I was surprised to hear that this doctor had firsthand experience with chronic pain, Mom continued to talk. The similarities in Sara's and my medical histories were uncanny. We had seen the same doctors, been to the same hospitals, and undergone the same procedures. However, Sara no longer took medicine since returning from Corpus Christi. She had gotten her life back and was living pain-free.

This stunned me. Thinking that a doctor fifteen hundred miles away held my miracle flabbergasted me. All I thought was how we needed to get to Texas. The drugs had been destroying my body. Unless I was willing to participate in some trial study or re-implant a spinal cord stimulator, I had no options. I did not want to have another invasive procedure. There were too many risks involved, and I did not feel my body was strong enough to recuperate.

I called the doctor early Monday morning, hoping I would be able to speak with him directly. The bubbly receptionist told me he was with patients and would not be available until that afternoon. She then explained how he had a routine of returning patient phone calls on his drive home from work. If I left her my name and number, she would see that he received the message. Although the receptionist was kind and sweet, I was irritated. I did not want to wait. Jaded by the medical field's constant broken promises, I took her comment with a grain of salt. *What doctor would actually return calls away from the office?*

That day seemed to drag on as I impatiently waited near the phone. I was about to give up hope when I heard a ring around 2:30 PM. *It was the doctor from Texas.* Doc, as I will refer to him, seemed down-to-earth and lacked egotistical superiority. He was inquisitive and asked many questions regarding the treatments I tried and the medications I currently consumed. While I tried to answer each question thoroughly, I noticed his voice becoming more distressed. Now I was self-conscious—what had I done wrong?

He believed from his own experience and research that the forms of therapy I sought out exacerbated the condition. Where most treatments required an invasive procedure to combat pain, his therapy was non-invasive and entailed no medications. He focused on both the quality and quantity of life. Doc's goal was to help his patients return to their normal activities.

In order to obtain those results, he had created and invented the Sympathetic Therapy System (STS). The Dynatron STS RX was a non-invasive machine designed to normalize the autonomic nervous system by stimulating and affecting the central nervous system. As his machine increased the production of certain neuropeptides like vasoactive intestinal polypeptide (VIP) and calcium gene-related peptide (CGRP), it reduced the production of norepinephrine and substance P, the two main transmitters of pain.

I was confused. Although I did not understand the medical terminology, Doc did not stop. He further explained the effects RSD had on the central nervous system from the over-stimulation of my sympathetic nerves. Many physiological reactions were occurring inside my body so I could continue to perform under such stress. Living in a constant fight-or-flight response increased the production of norepinephrine from the adrenal glands. This caused a change in the distribution of blood flow throughout my system.

During a time of the stress, the flow of blood focused solely on the large muscles, at the expense of the nerves, small muscles, and digestive tract. While this was helpful when being attacked, this same response became hazardous after long periods of time. Without adequate circulation of blood to the intestinal tract, mass productions of norepinephrine and substance P cause the body to deteriorate.

Alas, my body was stuck in an unending cycle. The increased stress my nervous system faced led to the greater supply of norepinephrine and substance P in my body. That abundance resulted in the progression of my disease and the other problems that followed. In order to regain my health, I would have to fight off those two substances that ran rampant inside my body. By using his machine, my body would begin to produce the missing VIP and CGRP. This would inadvertently decrease the over-stimulation of norepinephrine and substance P, thus enabling my central nervous system to relax and bring about pain relief and remission.

While it was difficult for me to grasp his theory, I was impressed with the time he gave me. He did not seem rushed and answered all my questions multiple times before explaining his typical treatment program. He asked patients to commit to a fourteen-day stay, although it could be longer, depending on the amounts of medication needing to be withdrawn. I already knew this because of Sara. It had taken her more than two months to return home. While sixty days felt like an eternity to be away, I knew it was a small price to pay to be pain-free. Moreover, I was confident that my visit to Texas would be shorter. She was on heavy medications that I believed to be more toxic and harmful than mine.

I then thanked Doc for his time and hung up the phone. Now I needed to speak with my parents for their opinion. That evening, the three of us sat around the kitchen table, discussing the conversation. The longer we spoke, the more convinced we all were that Doc would help me recover. *He was my answer.*

With my parents' full support, I made the ultimate decision to go to Corpus Christi, Texas. Dad was quick to make arrangements. Within hours, he had booked airline flights and made hotel reservations. Meanwhile, Mom took a leave from work so she could stay and care for me.

Five days later, Mom and I boarded a plane with no idea of what was yet to come. My life was about to change forever.

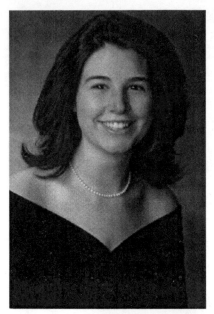

Professional photograph by Lifetouch

- My senior portrait was taken two weeks before my injury.

I still had many dreams and aspirations for my future, including attending college, studying abroad my junior year, and becoming an independent, self-sufficient individual.

Personal photograph by Unknown

- Meredith and me at a school function.

Trying to cope with my disease and school was difficult. I wanted to participate in many school activities, but being in pain made that nearly impossible. I had to drop two of my classes in order to visit numerous doctors on my quest to find a diagnosis.

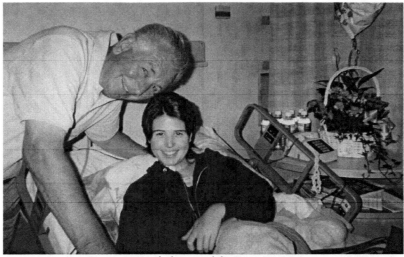

Personal photograph by Agnes Ruo

- My grandfather visiting me while an inpatient at Lucile Packard Children's Hospital at Stanford.

Hospitalized for five and a half weeks with an implanted stellate ganglion catheter IV, I spent most of my time in physical and occupational therapy, counseling or group sessions. (If you look closely at my neck, you can see the white gauze surrounding the catheter.)

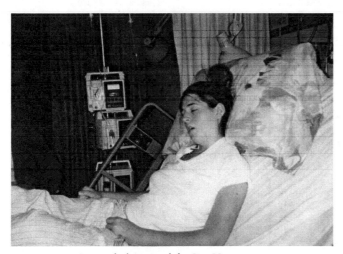

Personal photograph by Jim Hemmenway

Personal photograph
by Jim Hemmenway

- My life in the Pulmonary Care Unit (PCU)

Whenever I was hospitalized in the PCU, I would be heavily medicated in a last-ditch effort to ease my pain. This was one incident when my hand regained temporary mobility due to a drug.

- Texas and my ever-changing appearance

In October 2002, I arrived in Corpus Christi, weighing around 118 pounds. Within two months, my weight began to increase dramatically. Even though I had no appetite and ate sparingly, I gained more than eighty-five pounds in seven months. This was due to fluid retention from withdrawal.

Personal photograph by Catherine Hemmenway

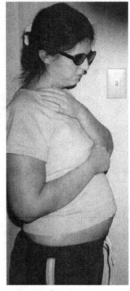

Personal photograph by Catherine Hemmenway

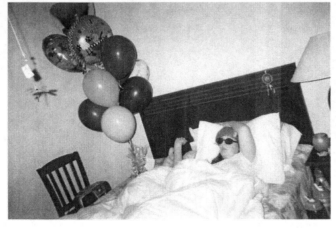

Personal photograph by Catherine Hemmenway

- This is me lying in bed helpless as the pain ravages my body.

Notice my right arm in the air and my sunglasses. I wore sunglasses at all times because I could not tolerate light.

- Body Changes

Due to my constant use of heating pads and hot-water bottles to ease the intense pain, I developed second-degree burns on my abdomen while my body became extremely hypersensitive. My skin even began to fold over the scar tissue left from the spinal cord stimulator.

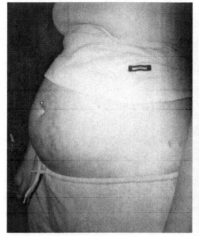

Personal photograph by
Catherine Hemmenway

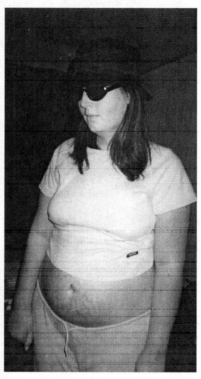

Personal photograph by
Catherine Hemmenway

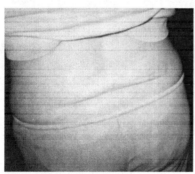

Personal photograph by
Catherine Hemmenway

Professional photograph by Thomas John Gibbons

- In September 2004, I spoke at the National Pain Foundation's Triumph Dinner.
That evening, I was presenting the Celina Field Award to my parents as Caregivers of the Year.

- On October 21, 2007, I ran the Harbor Half Marathon!
Nothing is impossible. Dreams do come true!

Professional photograph by RaceShots.net

Harbor Half: Mile Markers 9–12

"Okay, there is a slight incline coming up, so you need to push. I do not want you to give up now. Look toward that group in front of us and make passing them our goal."

I nod my head as I try to make sense of what Rick is telling me. With the sun shining overhead, my body temperature begins increasing and I know I need to be careful not to dehydrate. I need a Clif Shot before I make any move, so Rick unzips the pocket on his CamelBak and hands me the lemon-lime chew. I swallow it with some warm water as a gentle breeze sweeps across my face. Then I take a deep breath and focus on the four ladies in front of me. I am going to catch up to them…*I will catch them.*

As I have always thrived on challenge, inching closer to the pack exhilarates me. With a wave of confidence, I pass the group and notice I am at the exact spot where the first runner passed me on his way to the finish line. Giving myself time to absorb that only four miles separate me from the end of my long-awaited journey, a glow returns to my face.

"I will not allow the threat of a future flare-up to rule my life. From now on, I will not allow my disease to define me. I am far greater than that. Now *I* control my life!"

Rick grins as we exit the causeway to begin the trek on the boring, dreaded access road. "That's right, baby. Just keep it up. Let's go, Jillian!"

I look at Rick, who is chuckling at his own remark. While I always joke about being buff and fierce, just like the trainer Jillian Michaels on NBC's *The Biggest Loser*, I knew I was far from it. Yet as I think about her die-hard motto, I quickly retort, "You better keep up, big boy!" and dart down the road. Becoming one with the wind, I envision myself floating over the street. *I am fully alive and aware.* Swinging my arms, I move with gusto and ease…and for an instant, I am unstoppable.

Except just like everything else, the euphoric, carefree feelings of being powerful pass and reality returns. The pain is getting worse, the outside temperature is rising, and I still am running. Slowing down to a minimal jog, I sip water and pray to my angels. I think about the plague of challenges I have encountered over the past two hours. Even with the weather, physical pain, and emotional hell, I am running. I had every reason to justify stopping, but I continued. For the first time since the race began, I feel proud of myself.

"From this point on, every step you take is one step further than you have ever traveled before. Just keep your mind on that, baby."

While Rick's constant praise motivated me, it bothered me that he never said he is happy with my progress. That in spite of all the physical and environmental challenges, I am doing a phenomenal job. *Did he think I should be doing better? Were my best efforts not good enough? Why am I always searching for outward approval?*

The excruciating numbness, tingling, piercing, stabbing, and aching pains spread throughout my body. It was as if the nagging chronic pain knew I was fighting for full control. In a fierce game of tug-of-war, I began praying to my Higher Power for guidance. I needed to be surrounded with light so I could finally win the battle. Once I accomplish this goal, nothing would ever stand in my way.

Yet the closer the finish line is to my grasp, the more terrified I become. The fear of success cripples me more than the shame of defeat. I begin walking a slow, sluggish stagger. *Who am I without chronic pain?*

"What's wrong? Are you okay?"

I have no idea how to explain such strange, sinister feelings to Rick, so I do not even try. Instead, I try to ignore him. *He wouldn't get it—he couldn't understand.* "I just need a minute to breathe."

"You are breathing, babe. Come on, we are almost there. Running on the steep grade is what you like to do. If we keep going, we could easily pass that group ahead of us!"

I know what he is saying is true, but I cannot bring myself to run or jog. I feel emotionally paralyzed. It was not as if my body physically hurt any more than it did three minutes ago, but now I am less than twenty-five minutes away from my destiny: *twenty-five minutes away from my new life.* I just needed a minute to prepare for this life-altering, life-shattering moment.

"Rick, you are not listening to me. I need to walk …"

Chapter 19

Texas

We managed to arrive at the Corpus Christi airport during renovations and a torrential downpour. After following a mapped-out maze to reach the portable building designated as the temporary baggage claim, we then trekked back outside through the storm to the rental car section of the airport. Mom and I were drenched by the time we loaded our luggage into the trunk. It was total mayhem, but we did not care. All we did was laugh and giggle at the likelihood of this happening to us. *It was Murphy's Law again.*

Not having the slightest idea where we were going, Mom drove down the unfamiliar freeways as I read her the map. Navigating through the dark in an unknown place was difficult but fun. Since neither Mom nor I was scared being on our own, we saw this as an exciting journey. We both knew we would eventually find our way. Missing our exit twice, we pulled into the hotel's parking lot just as the rain started falling faster and heavier.

I stayed in the car while Mom hurried to the entrance to check in. When she returned, I began gathering the belongings we had placed in the back seat. Then I raced to the warm lobby as she held the hotel door open for me. She told me to sit on the couch while she got our suitcases out of the trunk. I did not object. Because of the plane ride and severe weather, I had to take additional medicine to calm the intensified pain. The swelling and agonizing burning were beginning to take their toll on me. I was exhausted and only wanted to rest.

As I entered the hotel room, I was in total disbelief. Stains covered the carpet, and a musty stench overwhelmed me. Holding my breath as I made my way into the room, I tried not focus on the negatives. I checked the bathroom and was relieved to see it was clean and decent. Then I looked at the kitchen. Although it lacked many basic utensils, it had what we needed: a dishwasher, stove, refrigerator, and oven. Across from the kitchen was a small desk, which was next to the pullout couch and recliner. On the opposite wall from the couch were the bed and nightstands. I exhaled as I looked at the bare and somewhat dirty room. We would make the best out of this situation.

Mom began to unpack as I wrapped myself in my Nikken Kenko Travel Comforter and sat on the grime-infested couch. She started by changing the sheets on the bed to the ones we had brought from home. This was a necessity, since my hypersensitive skin could only tolerate high-thread-count Egyptian cotton. She then placed my crystals on the coffee table next to my arrangement of healing books. Mom moved around the room quickly, stacking my favorite girlie movies next to the TV.

Soon she was in the kitchen, emptying the organic brown rice cereal, oat bars, and spelt bread onto the counter. I wanted to help her, but the pestering pains forced me to watch her hang coats in the closet and stack clothes in the built-in dresser. When she finished, the two of us looked at our newly transformed room. I finally felt at peace. I realized this was exactly where I needed to be. *My miracle was coming.*

∞

The next morning, we had to wake up early in order to make it to the doctor's on time. Doc had an unusual schedule of working Sundays, Mondays, Wednesdays, and Fridays. Yet because he understood pain did not retreat for weekends or special occasions, he made sure his clinic was open seven days a week, including holidays. Therefore, my first visit was Sunday morning.

I was petrified. Self-defeating thoughts bombarded my mind as I clung to my stuffed dog. The outcome of that day—October 20, 2002—had the power to change everything for me. Now I wondered if I might have prematurely put all my faith, hope and dreams in a man I had never met. My life was riding on this meeting. *He was my last and only hope.* What if he could not help me?

Heading east down a busy street, I stared googly-eyed out the window. Everything about South Texas seemed foreign to me. Whether it was the humidity, the freeway off-ramps, the Christian posters hanging on fences, or the "Don't mess with Texas" road signs, it was all so different from Northern California. While I checked the addresses on the passing buildings, Mom began preparing me that Doc's office lacked curb appeal. Seeing the small, worn-down building between a tamale drive-thru and a Jiffy Lube took me aback. *This did not look like a respectable or notable facility.*

My heart sank as we drove into the tiny parking lot filled with large potholes and double-parked cars. *Was this really it?* Reminding myself I had no other options put the seemingly desolate building into perspective. I was coming here because I was sick and I needed help. After putting on my brave face, I looked at Mom. Her eyes welled with tears, and I had to tell her everything would be all right. Then I took a breath and unlatched my seatbelt. This was it; now it was time for me to heal.

A foul, pungent odor overpowered me as we walked into the clinic. I was already feeling nauseated, but now I also felt faint. As the receptionist was on the phone, a beautiful blonde-haired twenty-something attached insurance papers to a clipboard for Mom to fill out. She introduced herself as the office manager, while profusely apologizing for the terrible smell. It appeared the extreme rain had caused flooding inside the building, and the stench was coming from the mildew-soaked carpets. She reassured us that Doc was having linoleum put in later that week, so this should never be a problem again. I liked her. Her cheery personality was just what I imagined from a true Southern belle.

Mom handed back the clipboard. My palms suddenly began to sweat as I stood up when I heard a tech call my name. *Everything was riding on this appointment.* She led us down the long hall and directed me to the third room on the right. It was a tiny area, probably no larger than two office cubicles, containing an overstuffed recliner and a combination television/VCR.

Mom wrapped me in my favorite blanket before I sat down, and looked up at the tech. She was holding a clipboard, blue ballpoint pen, and a pink and orange highlighter. My job was to fill out the packet by rating my pain. Seeing the depth of those four pages made my eyes widen. Doc had laminated to the back of the board the pain rating scale he wanted his patients to follow. It ranged from a 1 (mild aches) to a 10 (nonfunctional on the verge of tears).

The first page alone listed twenty-two different areas of the body, for which I needed to indicate the severity of pain. Just staring at the paper caused my head to pound. Tears welled in my eyes as the room started dancing. I had never differentiated my pain in this manner. I was overwhelmed. The only thing I wanted was for the doctor to help me.

Thankfully, Mom came to my rescue. She started at the top of the list and worked down, asking me to tell her my discomfort levels for indigestion, nausea and constipation. Then she asked me about colds, flu, allergies or asthma. We next discussed the different joint pains of my fingers, elbows, shoulders, neck, hips, back, knees, ankles and toes. After continuing to rate my generalized fatigue, headaches and memory problems, we were done with the top of the page.

I felt a weight lift off my shoulders as we moved to the second section. I now needed to record every medication I had taken during the past twenty-four hours, including the strength and dose. This was torture for me, because I had so many different drugs. As I pulled out the toiletry bag holding all my medications, Mom and I began sorting through pills. I had eleven prescriptions to list. The medications ranged from a diuretic and laxatives, all the way to nonsteroidal anti-inflammatory drugs (NSAIDs), anticonvulsants, anti-nausea pills, antihistamines, sedatives, narcotic pain relievers and opioids.

We were finally finished with the first page after twenty minutes of exhausting work. Yet, seeing a diagram of the right side of the body on the second page frustrated me. *How much more crap did still I need to answer?* Doc needed me to highlight the locations of the pain. The worst areas were to be shaded with the pink marker, while my minor aches were to be orange. I had Mom shade the entire right side pink, with the exception of my upper thigh, buttocks, knee and face. Those were colored orange.

The third page was the same, except it showed a diagram of my left side. This proved more challenging for me. Although I typically had less pain on my left side, the plane ride had intensified my symptoms. It was hard for me to decide whether to use the pink or orange marker, because I did not want Doc to think I was exaggerating my pain.

Luckily, Mom was with me to re-read the instructions. They specifically said to highlight current sensations. That would mean if my pain was high, I recorded it higher. Doc was interested in where I hurt now, not where I typically hurt. I decided to leave the buttocks, upper chest and face blank. Then Mom colored my upper thigh, calf and forearm orange, while the rest of my left side was pink.

I was glad to have finished three pages, but the fourth page contained even more columns of symptoms and body parts that needed pain ratings. I was flabbergasted. This was taking an eternity, and I wondered if it would ever end. *How much more could there possibly be to know?* I wanted Mom to finish it herself, but she refused. I just had a few more questions to go.

The first column pertained solely to my feet, with separate spaces for my left and right sides. Here I had to decipher the differences in the burning, numbness, tingling, pain, aching, discoloration, swelling, itching and stiffness between my left and right foot. The second row dealt with specific areas on the legs and arms. While this took some time, the third column went quicker. All I had to determine were the pain intensities for my abdomen, neck, chest, face and back. Finally, we moved to the last row. This section pertained to side effects such as diarrhea, constipation, indigestion, insomnia, mood swings, light-headedness and memory problems.

I looked at the clock when we finally finished. It had taken us a total of fifty minutes. While I re-examined my responses as we waited for a tech or Doc, I was shocked. This was the first time I had ever paid attention to every single sensation. I never realized how high my pain levels actually were throughout my body. There were only four zeroes, while the next lowest number was a six. I was dumbstruck. This pain was *really* bad, and I was *really* sick.

On the tech's fifth return to my room, I was able to hand her the clipboard and completed packet. She subsequently placed it on the counter so she could check my blood pressure and the temperature of my feet and hands. Measuring the skin's temperature and comparing the differentials between my left and right sides was a new concept to me. No doctor or therapist had ever done this before, so I had many questions. Doc's tech explained this was just another indicator of an autonomic nervous system (ANS) dysfunction. A lower skin temperature suggested a decrease in circulation to a limb. This resulted in an exasperation of chronic pain and its symptoms.

In order to get an accurate reading, I had to sit still for five minutes while I had sensory electrodes taped to the palmar surfaces of my thumbs and the plantar part of my big toes. I learned a healthy person had less than a one-degree difference between the left and right side. Standard temperatures for the thumb registered around 91 degrees Fahrenheit. Feet were naturally cooler, and therefore, considered normal at 83 degrees Fahrenheit.

I did not even come close to these averages. My hands were in the low seventies while my toes were in the mid sixties. This gave Doc tangible proof that the disease had compromised my nervous system. Moreover, it allowed him verify the success of his STS treatment. He would use these numbers and compare them to my finishing temperatures.

$$\infty$$

My first impression of Doc was pure confusion. I actually thought he was another patient who accidentally strolled into the wrong room. Doc wore Levi's, tennis shoes, and a homemade T-shirt that had a picture of his twin sons' faces. *He looked more like a soccer dad than a doctor.* As he introduced himself and held out his right hand, he started making small talk. He joked with us about the differences between California and Texas before talking about the roads in Rome. I was perplexed. While he was perfectly polite and attempted to be humorous, I could not get over the fact that *he* was now my doctor. I had never met a doctor so down-to-earth and country.

He then sat down on a stool and picked up my chart. I noticed his head nod up and down as he skimmed the pages. While he rocked back in forth, he mumbled, "Okay … All right … Yep … Okay."

After a while, he looked up and asked me to explain what happened three years ago. He wanted to know what actions I had taken to get better. As this was the umpteenth time I had to relay the high-five fiasco, I felt like I had memorized a presentation. I had mastered the story down to every word. *It had become an art form.*

Recalling the previous years of treatments always made me uneasy. Having had so many specialists question my pain made me fear no one would ever believe my suffering and angst. Yet, much to my surprise, Doc did not seem to question me, per se. He felt it was obvious that I had RSDS—as he referred to the disease—after examining my afflicted hand to my functional arm. Instead, he wanted to learn how I had ended up on such lethal amounts of medicine. I was stunned. *He believed me.*

Confident he had obtained sufficient medical history, he proceeded to describe how many diseases could trace their origin to a breakdown in the stress response system of the body. While I realized this was the same information he discussed with me over the phone, it was nice to have it reiterated. Lately, it took me a long time grasp concepts. I found myself repeating questions and still not remembering answers. Thankfully, Doc did not seem bothered by Mom's or my constant interjections, and patiently re-explained his theories.

Dynatron STS was a non-invasive sympathetic therapy system designed to normalize the autonomic nervous system. By placing electrodes in various spots along the nerves and using low-frequency electrical current, his machine stimulated and affected the central nervous system. It increased the production of neuropeptides like VIP and CGRP, while reducing the production of norepinephrine and substance-P. Therefore, the treatment allowed the body to return to a healthier, pain-free state.

While this was a lot of information to absorb, the purpose of this therapy was starting to make sense to me. I was beginning to understanding how the STS would be able to help me. It was not hocus-pocus—Doc based his treatment on hard science. Since I still had to undergo another set of tests to determine my personal intensity range for the machine, Doc left the room. He promised to return later with my results.

The testing was painful. All I could think about was leaping off the table in order to escape the static electricity running deeply through my veins. I remember shrieking and shaking on the table while the tech stood looking perplexed. Due to my extreme hypersensitivity and discomfort, we had to stop. I wiped tears from my face while wondering what was wrong with me. *Were they trying to torture me or was I just that sick?*

Mom and I next met Dr. Lane, a doctor of osteopathic medicine (D.O.) who worked in conjunction with Doc. As a D.O., she took a more holistic approach to preventing disease. She treated the whole person, rather than following a doctor's more systematic manner. As she would prescribe my drugs, possible herbal remedies and vitamin supplementation, she wanted me to know that we would work together in order to form the best program for me.

I immediately liked Dr. Lane. She explained how she had grown up in Denver and only moved to Texas to finish her medical internship at a nearby hospital. It was reassuring to know that she understood my desire to eat unprocessed, hormone-free foods. Corpus Christi did not have a Whole Foods Market. Having her explain where to shop for organic groceries and natural products eased my fears of not being able to follow my strict eating habits. She also listed a variety of ethnic and authentic restaurants for us to try. Dr. Lane connected our old, accustomed way of living to our new reality.

Soon Doc returned at the door to go over my results. As we said goodbye to Dr. Lane, she handed Mom her card with her pager and cell phone numbers. She told us to call if we ran into any problems.

My full attention was back on Doc. I felt my heart beat faster as I waited for him to speak. He started by telling us that my hypersensitivity was completely off the charts. Though he expected this, it meant he would need to progress slowly. In order to make sure we did not over-stimulate my nerves, the intensity of each beat frequency would need to remain low. I would be fighting an uphill battle.

Doc's first order of business was slowly decreasing my medications. Since I had undergone severe withdrawal before, I knew these reductions would be hard but manageable. I had stopped cold turkey last time, so I foolishly believed a gradual decrease would not affect my pain levels too much. I really did not think this would be that hard.

Glancing over my lengthy list of prescriptions, he chose the four that, in his opinion, were impeding my recovery the most. They were my diuretic, anti-convulsant medication, non-steroidal anti-inflammatory drug for arthritic pain, and my antihistamine used to relieve tension and anxiety while aiding in sleep. He explained how over the next ten days, I would dwindle these medications down. This would prepare my body for the actual hurdle: morphine withdrawal.

I thought my head was going to spin off. It surprised me that he would start the withdrawal process on the first day. I could not believe that *this* was actually happening. I was finally here. I was finally getting help I needed.

Had we really found my miracle?

Chapter 20

"Ten"

The next day, I awoke feeling worse than usual. I believed it to be a mixture of the lowered medication dose and the never ending storm. Arriving at the clinic with my stuffed dog, traveling quilt, and pillow, I went through what would become my usual routine. A tech escorted me to a room, where I immediately had my blood pressure and temperatures of my extremities taken. Then I began to fill out the lengthy pain-rating packet.

Although I thought the process of recording my pain levels would become easier over time, it did not. It still took Mom and me more than a half hour, and time passed so slowly when suffering. I thought I was going mad my second day at the clinic. All I wanted was Doc. I needed him to tell me why my pain had intensified. It was starting to reach unbearable levels, and he needed to do something to help me. When he finally came to the room, he reassured me that these new symptoms were expected. It was normal for the pain to worsen during withdrawal, weather changes, and the stress of being away from home. However, he knew I would begin to feel better after treatments.

The tech responsible for my therapy was Ruben. He had been working for Doc for a few years, and was Sara's angel. He had formed a special bond with her family after helping her through some of her darkest nights. Now he promised to watch over Mom and me too. I was touched that someone I never met could genuinely care so much about my well-being. While he was stocky in stature, his soulful eyes livened up a room and his grin was infectious. *He radiated love.* As he handed Mom his phone number in case we needed anything, I knew he would profoundly change my life.

He understood that my body was hypersensitive to touch, so before he began, he asked me where it was all right for him to touch me. This calmed all my previous fears over another flare-up. I watched him as he placed four electrodes in strange places on both of my feet.

The Dynatron STS RX itself was nothing fancy. It was the size of radio-alarm clock and had three visible display screens. Written next to the two smaller display monitors were the words "intensity" and "treatment." Printed next to largest screen was the word "time." On the right side of the three display boxes were two arrows pointing up and down. These changed the settings to fit one's specific needs. Chills ran down my spine as I recognized the utter importance of this simple box. *This machine would be my miracle…it would make me pain-free.*

As the STS device booted, Ruben switched the beat frequency to the one Doc had designated. I sat completely still, fixated on what would happen next. Instantly, I felt a surge of electricity rush up my spine after he hit the *up* arrow twice. I wailed.

Without hesitating, Ruben lowered the intensity one notch and in a calm voice inquired if that felt any better. The pulsating sensation seemed to become less intense, so he left the frequency at a half. I spent a total of eighty minutes connected to the STS machine and completed three protocols that day. While the treatments were tolerable, I did not notice any relief or comfort.

After adhering to the same strategy for two more days, I still had not seen any improvements. In fact, I was getting progressively worse. The pain was now more evident and prominent. I had constant headaches, a bloated abdomen, and ankles that were indistinguishable from my calves. While I continued to have partial mobility in my right hand, the increased inflammation made moving my joints difficult. I was miserable, and I knew the weather was not helping the situation.

With torrential rains and wind speeds nearing 100 miles per hour, the greater Corpus Christi area was under a tornado warning. Mom and I were both born and raised in California. Not knowing what to do during a warning, we followed the instructions from hotel management. The hotel had sent a memo to all its occupants that the safest place to be was in the bathtub with blankets, flashlights, water and food.

Mom gathered as much food and water as she could while collecting my medications and the STS machine. As she helped me move from the bed to the blanket-filled tub, thunder shook the building, while the lightning became more piercing and powerful. I sat in the tub as Mom left the bathroom to recheck that the windows were locked and curtains shut. Then she rejoined me to wait out the storm.

Hearing the gusting wind, booming thunder and crackling lightning terrified me. All I wanted was to escape the misery residing in my body. I wished I could flee from the hammering sensations that pounded my skull or the zinging pains that traveled up and down my spine. I prayed for an intervention from above—for my Higher Power to distract me from this hell. Yet there was nowhere for me to go. I was stuck living out this nightmare.

The worrisome part of the storm passed over us in thirty minutes. As Mom cautiously opened the door and peeked out, she surveyed the room for broken glass or leaking plumbing. Luckily, we were okay. Mom subsequently guided me to bed, where I lay in the fetal position, tightly holding on to my stuffed dog. Snot fell down my upper lip. My nose was raw and my red, puffy eyes stung from all the crying. *This was not what I had expected from this trip.*

Over the next few days, my appetite plummeted. This really worried Mom, who did not want a repeat of what happened six months ago. Although I drank a protein smoothie at Dr.

Lane's request, each day it became more of a challenge to swallow. My unwillingness to eat came from my overpowering abdominal pain. Nothing seemed appetizing; all food exacerbated my indigestion and inflammation. I was falling further into the abyss.

By day eight, my pain levels had reached ten. My world crumbled apart. Experiencing more pain and discomfort from running protocols, I was only able to stop taking two non-opioid drugs. Not keeping up with Doc's schedule discouraged me. I was regressing.

My parents decided it would be best if we moved into an apartment. If we were going to be here for an indefinite period, it made sense to rent and have our own space. It would bring a sense of stability to our frantic, sad lives. I bet Mom and I visited ten complexes before discovering the one-bedroom apartment at Harbor Landing. With its location on the ground floor, near the office, and closest to the parking lot, it fit all our needs.

Our move-in date was October 30, 2002. To prepare for the big move, we visited a local furniture rental store. Here we leased a bed, end table, pullout couch, overstuffed chair, coffee table and two lamps. Patients and techs from the clinic graciously lent us kitchen items, towels and a television set, so Mom only had to purchase a few items. She bought posters to brighten the walls, contact paper to line cupboards, and re-usable plastic dishes and cups. We were ready.

By now, I was too weak to stand, so Mom had to unpack all our bags herself. As she redecorated our new "digs," I sobbed in bed. Nothing was going right for me. I constantly felt nauseated, and my stomach was beginning to bulge out. The sensation of pins and needles puncturing the soles of my feet made standing or hobbling agonizing, and the sharp burning of my right hand killed me.

With my health continuing to decline, Doc took action. He developed specialized protocols just for me. For now, he wanted me to try placing only two electrodes on each leg or foot three times a day. Thankfully, this seemed to work, and I was again able to use the STS.

That did not stop the worsening aches and pains. With the torment spreading throughout my body, I became depressed. Even a nine-hour sleep did not excite me anymore. Everything seemed overshadowed by the stifling pain. The treatments were failing me.

Doc then suggested Mom run the machine while I slept. I was not keen on that idea, but I knew I had no other alternatives. We had to try something to calm this flare-up. However, anytime Mom turned on the STS, I jumped and yelled. The treatment somehow caused electrifying sensations to travel through my body while immediate pressure bombarded my right hand. Mom would then stop the machine and sit on the edge of the bed. She would pat my head and whisper, "It is okay. You are so brave and I am so proud of you."

∞

November 3 marked my second week in Texas. Despite it being a Sunday, Doc had a family emergency that prevented him from coming to the clinic. Knowing Ruben also had this weekend off put me on edge. I did not have a close bond with Doc's three other technicians. Doc had scheduled the eldest technician to work with me. While I was glad she did not get involved in the staff drama, my concern rested in her competence.

I remember she began chatting about ABC's newest bachelor, Andrew Firestone, as she untangled cords and adjusted the electrodes on my feet. She thought he was very handsome and hoped he would find a nice girl. As she continued to ramble, I saw her program the device incorrectly and turn my intensity to a staggering 7. Before I could even remind her that I only ran protocols on a 0.5, she had hit the start button.

My health instantaneously deteriorated. She sheepishly and apologetically looked at me as I hollered and cried uncontrollably. I could hear Mom bolt down the hall. By the time she entered the room, the tech had already stopped the machine. Yet the damage was irreversible. Static electricity ran haywire through my nervous system.

I refused to do any other treatments. I pushed her away from me and had Mom remove the electrodes from my feet. I knew she was sorry, but I did not care. What mattered to me was finding a way to stop the agonizing pain. As Mom gathered my blanket and pillow, I hobbled to the office's front door holding my stuffed dog.

On our drive back to the apartment, I sat in the passenger seat convulsing. I was in shock. My entire right arm burned and throbbed. By the time we reached the apartment, I could barely stand on my own or move my fingers. *Shit…it was happening all over again.*

Doc was extremely apologetic. He felt awful and in no way condoned or justified his staff's grand mistake. As he spoke to Mom, he told her to be patient. We were going through a rough patch, but he promised this would all get better. He saw me healed; it was just going to take time.

Despite having scheduled my first morphine decrease for that afternoon, Doc now wanted to wait another four or five days. He even held off evening treatments so my body had more time to recover. While there was nothing he could do to ease the elevated pain, he wanted Mom to call him if I encountered more trouble throughout the night. Otherwise, I just needed to get through the next few days.

I was worse by morning. What had once been constant droning headaches had now turned into piercing, unrelenting migraines. Unable to tolerate any form of light without a drastic spike in my pain levels, I was forced to wear a black slicker hat and sunglasses at all times. Mom also had to cover the blinds with blankets to block out the slightest of rays. We began using candles to move around the apartment and started talking in our library voices. There was no denying my decline. I was losing this battle.

The drive to Doc's office that morning was horrible. Now that my hand had returned to its closed and fisted position, I found myself in protective mode once again. In order to shield my hypersensitive limb from others, I elevated my arm in the air by bending my elbow at a ninety-degree angle. I would do whatever it took to avoid further agony.

I sobbed as we waited in the treatment room for Doc. He immediately appeared and asked me to describe what I was enduring. He needed to understand my worst symptoms so he could choose the accurate protocols to run. While I tried to explain my torment, I felt the tiny room cave in on me. It was as if I was sitting in a hot sauna, suffocating. Almost immediately, the room started to spin, and I turned cherry red. I was light-headed and confused as my head rolled from side to side.

Fearing I would pass out, Doc rushed to lower the office's air conditioning temperature and brought me a fan. He placed the fan in a corner so the air would not directly blow on me. Then he and Mom stood anxiously waiting for my breathing to stabilize. I began to feel better within minutes and was ready to start treatments.

Yet each time Ruben started a treatment, the burning and shooting worsened. I tried to breathe through the torture, but it was impossible. The pain destroyed me. Soon I found myself screaming for him to stop. We kept moving on to other protocols, but they were all the same. I cried in utter frustration and despair as Ruben began removing the electrodes from my feet.

He told me not to lose hope or give up. He had seen miracles walk in and out of these doors, and he believed Doc would help me. While I might have felt helpless right now, Ruben wanted me to hold on to faith. His support and encouragement meant the world to me. I realized I could not throw in the towel. *I had already come too far to let this experience be a waste.*

After spending more than four hours trying to find a protocol to lower my escalated pain, I was exhausted. I had had enough and needed to leave the clinic. With the aching misery now unmanageable, I could not hold back the tears. The water works fell, and I had trouble wiping away my tears when Doc entered the room. I looked at him with pleading eyes; I needed him to help me deal with this pain.

He turned toward Mom and said that we needed to hang in there. Doc did not know when this flare-up would subside, but he knew I needed rest. In order to calm my autonomic nervous system, he had prescribed the drug trazodone. Although trazodone was a commonly used anti-depressant, it also worked well for sleeping. My body needed sleep.

Mom and I went directly to the pharmacy to pick up the prescription and then followed Doc's instructions. Immediately, I took half a pill and saved the second half for later that night. Once I had taken the medication, I crawled onto the couch, where I rested my right elbow on a pillow placed in my lap. As I sat waiting for the drug to take effect, Mom hurried to check our mail.

Checking the mailbox had become my favorite part of each day. It was my only connection to the outside world. Receiving encouraging notes and care packages from family and friends seemed to make me better. It did not matter how discouraged or helpless I had previously felt; contact with my former life boosted my morale. The unbelievable outpouring of love gave me the courage to look past the fear and remember hope. This treatment was my hope drug. Doc would help me heal...*for good.*

While sorting through the mail that afternoon, I became hungry. I wanted strawberries. Since this was the first time in days that I had asked Mom for food, she wasted no time and hurried into the kitchen. I watched from the family area as she rapidly washed and cut the berries into small bites and brought them to me. They were so deliciously sweet that I then wanted toast with peanut butter and honey. Because I could not take large bites, Mom cut the crust off the bread while sectioning each piece into nine miniature squares.

I had to lie down as the food begun to settle in my stomach. It was time for me to rest in darkness. I managed to sleep for an hour before the extreme pain woke me. Hobbling into the family room, hunched over like a ninety-year-old woman with osteoporosis, I noticed that objects in the room were blurred. The television screen, magazine covers and Mom's face started to fade into black-and-white dots. Then I felt gurgling and churning in my abdomen. My face flushed. I had to get to the bathroom...and fast.

My last bowel movement had been eight days ago. Unable to release the medicines' poisonous toxins on a regular basis was posing major complications. Doc said this was what caused the inflammation and drastic weight changes. It was also the reason my liver and kidney function were impaired. Those contaminants stored in my system had weakened my body almost to the point of no repair.

Another not-so-obvious problem was the additional pain and torment my body endured going to the bathroom. I always felt blocked and constricted, and pushing only caused more strain that tore my delicate skin. I found myself stuck in the restroom for a lengthy amount of time, trying to release my hardened bowels. Pleading with a Higher Power to help me pass the rock-solid feces, I would grunt and sweat. My inflamed sphincters were raw and sore.

Constipation was not a topic I felt comfortable speaking freely about, and yet I had to. I recognized the seriousness and gravity of the issue. Understanding the potentially life-threatening problems that could arise helped me begrudgingly speak with Doc and Dr. Lane about my "pooping" issues. Explaining the frequency and dark, rough appearance of my stools scared me. I knew something had to be seriously wrong after discovering my bathroom visits had caused plumbing issues for my entire apartment building. *How could my bowels plug up every toilet in my complex?*

Doc was obviously concerned. The increased water retention and significant weight gain were a problem, but he felt withdrawal was to blame. He still believed that once I was off my medications, I would improve. Dr. Lane, however, wanted me to take acidophilus, a group of probiotics used to aid in digestion by supplying the body with healthy bacteria. She hoped this supplement would naturally regulate my system.

That evening, I had trouble staying comfortable. No matter how I maneuvered my body, I could not find a position that did not inflict extreme agony. As I screamed and cried over the piercing pains in my right hand, I kept my arm jutted up in the air about six inches away from the rest of my body. I just wanted out of the misery. Unable to set my arm on blankets or sheets meant I could not sleep. Even if I drifted off for a second, I would be jolted awake as soon as the arm made contact with my duvet. As I fought to survive another minute, my right leg rapidly convulsed and my body started to shake. *I had entered hell.*

When the hypersensitivity finally calmed at six in the morning, I was able to get some much-needed sleep. Exhausted, Mom called Doc. He told her to let me rest for the remainder of the day. He did not want me coming in to the office or even attempting the machine. My body had needed a break; this was just part of the healing process.

The higher pains were normal for drug reductions. As my body battled withdrawal, I would need constant reassurance from my parents that I would be all right. Doc understood that this would be challenging for them, but it was crucial to my healing. In order for me to overcome this ordeal, I needed others to be upbeat and positive. I needed to be able to cling to hope.

After sleeping for five hours, I woke to the bitter realization that my pain was real. As I looked more closely at my hand, I noticed a slight change in the swelling and discoloration. It still resembled a blown-up latex glove from the doctor's office, but it was visibly smaller. The color seemed pinkish instead of its usual glossy white and peach tone. I could even bring my arm within three inches of my torso and was able to rest the limb on a pillow. This might not have been overwhelmingly great progress, but it still classified as minor improvements. It was another baby step, enabling me not to feel so defeated.

Although I had wanted to appease Mom by eating, my nausea and severe abdominal cramps made that impossible. Even the foods I usually tolerated like soup, strawberries, clementines, smoothies, ice cream, peanut butter toast and mashed potatoes were now unappealing. Drinking peppermint-and-ginger tea to soothe my sour stomach did not help me anymore.

Even though I was not eating, I found myself still getting wider and bigger. Each day it felt as if I gained another five pounds. I had arrived in x-small and small clothing, but my body had expanded and swelled so much that I needed larger sizes. As Mom had to keep going to Old Navy in order to purchase pajamas and T-shirts for me to wear, she always cut out the tags so I would not know that I now needed a men's large.

Whereas all of this was soul-crushing, not being able to bathe destroyed what little self-worth I had left. The water pressure felt like hypodermic needles puncturing the entire surface of my skin, while the warm temperature felt like scalding oil on half of my body. These sensations were so intense that I had no choice but refrain from showering. It was as if I had reverted to infancy. With no control over my own body, my sole existence depended on others caring for me.

Although my pride was shattered, I refused to be decrepit. Instead, Mom bought baby wipes so I could clean myself from bed. We then searched for a local salon to wash my dirty, mangled hair. In a pure moment of fate, the first shop she called was a family-run day spa and salon. After hearing about our situation, the family did everything they could to help accommodate Mom and me. This included them scheduling my appointment near closing, so they could turn off lights and lower the background music. It was as if I received another sign from above, telling me I was not fighting this alone. *I could do this.*

I visited every two weeks or whenever my health permitted, to have a pedicure and my hair washed. This family was exceptionally gentle with me. The father helped me walk back to the shower bowls, so I would not fall. One of the sons gave me water with frozen fruit balls when I became flushed or light-headed. The mother offered me peppermints or tea to ease my nausea. As they strived to make me feel comfortable, I felt more like a family member than a complete stranger. With most of the world ignoring my existence, this family accepted me and made me feel normal again…and that was the greatest feeling.

However, finding this amazing salon did not end my suffering.

∞

Dad visited us for the first time three weeks after we had arrived. By then, I was not doing very well. In fact, I was miserable all the time. I only wanted my nightmare to end so my life could begin.

Even with the horrendous tingling pain traveling up and down both of my arms, I was ecstatic to see him. Dad had always been my favorite cheerleader, because his humor made me feel better. Whenever I felt distraught or wanted to give up, he knew the exact words to lift my spirits so I would keep fighting. His presence had the power to shift my thinking.

Dad helped free me from the devastation that had recently consumed me. The quicker I could accept that I would not be better in a matter of weeks, the better equipped I would be to handle my current situation. Overcoming chronic pain would be a huge feat that would require time and energy. I had to be tolerant and less discouraged by the process. I needed to continue to move forward with optimism. I had to remind myself this was happening for a greater purpose, and in the end, I would be pain-free and healed.

With a better attitude, my whole outlook on this journey seemed to change. To say I embraced the pain might have been an overstatement. Yet I had accepted this life-challenge and was beginning to take ownership of the recovery. I was determined to heal and finally prove everyone else wrong.

Throughout my illness, doctors had told me my health was a lost cause. I viewed my pain differently. I believed if I never gave in to the specialists' unmerited opinions in the past, then I could not throw in the towel and accept defeat now. There was just too much research left untapped. I would fight until my last breath. I overcame this disease once, so I would find a way to beat it again.

As this would be the greatest obstacle I would have to overcome, I wanted it documented. I needed tangible proof that despite such misery and grief, I had won my battle with chronic pain. I tried writing as a way to keep daily records of my feelings and emotions but found it to be too difficult without my right hand. Then I thought about photography. Pictures would be the perfect way to capture my journey. As Mom bought disposable cameras, I explicitly instructed her to photograph my stay. No matter how much I might be suffering, she had to take pictures. I had to do this for my fellow comrades living in pain; she had to make this experience real and authentic.

While this new outlook allowed me to face the demons that haunted my soul, the pain persisted. Doc scheduled an appointment with my parents and me to explain why I had such a difficult time responding to the therapy. I had an over-stressed autonomic nervous system from the opioids semi-permanently altering my nerves. This resulted in a tendency to react poorly to any type of stimulation, including the STS therapy. Doc was confident that I would heal, but it was just going to take longer to do so. It was imperative that I rid myself of the narcotics.

For my parents and me, this whole ordeal was terrifying. We felt as if we were treading on unknown waters. Yet Doc had been in these situations before. He had other patients who needed more time to get well. Although he was frustrated with my current progress, he knew the situation was not hopeless. As long as we were willing to stick it out, he knew I would recover. Since we had no other options, we had no choice but to believe him. *I had to put my full faith in him.*

Doc continued to share with us how challenging my case was because of the amount of medications I was taking and the dosage strength. He was amazed that in spite of the severity of my condition, I was still functioning. Not only were the prescribed amounts too severe for a person my age, height and weight, Doc felt they were inappropriate for any human being. With that said, Doc knew he would have to proceed more slowly and more carefully. He then worked out a tentative medicine reduction schedule where I only dropped fifteen milligrams every five to ten days.

Hoping to bypass some of the most horrible withdrawal symptoms, he needed me to increase my protein intake. This was crucial, since RSDS thrived in a protein-deficient body. While insisting my parents sprinkle whey powder on everything I ate, he also wanted me to start having a bowl of ice cream each night. This was strange to me. I could understand the need for protein in my diet, but I had never heard another doctor say, "Eat ice cream."

Doc told us that ice cream coated my stomach for medications and contained Morpheus. Morpheus was the protein found in milk that induced sleep. Therefore, while he might not be able to stop the pain, he could try to ease some of the excruciating withdrawal with sleep and protein.

∞

The day I had been dreading since I arrived in Corpus Christi had finally come, and it was worse than I even imagined. I would not only have to drop the first fifteen milligrams of morphine, but I also would have to say goodbye to Dad. With the reduction planned for the afternoon, my physical health and mental state progressively declined as the day wore on. I decided to stay behind while Mom drove Dad to the airport, because I was just too upset. Tears fell relentlessly down my cheeks, and I found myself falling further into the void of despair. *This was never going to end.*

Despite it being only hours since I lessened my morphine, I had already begun to experience intense withdrawal. The sharp contractions in my abdomen strengthened, causing me to lie in the fetal position with pillows thrust against my midsection. Doc thought Pepto-Bismol might make the ruthless abdominal pains more manageable. I took the over-the-counter medication advertised to relieve heartburn, indigestion, nausea and upset stomach. Yet the improvement lasted briefly.

When the angst returned, I began forcing myself to eat, in an attempt to ease the feeling of my intestines shredding apart. I had smoothies in the morning, toast with peanut butter for lunch, scrambled eggs for a snack or dinner, and ice cream with whey powder as snacks. Nothing eased the brutal pain.

Once my headaches intensified to migraines, they began to override my life. These paralyzing, sidesplitting pains now took precedence over all my other complaints. I felt like my head was about to burst open. Since I could not live with the agony that kept me begging for mercy at night, Doc prescribed a narcotic analgesic nasal spray used to treat, control and relieve migraine symptoms. *I just hoped it would work.*

I had never used a nasal spray in the past, so using one correctly was a challenge. After my first attempt at priming the bottle by pumping the sprayer several times, a fine mist appeared. Then I inserted the tip into my left nostril while I blocked my right nostril with my fist. As I took in a breath through my nose, I tilted my head forward slightly before re-shifting my head backward in order to sniff.

While I felt a small change in my headache, I was unsure if I received a full dose. Mom called Doc to see what we should do. He told her to wait an hour and repeat if necessary, using the opposite nostril.

Waiting the next sixty minutes was grueling. I wanted immediate relief, and not receiving that made me impatient. When I primed the pump again, I noticed a significantly larger stream emerge into the air. I instantly felt light-headed after my second attempt. Although consciously aware of what was occurring around me, I was incapable of reacting to any stimuli. It was as if my own body was holding me hostage.

I was unable to open my eyes or form words for nearly ninety minutes. As I finally regained control over my speech and limbs, I remember being terrified. I panicked and began to cry. My skin turned clammy while my heart raced. I was confused. *What was going on?* Mom called Doc, who told her that she needed to take me directly to the emergency room. I was going to need a katabolic injection to reduce the inflammation and prevent the chemicals from spreading further in my body.

Nurses placed me in a wheelchair as soon as we arrived at the ER. It was controlled mayhem where everyone diligently worked together, knowing the importance of time and efficiency. As one nurse connected me to monitors, others took my pulse and blood pressure and started an IV line. I was overwhelmed with fear. This type of reaction was new to me, and I did not like feeling so anxious and inebriated.

The ER doctor promptly ordered the injection; it had no effect on the allergic reaction. Now I was inconsolable and completely paranoid. *Why had it not worked? What was wrong with me now?* I started to lose control on the exam table, scared that I might die. The doctor found it essential to try another shot. This time it was an antihistamine. While injecting ten milligrams of a different drug into my system, he explained to Mom how antihistamines could relieve and prevent symptoms of medical problems. Since it would take time for the medicine to enter my bloodstream, the waiting game began. Time was the only way to determine the success or failure of this drug.

My heart beat ferociously while I sat propped up in my hospital bed. The pounding in my head intensified from the blaring lights and loud frenzy. Exhausted, I looked around the room and tried becoming aware of my surroundings. But my senses were garbled and I felt as though I was living in an altered state. Voices soon seemed strange, and faces became indistinct. As I repeatedly opened and closed my eyes, I found myself staring out at a foreign world. Passersby reminded me of cartoon characters. Unless I focused all my attention on an object, everything seemed distorted and hazy. *I was afraid I was having a nervous breakdown.*

Although I detected minor improvements in my right arm an hour after my last shot, I was still restless. An ER attendant scanned the monitors, took my pulse, and looked at my pupils while I sat clammy and shaking. Wide awake and jumpy meant it was time to try another type of medication.

For this injection, I would be administered a shot of an analgesic. This type of drug blocked certain receptor sites in the central nervous system. Instead of a decrease in pain, I felt hot and flushed. An intense, ravaging heat swept through my body, smoldering my intestinal lining and stomach. My right hand turned tomato red and burned. Then my body went limp from my arms down. I looked like a bobble-head.

I was terrified, especially after trying to speak and only hearing maddening laughter filter from my mouth. While unable to communicate, the doctor tried to assure Mom and me that this side effect was considered normal.

I was in hysterics. Since the ER doctor had to visit his other patients, he instructed a nurse to monitor my breathing and heart rate. Knowing that a trained medical professional was checking me for any unforeseen complications calmed me. Soon I was able to relax and use the breathing techniques Sharon had shown me at Stanford, and the guided imagery lessons Maureen had taught me from Healing Touch.

Just by concentrating on these two therapies, I felt my body loosen. I began to breathe easier and eventually regained control of my motor skills. I was stabilizing, and finally at one thirty in the morning, the ER released me to go home. *I was there for four hours.*

Chapter 21

New Coach, New Approach

I felt as if I was bordering on a complete meltdown. I had come to Texas with such high hopes, but they had all been shattered. With the disease spreading rapidly through my body, it left Doc scrambling to put out the flames before the fire fully ignited. I was lifeless and questioned how to move forward.

In order to handle the ever-escalating agony, I found myself withdrawing from the world. Since I had come to Texas hoping to become pain-free, my body had been physically pushed to the ultimate limit. Disconnecting from those around me was the only way I could cope with the horrific aches and symptoms. I learned to silence the outside environment and focus inward. I had to become despondent so I could survive.

With Thanksgiving only days away, Dad returned to Texas so Mom could go home for a week. Although I liked having Dad with me, things changed with him in charge. I had grown used to Mom preparing my food to my liking, so it struck me as rude when Dad resisted following suit. His new phrase soon became, "New coach, new approach."

It was not that he wanted to be mean, but he believed cutting my strawberries or bread in a particular manner only fed into my **need** for control. Dad felt my mindset of needing to control the outer world to counteract the lack of power I had over my own life was detrimental to my recovery. He did not want me to associate with the negatives in my life but to look toward the positive outcome. Although it might seem as if life was crumbling, my life was actually just taking shape. *From this darkness would come light.*

Thanksgiving had always been my favorite holiday. I loved how it centered on family and good food. It was a time to give and embrace while cherishing moments spent with loved ones.

This year, my Thanksgiving would be different; this year, my family would be not be together, because I was sick. While I would have done anything to see Dan and be with my extended family, I knew I had to stay strong. My life's purpose right now was to heal, and I was in Texas to get better.

Much to my surprise, Doc invited Dad and me to spend the holiday with him and his family. Doc lived in the country with acres upon acres of land separating him from his neighbors. As we drove down the long dirt road to reach his house, I could not believe the amount of open space surrounding him. He literally was miles away from everyone, secluded in a remote area with livestock and a large pond.

After greeting us at the front door, Doc gave us a personal tour of his home. Then we convened in the kitchen, where his wife was cooking. I was sure having company four months after giving birth to twins must have been stressful. Yet she seemed genuinely glad to see us. She never once made us feel as though we were imposing. Instead, we were just an extension of their family circle. Their love and generosity toward us was real, and it made me wonder if any of my previous physicians would have extended this same invitation. *Probably not.*

I did not have an appetite, but the aroma of the holidays overpowered my senses. Soon, smells of sage, cinnamon, nutmeg and pumpkin made me salivate. This was the first time I truly felt hungry in weeks. The food was delicious, and I even asked for seconds on the stuffing and green bean casserole. While the atmosphere was nothing like home, I laughed and enjoyed myself. We all shared family stories, discussed newsworthy events, and talked about my health.

Part of me did not want to leave. Just getting away from a medical environment for a few short hours reminded me of the person I was before Texas. Normalcy somehow returned to my out-of-control life. I was able to see myself as *me* again. For a brief moment, I was no longer *"the patient"* but simply *"me."* And I liked that.

Unfortunately, that Zen feeling did not last long. As November pressed into December, I had grown more dependent upon a wheelchair. Having a wheelchair made life less complicated. Now Mom and I could leave the apartment and visit a store. On the flipside, I had become the sore thumb. I either received pitiful stares or complete avoidance wherever we went. It was as if not acknowledging my presence made it easier for others to go about their daily lives. If people did not look at me, then I did not exist, and therefore they did not have to think about the unfairness and injustices of the world.

Although the darting glances made me uncomfortable, I learned to accept my situation. People were ignorant. I knew getting upset would not change the problem, so I had to let it go.

Mom, however, had a much harder time forgiving people. I believed this had to do with the stark contrast between the person I used to be and the person I had become. In the past, when I weighed forty pounds less and walked, people initiated conversations with me. Yet now that I was "handicapped" and overweight, people seemed to avoid me like the plague. It was almost as though they were afraid they might catch it.

Trying to make her see that we could not let others affect our lives was impossible. *I was her daughter.* It was in her maternal makeup to shield and protect me from the pointing fingers, the laughs, and the disrespectful, dashing eyes. Although I believed that was part of her issue, I also felt she could not handle the tactless avoidances because it made my illness real. Forced to see me through the eyes of another meant she could no longer deny the inevitable. *I was sicker than anyone wanted to accept or believe.*

I then faced another disappointment in mid-December. Since I had only decreased my narcotic intake by forty-five milligrams, I realized my goal of being home for Christmas was not realistic or feasible. I was absolutely distraught.

Reminding myself that my attitude mattered to my overall well-being, I began to set my sights on Easter. Easter was four months away, which gave me plenty of time to get better. While having this new plan in order motivated me to keep fighting, I still felt ashamed for destroying my family.

I had placed next to my bed a beautiful beaded journal that Mitzi had given me before I left California. She wanted me to have a book in which I could chronicle my time in Texas. I had meant to write daily but found myself too tired and in too much pain. Yet for some reason, I finally decided to open the indigo book on December 15, 2002. I felt compelled to express my deepest feelings. While it took me some time, I entered my thoughts in my most legible left-handed inscription.

Today marks my eighth week here in Corpus Christi—and I know that I still have a long road ahead of me. I never would have imagined that it would take this long to get off narcotics. It is so hard on my body that we have only been able to drop 15mg every ten days or so. Since arriving on October 20, 2002, I have only been able to decrease my morphine by 45mg—leaving me 175mg to go... He [Doc] just wishes that he had reached me earlier. But I always tell him that there is a reason I am here now—I think it gives me much more validation when I'm speaking to others in the medical field because I did mainstream medicine...

Lately I've been in a whole lot of pain. Slowly the RSD is spreading and I'm off my diuretics so my whole body is swollen and very sore. My skin literally cannot stretch anymore. I arrived here in 'XS' and 'S' clothing and now I am in 'Larges.'

This is really hard for me to handle...

Writing lifted a weight from my shoulders. I had finally found a constructive way to channel my grief and be honest with myself about what my body was enduring. Being able to write the things I could never say aloud was healing. This was me unscripted.

∞

As the holiday approached, Corpus Christi turned festive. Soon, Christmas decorations of lights and trees adorned the streets. While I usually enjoyed driving through neighborhoods to look at twinkling lights, this year, that tradition seemed trivial and cliché. *These houses and these lights were not home to me.*

Mom did her very best to make this holiday normal by trying to create a sense of *home* here in Texas. She purchased a small, fake tree and decorated it with strands of lights and our personal ornaments that Dad mailed to her from California. Resting the tree on top of a large box in the corner of the family room made it appear radiant. It looked perfect.

Although I was excited to have both Dad and Dan here for Christmas, I still wished things were different. I was missing the many rituals that made this time of the year so special to me. It devastated me that I would not see my high school friends on break from college or be able to attend the annual Callaghan Christmas party. Life had completely changed for me, and I still could not grasp how it went on for everyone else. *I was only twenty-one.* I should have been partying, dating and having fun. Instead, I suffered and relied on others to care for me.

Dan's first quarter of college ended on December 18, so Dad and he scheduled their flights for the twentieth. As Mom went to the airport to pick them up, I stayed in the comforts of the apartment, where the lights were off and the room was quiet. My mood had improved over the past few days. I think it had to do with the anticipation of seeing my family. It had been three months since I had last seen Dan, and I could not wait for him to arrive. I had missed him so much.

I remember I was lying on the couch when I heard the key turn in the lock. I sat up and tried to look happy and healthy. But as Dan looked at me, I saw terror sweep across his face. Even my parents' forewarning about my drastic change in appearance did not prepare him. He appeared downright frightened. It saddened me to have to witness his internal pain. I knew how agonizing Mom's illness was on me years earlier. Seeing Dan struggle with my own disease brought back the haunting feelings of helplessness. *How could I put my family through that same ordeal?*

In an effort to make this Christmas more bearable, my parents had rented two beautiful rooms at a waterfront hotel. Even though I did not have energy to move around, it was nice being away from the apartment for a few nights. Just staring out the window at the incredible views of the Gulf was comforting. Watching the waves hit the sand and loll back out in the water soothed me. *I was part of the circle of life.*

Christmas Day was low-key. We followed our typical family routine of seeing an afternoon movie. I soon discovered that the sense of *home* had nothing to do with the location but everything to do with the company. The holiday was meaningful because we were with each other. As long as I had the three of them, I was home.

That night I found myself unable to sleep. My mind would not stop racing as I lay awake in my hotel bed. Knowing how my parents kept sacrificing on my behalf made them my heroes. I was so lucky to have that unwavering love and support. It would have been very easy for them to question or blame me. Yet they never did. Instead, they always told me that I would heal despite how long it might take. We were in this together, and we would work as team to overcome this hurdle.

We checked out of the hotel the next day with Mom and me returning to our apartment while Dad and Dan left for California. I did not like goodbyes, so I opted to stay at home while Mom took them to the airport. I remember sobbing on the couch, waiting for her to return. I did not want to see them go. These past six days had rejuvenated me. I felt as if I needed Dad and Dan more than ever right now. I clung to them to help me get through my personal hell. I hated constantly being left behind. All I wanted was to feel normal again. *What did it feel like to feel nothing?*

New Year's Eve was horribly discouraging for me as well. I remember Mom and me sitting in the dark, watching Dick Clark's countdown to 2003 live from Times Square. We were silent. We both knew there were no words to mend this type of heartache. Another year had passed and I was still in pain. I went to bed right after the ball dropped, needing to be alone. It became harder to stay positive when every day that passed I seemed to worsen. My body was exhausted and I wanted this battle to be over. *How much longer could I possibly keep hope alive?*

Chapter 22

Unnecessary Antics

I faced another roadblock as we moved ahead with the tentative drug-reduction schedule. Doc soon discovered he could not lower my morphine without the assistance of other medications. This turned into a long, drawn-out ordeal, since he exclusively based finding the right medications on the trial-and-error method. That meant Doc would make an educated guess on what to give me, and then I would have to test the prescription to determine its effectiveness at bringing me relief. Since nothing seemed to help me, Mom had to visit the pharmacy multiple times each week for new medications.

It was during these tedious trips back and forth to the drugstore that Mom began facing questions from the pharmacist. The pharmacist was concerned at the amount of medicine being prescribed to one individual. In his professional opinion, it was way too much.

As Mom felt attacked, she began defending Doc's ethics and medical practice. She thoroughly explained my situation and the severe morphine withdrawals. Doc was not supplying medicine without merit, but he was trying to save my life. He was getting me off the drugs so I could live.

Although the pharmacist eventually apologized, that was not the end of the inquiries. Mom faced the same harassment and skepticism every time she picked up a new medication. It was draining on her to have to justify Doc's actions and re-explain my health condition to complete strangers. Yet she realized the strength of the drugs and the frequency of her visits could cause reservations. She just figured it was something she needed to get used to, because they were only doing their jobs.

During the last week in January, Doc seemed edgy, bothered and concerned. He quickly reviewed my chart before having Ruben run protocols. Sometimes I wondered why I even went to the trouble of leaving the apartment for a couple seconds of treatment. It felt like a cruel joke to have Ruben stop the STS machine and retrieve Doc minutes after arriving.

I knew something was terribly wrong when Doc returned for the second time. His face appeared serious; he needed to speak privately with Mom and me. The police had contacted Doc the previous evening to verify his frequent prescriptions of a narcotic analgesic nose spray to a Nicole Hemmenway. He told the officer he had only written one script for that particular drug, since I had suffered an adverse reaction. The detective then informed Doc that the head pharmacist had contacted local authorities after noticing an increase in the regularity of this particular drug's refill. He suspected drug abuse.

Doc told us that the news shocked him. Since he could not offer the police any explanation, he promised to speak with us to determine what might be happening. He then looked straight at Mom and said he was worried. Doc knew how emotionally disturbing it was to watch your child suffer, and he only wanted to make sure Mom was handling my illness all right.

Hearing the story unravel completely stunned us. Not only had the medication in question landed me in the emergency room for half a night, but we also had never been to the pharmacy where the drug was refilled. Mom thanked Doc for his concern over her well-being, but she said there was only one logical explanation. Somebody in his office must have been using our insurance to obtain medicine.

Mom was adamant about clearing our name, so she went straight to the store to speak with the pharmacist. He took one look at Mom and laughed. The person in question was a woman in her late twenties with shoulder-length, dirty blonde hair. Mom was in her early fifties with short salt-and-pepper hair. While we drove a blue Jetta with California plates, the woman picking up prescriptions had a brand-new white car with a Texas registration sticker. There was no way it was Mom filling this prescription.

While relieved to know this matter would be resolved, Mom was saddened. She instantly knew that the receptionist who had quit last week was ordering the medication. This devastated Mom and completely troubled Doc. Although he had not personally stolen from us, he recognized the role he played. He was responsible for hiring her, so the blame fell directly on his shoulders.

Though I continued to see Doc, my trips to the office became less frequent. For some reason, I found myself at conflict with his staff. He had three technicians who I believed perceived me to be spoiled and demanding. I will admit that I was very assertive and particular when it came to my health. If I did not feel comfortable with a specific tech setting up my protocols, I would make it clear to Doc that I did not want that person working on me. That might sound arrogant, but I felt I had to protect myself. After my previous encounter with an inexperienced and inattentive technician costing me mobility in my right hand, I needed to be cautious.

By this point, I was completely hypersensitive to touch, fabrics and magnets. It felt as though third-degree burns covered my body while waves of shooting pains traveled up and down my spine. Doc tried his best to accommodate every patient's needs so he scheduled my appointments for the afternoons. This way he could lower the thermostat to make me more comfortable. Nevertheless, some of the staff felt this was unnecessary and ridiculous. They thought I was crying wolf and exaggerating my pain for attention.

I noticed the first inclination of retaliation when the office itself felt cool but my room was hot and stuffy. After two days of unbearable warmth that caused my skin to radiate and throb, Ruben discovered the air vent in my room had been closed. Although I did not want to seem paranoid, I knew it must have been members of his staff. It seemed too suspicious that the only vent tampered with was mine. I had hoped casually mentioning this problem to Doc would end the mean pranks: it did not.

Magnets greatly bothered me. Anytime I was near them, I would feel as if a farm of ants was crawling all over my bare skin. Then waves of electrical current would sweep down my spine before I began to feel lightheaded and hear droning sounds in my eardrums. Since Doc understood my hypersensitivity to magnets, he made sure my treatment room and the ones adjoining mine did not contain magnets. Not his staff. Instead, they purposely hid magnets to test my pain levels.

I remember the first afternoon when my entire body began to burn in his office. I had just sat in my chair when I immediately felt intense agony. As Mom checked the room for magnets, I prayed it was just my paranoia getting the best of me. Not wanting to believe his techs would want to harm me, it felt like a head-on collision when Mom pulled the magnet out from the inside of my recliner. I just did not understand. It was so disheartening to think his team would willingly jeopardize my health for a laugh. *Did they really think that little of me?*

With the pain increasing, I asked Mom to help me back into the car. I just needed to leave. I had to get away from the stupid clinic. Mom immediately called Doc on his cell phone. She was furious at such inexcusable behavior. Doc seemed mortified and baffled, and assured us both that this type of conduct was intolerable.

Although I wanted to believe him when he promised me it would not happen again, I was still hesitant to return to the office. How could he be so sure? Therefore, Mom devised a new system where she would check my treatment room before I even got out of the car. This seemed to work well, because it protected me from additional stress and further pain.

Several more days had passed. Despite my health declining and the STS not working, I still found myself visiting the office as much as possible. My focal point was healing, and this clinic was my last hope. I knew I needed Doc and his machine in order to get well, so I had to trust that these antics had been nipped in the bud.

A few days later, Mom and I arrived at the office to discover another patient was occupying my usual treatment room. Therefore, the techs moved me to the back room. This was the largest room in the office, as it had two treatment chairs, a huge black exam table, and many air vents. Mom was worried because she was not accustomed to searching this space. Doc personally assured her that he had already checked the room for magnets and closed vents. He found nothing.

I started to feel dizzy and lightheaded as I began to fill out the tedious pain grid. I noticed that my arms and legs stung, as if I had a fresh sunburn. I told Mom about the uncomfortable sensations, wanting to make sure she was positive that there were no magnets in the room. Mom did not hesitate. She quickly went across the hall to Doc's office, where he was talking with his wife. Although she hated to interrupt their conversation, she knew they had a limited amount of time before my symptoms would begin to flare.

I was in tears when the three of them returned to the room. The pain was increasing. Doc tried his best to calm me down, but I was convinced there were magnets hidden. While he and Mom repeatedly told me the room was clean, Doc's wife was not so sure. She kept saying she felt different near the exam table. I then looked up and saw the metal lamp above her head. Placed inside the fixture near the light bulb was a magnet.

Why would they do this to me?

That was the last straw. I had had enough. Refusing to be hurt for someone's sick pleasure, I told Doc I would stay at the apartment unless he took permanent action. I was just too sick to have to deal with these unnecessary pranks. I was at a total loss. Already in a downward spiral, I now believed my trips to the clinic were detrimental to my health. I felt like a victim unable to defend myself. While I knew I could not let the hate of three people cause me to leave, I did not know how I was supposed to go back. I was deeply hurt. How could Doc let his employees get away with treating a patient in such a disrespectful manner?

My health rapidly declined over the next few days. Since it was impossible for me to get out of bed, I spent my time thinking in the darkness. This was when I truly realized my predicament. If I continued reducing medications at my current rate, it would be another ten months before I finished. Just thinking about almost another year of hell was more than I could handle. I needed to seek outside help.

When I was finally strong enough to return to the clinic for a visit, I spoke candidly to Doc about the tremendous suffering I had endured over the past four months. I had only made a minimal dent in decreasing my medications, so I wanted to visit a doctor who specialized in drug withdrawal. Much to his dismay, Doc listened to me. He had to; he *knew* I had been through the wringer.

A weight lifted from my shoulders when he agreed to help. I was not trying to demean Doc's intelligence or criticize his treatment plan. I understood that I had to be off narcotics before his STS machine could help me. Therefore, I wanted to search for a more effective way to speed up the withdrawal process. I had to make necessary changes so I could fully recover.

After making a few phone calls, Doc thought I should visit a local facility dedicated to drug and alcohol rehabilitation. He believed their specialist could positively assist me through the next few weeks of withdrawal. Doc asked if he could come to the consultation. He was interested in the suggestions this doctor might provide for future patients. We eagerly said yes. Because he was my doctor, he would know the right questions to ask.

I was overwhelmed with the lush, manicured lawn surrounding the behavioral hospital. The place was pristine and beautiful. A large fountain and nicely shaded bench areas lined the grounds, along with many mature trees. As we drove down the road to the entrance, I was determined to walk into the appointment. I did not want the doctor to judge me as the decrepit girl.

My refusal to use the wheelchair meant Mom had to drop Doc and me off at the front. It took some time, but I managed to hobble to the nearest chair and sit down. Soon the doctor came to greet us and led us down a short hall to a large office. He immediately began firing questions at me. However, I quickly got the impression that he was uninterested and unimpressed with my answers when he cut me off to explain the philosophy of his facility. I felt the hairs on the back of my neck rise as I awaited his recommendations. My life's happiness rested entirely on him.

When he started to speak in an authoritarian voice, I knew I was in trouble. It was as if I was just another case study to him. He was not interested in talking *to* me but rather *down* to me. Who I was as a person meant nothing to him. He only viewed me as "sick" and "in need of saving."

The doctor continually refuted the notion that my body had a chemical dependence on opioids because of two years of medically prescribed use. Instead, he was convinced that I was a drug addict in need of an intervention. He had seen people just like me before. He was used to docile, polite, intelligent people complaining of pain for the primary purpose of receiving drugs. In his opinion, the time had come for me to face the lies and deceit. The only way I could begin to heal was by accepting and acknowledging my own addiction.

Despite my best attempts to talk to this man rationally, it was useless. He just continued to talk over me, while berating my very existence. My face felt as if it was on fire. Fuming with rage, I raised my voice and pointed to my hand. *Where did he get the audacity to say I did not have RSD? Who was he to suggest that I exaggerated my pain for the sake of abusing drugs?*

He brushed my question aside as if I was a child, directing his comments only to Mom and Doc. If they did not insist that I obtain proper medical attention, they were enablers to my sickness. It was up to them to choose whether they wanted me to heal or continue down this bleak road.

The hospital followed a precise approach with every individual: comprehensive counseling and a three-day withdrawal program. During those three excruciating days, patients stayed in white padded rooms while being administered different oral medications to help deal with the terrible pain. Patients could not have visitors and were on a twenty-four-hour watch. Since he also felt I was in denial, I would therefore require extra psychological exams.

I was livid and found myself biting my inner lip to hold back the tears. There was absolutely no way I was going to spend one second alone in this facility. Although I understood that there were people who suffered from true drug addictions, I knew I was not one of them. In disbelief over what this man was saying, I looked over at Doc. He had been silent throughout the consultation but kept nodding his head as the idiot specialist talked. Did he agree with this asshole?

I had had enough of his judgment and professional opinion. Not once had the arrogant jerk listened to what I had to say *or* taken into consideration my diagnosis. Instead, he pegged me as an addict before I even entered the building. I abruptly stopped the meeting by saying we needed to leave. It took all my strength to thank him for his time and not deck him. Then I turned around and headed toward the door.

Despite the tremendous pain in my legs, I walked out of that office as fast as I could move. Tears streamed down my face as we drove back to the clinic. I was upset—had that really happened? It was a relief to hear how furious Doc was with the specialist's findings. In no way did he condone or agree with his suggestions. While I felt somewhat better, I still did not understand why he had not come to my defense. Doc apologized. He told me that it was hard for him to stay quiet, but it was not his place to challenge or ridicule another doctor.

This made sense to Mom but not to me. Both of them had left me to fend for myself. That specialist had not only questioned my pain but also held suspect my character. It was difficult for me to accept that neither of them had come to my rescue. But after being demoralized for an hour, I was just glad I would never to have to see that man again.

Chapter 23

Visitors

I became weaker and more detached from the outside world shortly after that horrid experience. I once again found myself unable to get out of bed or walk. Spending the next few days alone in my bedroom, my hopes of finding a faster and less painful withdrawal process had been extinguished. Now I would have to deal with the unrelenting misery. I struggled to keep my head above water as the disease continued to spread like wildfire. I could not believe my life had come to this. I was in bad shape.

I was lucky to have a temporary distraction from the negative events surrounding me. Instead of returning home for spring break, Meredith had chosen to visit me in Texas. I was very excited to have my best friend with me. Although I hardly shared my real feelings regarding my health with others, she was one of a handful of people I trusted. I knew I could count on her to make me smile and lift my spirits.

It was obvious that my drastic change in appearance stunned her as she exited the baggage claim and found Mom and me waiting outside the airport terminal. She tried not to stare at me by forcing her eyes to dart around the car or outside the window. Yet she could not hide her horror; my considerable weight gain startled her. *I think it worried us all.*

Once the initial shock subsided, we were able to pick up our usual banter and enjoy each other's company. It did not take long before she was even joking about my plumpness and referring me to as Violet from *Charlie and the Chocolate Factory.* While I did not find this amusing, Mom thought it was hysterical. After all, the few outfits I fit into were mostly blue or indigo, and I was swollen and engorged. In all honesty, my appearance put Violet to shame. I was a massive blimp.

Everything we did over the course of the next three days had to be slow-paced and quiet. The first night, Mom just ordered Mexican takeout from a local restaurant, and we watched TV by candlelight. We ventured out on mini-trips during the day. The three of us took a thirty-minute drive to Padre Island in order to have lunch at a secluded place overlooking the Gulf. We drove along Ocean Drive to look at the gorgeous homes and the crystal blue water. Mom made sure we ate at Whataburger, the famous hamburger chain in Meredith's favorite movie, *8 Seconds*. Even though we did not do much else, it was okay. All I needed was my friend.

I became hysterical the day before Meredith left. My pain had intensified again and I did not want her to leave me. Then I would be alone, and I hated being alone. I remember begging her to stay longer, although I knew she could not. I just fell apart and sobbed. Having her come to Texas only made me realize how much I was missing.

Instead of living with college roommates, I roomed with my mom. Instead of attending crazy parties and flirting with boys, I attended the pain clinic and sometimes said hi to our cute marine neighbor. Instead of worrying about a test or a grade, I worried about my temperature differentials in my hands and feet. Meredith's life was progressing forward while mine was at a standstill. While I was glad to see her happy, I could not deny the pain I felt wishing I could do those things too.

In order to move past this setback, I had to concentrate on the positives. This was why I once again returned to journaling. Much too frail to write full entries, I was left to jot down simple phrases. I followed Shelley's technique of keeping a gratuity diary. For every struggle and frustration I recorded, I needed to write three encouraging and optimistic points. While this was difficult to do, I soon saw its significance. *I realized where I focused my attention was what thrived in my life.*

I named my journal "Waiting for My Miracle."

Waiting for my Miracle:

-Thursday, 2-27-03
  +'s: Daddy came today. I sat up for 5 hours.
  -'s: Pain high because of weather. I can't use STS.
  Inspiration: Sara "Celine Dion CD"

-Friday, 2-28-03
  +'s: 5½ hours of <u>good</u> sleep. Smiled and laughed a lot. Dropped 5mg of MSIR.
  -'s: Pain is high in body. Terrible Indigestion.

-Saturday, 3-1-03

+'s: Smiled and laughed. Gave mom b/day gift. Daddy and I talked awhile.

-'s: Pain is worse. Every muscle aches. Miss my friends and family.

-Sunday, 3-2-03

+'s: Mom and I watched TV. I love my mom and dad.

-'s: Daddy went home—miss him and Dan a lot. I can't even get out of bed. Hand is on fire. Eyes burn. Feet tingle. Very weak and dizzy.

Writing about the more constructive moments led to an epiphany: while my life might not be the same, I was still living. I had to believe this pain would someday be my gift. I had to keep faith that a Higher Power was guiding me along this arduous journey. If I allowed myself to feel the discomfort, then this experience would become my greatest success.

Yet even in the midst of such enlightenment, I became increasingly weak. My symptoms soared to unbearable heights as my nervous system was in a state of chaos. Soon I could no longer walk or stand. I would instantly go from hot to cold, clammy to shaking. Smells would make me so nauseated that I would dry heave. Lying in bed, I spent my time counting seconds, grateful for each added minute to have passed with me still alive. My body was literally fighting to survive. This was torture, and I had no idea when I would escape.

How could the medicines I had been prescribed lead me down this path?

Thankfully, Mom and I had another set of visitors. My aunt Janice and her best friend Toni had planned a trip to Texas to visit Toni's son stationed in the marines. They decided to extend their stay in order to see us. Janice and Toni stayed at the same waterfront hotel we had during the holiday season. Arriving at our apartment each morning, they took turns watching me so Mom could escape for a few hours. I sensed Mom was grateful to have time to herself. These past six months had not only tested her faith but also her strength to carry on and persevere. It was apparent to everyone—*but me*—that Mom was acting on autopilot.

Having Janice and Toni, a registered ER nurse, with us changed our typical routine. Company forced us to stay positive. The two of them lifted our morale as we frequently laughed and smiled. Having family who understood the severity of my disease but saw past my limitations and envisioned my former self comforted me. They were cheerleaders in the best sense of the word; they knew when it was appropriate to be silly and outrageous and when to be serious and quiet.

However, once they left, reality set in again. Life continued as it had before their visit—with me stuck in bed all day. I resorted back to my old ways of passing the time by counting. As long as I kept reaching the number sixty, I knew I had survived another minute.

My life had become lonely and tiring, tormenting and torturous. Days turned into weeks as I continued to decline. While I understood the gravity of my condition, I rejected the belief that I would be sick forever. I refused to lose hope in a pain-free future…until I realized that seventy hours had passed since my last urination; then I became frightened.

How could my body handle such stress? Where did the liquids and waste go? Would I die because I had not had a bowel movement in nearly three weeks?

Although I moaned and pleaded for salvation, I had a strong feeling that I was not alone. I still felt an overwhelming sense of peace. It was as if a heavenly healing energy filled my room. Despite being by myself in the dark physical world, I knew light surrounded me on the spiritual plane.

Being fully aware of a Higher Presence eased my fears regarding my future. While I desperately wanted to live, I accepted the alternative. I knew if the disease and withdrawal ravaged my body much longer, I would not be able to continue fighting. Yet I was no longer afraid or angry; I had somehow come to terms with passing on. *I had come full circle.*

Chapter 24

Ultimate Decision

I was in bad shape three days before Easter. It had been more than twenty-four hours since I last moved, and darkness engulfed me. All I could do was lie on my right side with both arms outstretched in front of me. Having my right elbow bent at a ninety-degree angle, I gently leaned against a mound of pillows while tightly curled in the fetal position. There were two other pillows resting under my swollen feet, and another wedged between my thighs. Thrusting my stuffed dog into my abdomen, I hoped the force of pressure would relieve some of the deep pain.

Anguish filtered through the room as I took note of my surroundings. While I had once been vibrant and full of energy, I now was a recluse who lived in the shadows. Sadness filled me as I shifted my eyes upward and noticed the fan light. It had not been used in nearly seven months. Facing the window, I remained motionless and bewildered. What had become of me?

Although incapable of turning over, I knew exactly what was placed to the left of me. Resting on the nightstand was my journal and an unlit grapefruit-scented candle that Mom used when she needed to see. The "Angel of Strength" statue created by Willow Tree and Mattie Stepanek's book, *Heartsongs* were there as well. I also kept a small cluster of a cellestialite crystal next to my bed, hoping that its healing powers would heal me.

Directly in front of the nightstand was the lone chair that held my water bottle, ChapStick, Kleenex and two Dixie cups containing melted Gatorade and iced tea chips. Mom had positioned next to the chair a plastic lime green and hot pink can in case of a vomiting emergency. Further to the left lay the AeroBed mattress that she slept on when I had bad nights.

Then there was the small hallway leading to the closet and bathroom. Two bright posters of flowers and one with inspirational quotes adorned the bare white walls. In front of me was the closed door that opened to the kitchen and living space, and a wooden table holding the TV and VCR. This was my life. *I was isolated from everyone and everything.*

∞

The sheer torture ravaging my body made it impossible for me to concentrate. Nothing could deter my attention, and I physically did not know how much longer my organs could fight this battle. I literally lived each day moment to moment. As the past twenty-six weeks had wreaked havoc on my immune system, just surviving another minute of the fiery hell had become a huge feat; yet I worried how much more damage my body could take before it just shut down.

The pain had become indescribable and monumental. Severe, relentless migraines seemed to paralyze me. It felt as if someone was actually smashing and crushing my skull. With the entire circumference of my head pounding in overwhelming agony, I thought shutting my eyes might bring some relief. It did not. Whether I had my eyes opened or closed made no difference. I was trapped; there was no way to escape my pain.

By this point, I was certain my abdomen had stretched to its ultimate limit. Having heard childhood horror stories of people's skin splitting apart terrified me into believing my own stomach would burst if it expanded any further. Red lines covered the width of my belly, along with second-degree burns and open sores. Doc had told me this was a direct result of my constant use of hot water bottles and heating pads to ease the searing discomfort. He promised it would all go away once I was better. I just hoped he was right.

I could not find a comfortable position that alleviated the tension in my weak back and brittle spine. It always felt as if a rusty knife was jabbed into my spinal column as white vinegar poured into the fresh wound. Having so much scar tissue in my lower back from the removal of the SCS battery caused problems too. Hypersensitive and inflamed, even the minimal amount of pressure caused me to scream and feel a bone-deep burn. The jolts of electricity and shooting pains continuously traveling up and down my vertebrae were excruciating. Any movement seemed to intensify it tenfold.

My hips had locked into place and my buttocks tingled as if pricked by thousands of threading needles. While the only way I could handle the horrendous pain was by clenching my muscles, this also exacerbated my symptoms. Soon my tendons became taut and rigid. I did not feel twenty-two. Instead, I felt ninety-two. My life was out of control.

Constant throbbing bombarded my legs. The tightening, cramping, and muscle spasms in both of my calves made me want to shout out in misery. My knees were red and sore and took on the shape of ripe cantaloupes. Blood vessels began popping behind my kneecaps and on my upper thighs due to the edema adding pressure to my fragile veins. My thighs looked like a road map marked with hundreds of red and blue lines. Soon the veins began to protrude outward, and this mazelike pattern became sensitive to touch and extremely uncomfortable.

I no longer recognized my own reflection. With my body destroyed and altered, my feet were three times their usual size. They were discolored and swollen, whitish-red and shiny. My heels seared anytime I placed the slightest amount of pressure on them. The two pillows I placed directly under my anklebones did not ease the stiffness and rigidity in the area. My ankles still felt as if someone was stabbing them thousands of times with ice picks. Movement only increased the profound burning sensations radiating outward from the anklebone. I even started to fear that the bones had shattered from all the strain.

Yet the most horrifying pains came from my ribs and chest. Each inhale and exhale was torture. It felt like I had fractured my entire rib cage. Thinking my ribs would collapse into my chest cavity made me want to cry out in desperation. However, I never did. I could not even moan. Every shallow, non-rhythmic breath brought the burning to insurmountable levels.

The unfathomable aches and scalding pains continued to seethe and intensify as the hours progressed. I wanted help, but I was completely alone. How could I escape this hell, unable to speak or move? All I could do was pray for mercy. Time was not only my best friend but also my worst enemy. Whether I succumbed or survived depended on how long I could outlast the pain.

I plummeted further into the abyss as the days faded into one another. As I felt a distance separated me from the physical world, I realized these next forty-eight hours would be the most critical. With my thoughts no longer centered on healing, I was now concerned with living. How would this nightmare end? Would I lose the battle or persevere?

For years, I had relied on medicine in order to get through the day. Pills were my crutch, but they now had become my downfall. When I began taking opioids at twenty years old, I had no idea what type of damage these drugs would inflict on my immune system. I did not realize I was jeopardizing my body's ability to function. *Now I did.*

At the age of twenty-two, I finally saw what could happen. The disease was currently winning, since my kidneys were in the beginning stages of shutting down. Although I was fortunate to still be breathing and semi-coherent, I knew my outlook was grim. It did not matter if I wanted to attack this disease full-throttle; my strength was gone.

There was something about the power of faith. While I had grown up believing in God, I had never prayed for my healing. I believed it was selfish of me to ask a Higher Power to intervene, because I viewed my suffering as a teaching tool. Yet my opinion changed, the closer I came to death.

Soon my room felt like a vortex. A vortex was an abundance of spiritual energy flowing in a particular space that caused enlightenment. With my sixth sense heightened, I began to hear loved ones who had previously passed, telling me to hold on. These soft voices reassured me that my life was only beginning. The energy of Spirit consumed me, and I knew I was not alone.

Feeling a profound connection to a Higher Being led me to make the most important decision of my life. I knew the drugs were poisoning my body, and my chances of recovering were dwindling. Nearing the point of no return, there was only one question left to ask myself: *could I allow myself to die without giving it all I had?*

This was my last chance to take a stand. Whether I survived or not depended solely on if I stopped taking the rest of my medications cold turkey. I intuitively felt that the angels surrounding my bedside would keep me safe. Therefore, on Easter Sunday, I chose not to swallow another pill.

I heard a slight creak as the doorknob turned. Mom tiptoed near the bed to place my next dose of medicine on the pillow in front of me. Then she quietly retraced her steps out of my room. I did not flinch or move. As I stared at the circular tablets that had once been my lifeline, I began to feel queasy. Just thinking about taking one more drug made me salivate. I was done. My body had finally had enough and was saying, "No more."

I could not say how much time elapsed before Mom re-appeared in my dark cave. She panicked as soon as she noticed the medications still lying on the pillow. I knew these past seventy-two hours had been painstakingly hard on her; it had to be devastating to see her daughter unable to move or speak. Mom broke down in tears, no longer knowing what to do with me. Realizing that my silence was slowly killing her, I mustered up the energy to formulate a sentence.

I told her I was not going to take them. In fact, I told her I was never going to take them again. My own frank insistence over not taking medicine shocked even me. I quickly turned my head to face Mom for her rebuttal. Much to my surprise, she said nothing. She only walked out of the room, to return with the phone in tote. Doc was on the line, and he wanted me to understand the repercussions. "Was I really willing to face that agony?"

This was my defining moment. It was as if an illuminating light clicked inside my head. *The miracle I had been waiting for was saying "no" to morphine.* "Yes," I told him. "Yes, I was willing to face whatever agony I might endure."

Doc seemed pleased that I wanted to forgo all my medicine, but he had to explain what would most likely occur as the withdrawal intensified. While he forewarned me about the pain and symptoms intensifying, I brushed his comments aside. I was ready to do whatever it took to heal. I did not believe there was any way things could get worse.

I was wrong.

I made it through the first hour without any increase in pain. The second hour promised to be more alarming. This was when my head began to feel as though it were being beaten and thrashed with a club. My ribs felt as if they had collapsed into my lungs, and my sternum raged in blistering pain. By the third hour, I started to think my grand idea was an awful mistake. No one as sick as I should ever be allowed to make such critical decisions regarding health. *How could Doc let me do this to myself?*

Because it had been years since I had last been pain-free, I no longer recalled the sensation of nothingness. This depressed me. How I could reach my goal of healing if I did not have an idea of what nothing felt like? I therefore started to create a mental image of a life without pain. In my mind, I envisioned the sun shining while daisies and sunflowers blew in fields. I could taste cold lemonade sweating in a tall glass. I saw a wrap-around porch with a swing, and me in a long, flowing dress.

Although I tried focusing on my newfound paradise, I could not escape my hell. Pure agony swept over my body as I screamed for Mom to bring me my drugs. The pain proved to be more than I could handle, and I did not want to do this anymore. It was ludicrous of me to think I could stop seventy milligrams of morphine all at once. I reached out for the tablets with a trembling hand and threw them into the back of my mouth. As I took a sip of water, I waited for the medicine to take effect. Instead, I threw up within seconds. I was physically unable to swallow any more drugs. This was my body telling me it had had enough; now I had to face my demons.

As the withdrawal intensified, my chances of bouncing back crumbled. I was a time bomb ready to explode, while my caregivers—my SWAT team—desperately tried to disarm the blow. The debilitating pain had complete control over me, and I could not pretend to be strong much longer. I was weak and needed Mom to make the pain stop. Yet even as I cried and pleaded to Mom, I knew she was helpless. This was out of both of our hands. We just had to hold on to hope. We had to believe a Higher Power would guide us.

Mom was overwhelmed, and I sensed she did not know what to do. This was only the beginning hours of final withdrawal, but my health was already headed in a fatal downward spiral. I was scared we could not do this alone. What would happen if Mom was too tired and I became worse? This also worried Mom, who called Ruben.

Mom looked ghastly by the time Ruben arrived at our apartment at three in the morning. It had been days since she last slept, so her face was puffed and swollen, and massive rings circled both of her eyes. Ruben knew she was physically exhausted and told her he would take over so she could rest. Then he left her alone and came to me.

I remember the light from the grapefruit candle flickered as Ruben entered the room. He had become my main confidant over the past seven months. I relied on him for everything, especially encouragement. It was easy for me to share with him how much I hurt, because he was empathetic to my pain and familiar with my symptoms. Now I needed his support more than ever. As he gently patted my head, he told me everything would be fine. He had watched others go through this before, and he knew Doc would get me better. He reminded me of Sara; Sara was pain-free and healthy, and I would be too.

When Ruben asked me if I would do him a small favor, I naturally said yes since I would have done anything for him. Then I learned that he wanted me to run the STS machine. I instantly became nervous. I did not want to feel more pain, and the treatments always made me hurt more. Yet Ruben kept on asking me. It was not until he assured me that the machine would bring me relief that I agreed. As he set up varying protocols to ease the horrific symptoms, he repeatedly told me this suffering would cease. I just took a breath and hoped he was right.

I ran treatments for seven minutes until the stimulation became too intense. It felt as if electric currents were running through my bloodstream. I started to cry more as the pain worsened. Ruben remained calm as he softly whispered that I would soon live a normal life again. "You just have to believe. You have to hold on to hope." Then he was silent. It was time for me to rest.

My next memory was feeling mind-blowing pounding besiege my skull. I screamed in sheer terror that this was the worst migraine of my life. Ruben just shushed me and soothingly asked if I would do him another favor. Again I said yes, so he quickly went to my feet to place electrodes. I yelled for him to stop. All he ever wanted was to run the damn machine that only made me worse. Why did he always ask me do him a favor that hurt me?

Yet before he could answer, the room went completely black. I thought my candle had blown out, but that was not the case. *I could not see;* I was blind. Thrashing my head from side to side, I tried opening and closing my eyes. Nothing changed. With my world still dark, I began to panic. Fearing I would be blind forever left me in hysterics. I cursed Doc aloud for never telling me withdrawals of this magnitude included blindness. This was not what I signed up for; I did not want to die like this.

The next voice I heard was Ruben. He spoke forcefully and strongly. "Nicole, you need to listen to me. This is a blinding migraine. I know you are terrified, but you have to trust me. *This will go away.* Your vision will return as the drugs leave your body."

Then his voice softened as he told me we needed to run another treatment. He understood that I had reservations about using the STS, but there was a protocol designed to lessen throbbing headaches. I reluctantly obliged after he said it might help restore my sight. Hearing the machine beep made me sob. My life was no longer mine. With each passing minute, I felt my spirit fading further from my human body. *Please save me, angels.*

Miraculously, I felt a shift. My beating temples did not feel as if they were imploding. My clenched jaw loosened, and my neck was not as constricted. I felt strangely at peace, and when the blinding migraines dispelled three hours later, I knew a Greater Power was watching over me. This was just another sign from above that I had to keep fighting. There was a reason I needed to live.

∞

Ruben did not leave for the next three days. He and Mom took turns sleeping and caring for me as the pain continued to intensify. I cried during the day and wailed at night. Soon I questioned the meaning of life. Since I could not believe that God would allow me to suffer in vain, I wondered if there was an explanation to my misery. If I truly believed everything happened for a greater purpose, then what were the lessons I needed to learn?

I recognized that this journey was my rebirth. For some unknown reason, I had to experience deep pain and doubt. Oddly, this realization comforted me. With my inner strength triumphing over every test, my belief in a miracle overrode all the doubts planted inside me. I was a true fighter. It did not matter how weak or frail I became; I always continued to attack this disease head-on.

However, even my epiphany could not keep my agonizing pain at bay. As the torment worsened, all I wanted was my daddy. In fact, I fundamentally needed him. Dad had always been my pillar of strength and my reassuring voice. If anyone could help me emerge from this misery, I felt it would be him. This was not to say that I did not need Mom. I admired her more than I admired anyone. She had become my prime example of how to manage a life-altering disease with courage, grace and dignity. I felt blessed to have such an incredible mother, but I relied on Dad to make things better. I needed him to come to my rescue.

Dad arrived in Texas three days after Easter. I remember that my whimpers stopped the instant I saw him. It was not as if the pain had changed within those mere seconds, but I could breathe again. He was the solid rock in our family, and I knew he would take care of me.

It surprised me when Dad wanted to watch a video his first night in Corpus. Little did I know that my aunts had organized and videotaped a prayer service on my behalf. Watching the tape left me speechless. No one had ever done anything so kind.

The heartfelt prayers and raw emotion in the room astounded me. Seeing my friends and family crammed in the filled-to-capacity chapel sent chills through my body. *People actually cared…they had not forgotten me.* I felt awe-inspired watching my loved ones laugh, cry, sing and pray. Even the woes and horrors of chronic pain could not dampen my spirits.

My aunts felt it was important for me to witness the energy of the group. They had arranged for those in attendance to send personal greetings after the service finished. Hearing my friends' encouraging words awakened my soul. I loved how each cheerful message was unique. Some were funny and sweet, while others were more serious. However, there was one person who talked repeatedly into the camera, one who really pulled at my heartstrings.

He was a cousin of the Callaghans who wanted me to know that he understood what I was going through. His little sister had been in and out of hospitals, and he knew how scary that could be. He kept sharing how Kate, his recently deceased sister, would watch over me. She would make sure I got better. Kate would be my guiding angel. Tears poured down my cheeks as I broke down. His message resonated with me. I asked Dad to play it again so I could fully grasp his profound statement. Kate was on my shoulder.

We watched the tape twice that night and numerous times over the next few weeks. I felt saved each time I saw the service. Now I was on a mission. I had to heal for each of them.

∞

The effects of withdrawal lingered into the following week. I still could not move, so I would just lie in bed motionless. Sweat poured off me as if I was running a marathon. I would shake and quiver, watching the room spin around me. My pain was extreme. This was worse than anything I could have ever imagined.

Nausea was a huge problem for me as well. All the peppermint, ginger, and anti-nausea pills in the world could not have eased my unsettled stomach. This was why I made sure my vomit can was within arm's reach. Unfortunately, I misjudged my body's position in the bed when I began feeling queasy one afternoon. While the loud thud of my body slamming against the floor startled me, having my pain instantly jump off the charts worried me more.

When my parents barged into the room, Mom panicked while Dad tried to lift me up. I screamed. It hurt too badly to be touched, but I could not move myself. I was a dead weight. Dad looked nervous. Thinking of alternative ways to get me in bed, he tried lifting me by the waist and scooping me in his arms. When those attempts failed, I tried rolling onto the AeroBed. That did not work either. My parents were out of options, and Dad said we needed paramedics to lift me. I felt pathetic. It was humiliating to be *that* heavy that both of my parents could not pick me up.

I knew I needed to step up to the plate. Pleading with both of them to try one more time, I willed my arms onto the bed. I then had them each grab a leg and push. It was unbearable to feel my joints sharply push into my hip flexors. Tears fell down my face as my anklebones crushed together. I cringed and yelled, thinking they were dismembering me. *When would this pain stop?* It took them a few more jolting pushes before I was back in bed sobbing. I hated life.

My next ordeal was just as mortifying. I had gained roughly eighty-five pounds in the past seven months. This was due to my liver and kidneys being unable to process or break down substances. The poisons trapped inside me were finally on the loose as the withdrawal overtook my nervous system. With my body beginning to awaken and respond, these toxins wanted out of me.

Not knowing when the next urge to relieve myself would happen made me anxious. I knew I only had a small amount of time from my stomach's initial uneasiness to the moment I lost control of my kegel and sphincter muscles. Since my parents had to push my wheelchair seven measly steps from the bed to bathroom, I had many accidents. This was hard for me to handle. I just wanted a body that functioned normally. I did not want Mom to have to continue changing my pajamas. I was too old to be defecating and urinating on myself.

If I did make it to the bathroom on time, I would spend hours discarding abundant fluid and watery waste. I choked back vomit as my intestines released the chemicals that had nearly killed me. It felt like tiny needles were pricking my urethra as my anus seared in misery. The stinging, raging discomfort was hell. All I could do was sit on the toilet and scream. Montezuma's revenge had to be paradise compared to what I was enduring.

I started to see slight improvements on the eighth day without any medication. I could walk from the bed to the bathroom and then to the kitchen without my parents' assistance. Soon I even started initiating light conversation. Having believed days earlier that I would be leaving this Earth prematurely made these baby steps seem like milestones. While I was not ready to venture outside the confines of our apartment, I was relieved to know the worst was behind me. The human spirit could persevere through anything.

I had a breakthrough around day ten. I suddenly woke up and wanted to get my hair washed. This was a big deal, since I had not been outside in over seven weeks. I felt like I had finally been reborn. Life opened up, and I wasted no time jumping in. When I told Mom and Dad, they both smiled excitedly. I was breaking out of the darkness, and none of us could be happier.

My hair was oily and matted up in a ponytail when we arrived at my favorite salon. I remember I had to take tiny steps to the shampoo bowl while leaning on Dad for balance because I was so frail. Feeling the warm water touch my scalp was incredibly invigorating. I envisioned the water rinsing out the pain as the soapsuds cleansed my weakened body. This wash symbolized my return to the land of the living.

I finally showered a week later. Although I was anxious, not knowing how my body would respond to the light sprinkling drops, I knew I had to do this. I was only able to handle a quick five-minute rinse, but that was fine with me. It had been eight months since my last shower, and this was another step toward health. Withdrawals were ending, and I was back on the road to recovery. *Or so I thought.*

Harbor Half:
The Final Mile of the Journey

As I make my way into the home stretch with only a mile left to go, my body begins to decline at a rapid speed. It is impossible to deny the intense pains jetting down my spine or the radiating throbs besieging my feet. Seeming like déjà vu all over again—as if I were back in the heat of withdrawal—I emotionally and physically fall apart. Losing the willpower to continue, I feel I need a pep talk…or a good kick in the butt.

"Look to the right, Nicole. Do you see your mom and Mary waving?" Wiping sweat from my forehead, I squint in the direction Rick points. I see two very excited women jumping up and down, waving their arms in a field. I reckon if they can see me that I must be close to the end.

I know I have to keep going. Surely I can finish the last mile of a half marathon if I can overcome chronic pain. As this race summed up my entire battle living with pain, I must keep my thoughts on how far I have come, how much I have suffered, and how I am now going to thrive.

Yet with my dreams in reach, my anguish intensifies. Each time my foot pounds the surface of the pavement, the sharp, stifling pains of my hip flexor increase. I desperately want to quit, but Rick will not have it. Forcing myself to put one excruciating foot in front of the other, I see there is a curve in the upcoming road. Peppiness returns to my step as I realize I will soon be on the main drag. Except as I begin to turn the corner, a volunteer directs us to go down one more block.

Not wanting to go further down that road causes me to have a huge temper tantrum. Tears stream down my face as I just stop, walk and scream, "I hate life and this damn run. I hate myself for not being strong enough. I hate my body for being frail. I hate everything about my pathetic self. *Why is this so hard for me?*"

As I begin to sulk and pout, Rick begins his last motivating speech. "This is your moment, baby. Here is your time to shine and continue to inspire so many people. Let's finish strong, just like you ran strong throughout the race. You have less than a half mile to go, and I know you have the inner power to move faster than this. Let's finish like a champ."

I take a sip of water while thinking how I would love to beat the crap out of him. I thought it was easy for him to say "let's pick up the pace" because he was a college athlete. He had inadvertently been training his whole life for a half-marathon, and I had just started four months ago. I wanted to shout and curse and throw my hands in the air, but for some reason I did not. Somehow, I know what he is saying is true, so I turn my anger into action and begin jogging. *I have to do this.*

With Heather Small's "Proud" blaring from my iPod, I get a surge of energy. As I attempt to take another drink of water, I find my CamelBak is empty. Desperate for fluids, my throat swells, and I gasp for air. With my mouth as dry as sandpaper, I worry I may collapse with four hundred meters left.

Chapter 25

Needing a Break

Despite successfully overcoming my personal battle with morphine, I could not tolerate the STS machine. Doc had told me that once off narcotics, I would improve. Yet I had not noticed any progress except for a decrease in my weight. This disheartened and confused me. It did not make sense that I still had pain and could not move my right hand. How could I have endured so much, and still see no results?

Doc just kept repeating that my body had undergone a lot and morphine semi-permanently altered the nervous system. I had a severe case of RSDS, so it was going to take time to recuperate. He believed I was making progress. After all, I was walking again and starting to have an appetite. I could shower and leave the apartment. I could tolerate sunlight and visit his office. These were all positive signs that I was improving, and yet I was not convinced. I was on a seesaw ride of emotions. I continued to feel as if normalcy was slipping out of my sight.

Thankfully, Mom and I had another distraction: visitors. Kristin and I had gone to school together since second grade. Our families were close, and her dad had been a huge advocate for me during my first episode with RSD. Being a prominent cardiologist in our area, he and my amazing family practitioner had been able to connect us with the right doctors, who saw me immediately. Having her and her mom around was not only a comfort but also a great diversion for me. The four of us took small outings during the day, like a drive on the beach or lunch near the water. While it was nice to have them visit, I hated being sick in front of people. Part of me was actually relieved when they left. Then I no longer needed to hide my anguish.

∞

By August, I had had enough. Each time Mom drove to the office, piercing pains bombarded my stomach, and I would become light-headed and nauseated. All I wanted was to throw my hands in the air and shriek. Despite believing in Doc and his therapy, the pent-up animosity I had toward the staff made the clinic a non-healing environment for me.

I realized I had to leave but was terrified to speak with my parents. They had invested so much time and energy into my recovery that I did not want them to think it was all for nothing. I remember my stomach had butterflies the afternoon I told Mom. We had just left Doc's office when I blurted out that I was miserable. Soon every feeling and thought spewed from my mouth and I could not stop talking. While I was able to hold back tears, my voice quivered as I told Mom how I was beginning to question the STS treatment. Then I shared my anger and discontentment. I had mentally shut down, and I needed a break. *I felt like I was going insane.*

Thankfully, Mom agreed with me. She could see from my murky eyes that I had lost the willpower to continue. It was obvious that I needed a vacation, but where to go proved to be challenging. I refused to return to my hometown unable to move my hand and seventy pounds heavier. There was no room for discussion either. I had made a conscious pact with myself ten months ago not to go home until I was better, and I was not any better. I just could not face friends when I felt like a fat, ugly failure.

What I needed was a quiet place to meditate. My heart had been broken, and I yearned for solitude and serenity. It was time to make myself my number-one priority and deal with my recent experience. I had to regain my strength, begin to exercise, and learn to care for myself. I needed to find a place where I felt safe.

Palm Springs, California fit my needs. It had hot mineral springs, healing centers, and a dry climate. I felt called to this tranquil desert surrounded by pristine nature. Knowing that deserts were healing areas only sealed the deal. Palm Springs was the epitome of a spiritual haven to me. This was where I would regain control. I could receive a new chance at life.

Even though I was only going to be gone nine weeks, saying goodbye to Doc was harder than I expected. He had become the thread that held my family's hopes and dreams together. I had grown to rely on him, and not seeing him every day would be strange. However, I knew we would be in constant communication. Each week I would fax him a pain grid so he could send me new protocols. If I needed to talk to him, I had his home and cell phone numbers. Right now, it was important that I work on my inner self. I needed to redefine what mattered in my life so I could feel complete again. *Then* I would come back.

I sensed his disappointment. It was not as if he was directing his frustration at me, but rather at the situation. He just felt helpless, watching me suffer. Being unable to heal me weighed heavily on him. I wished I could take away his internal guilt, but nothing I said would matter. Doc was a typical type-A personality: he wanted to succeed at everything. I had to respect this, since I was the same. I wanted to be pain-free yesterday.

The drive from South Texas to Southern California was long and tiring. Since we had to move out of the apartment, our Jetta was totally packed. Mom had to squeeze behind the passenger seat with items under her feet and on her lap as Dad drove. She looked uncomfortable, while I had never been more excited. This was the start of my big adventure. It would be the first time since leaving Creighton University that I would be living on my own. I was ecstatic. This was my chance to find out what I wanted in life, and I was going to embrace it.

I quickly viewed Palm Springs as my new beginning. In the desert to retreat and start fresh, it was important for me to create balance. With my focus entirely on regaining health, I knew I needed a daily routine, something that would bring order and stability to my life.

Starting each day with a brisk one-and-a-half-mile walk reconnected me to nature. I enjoyed listening to birds chirping overhead as squirrels ran along the tree branches. I loved watching the sun rise and seeing the morning dew glisten on the freshly cut golf course greens. These morning strides opened me up to the beauty in the world. Nothing seemed mundane to me anymore.

Next on my agenda was a nutritious breakfast. Knowing that there were many chemicals trapped in my body greatly bothered me. I felt I needed to cleanse my body. Believing that what we eat is just as important as what we do led to me to consume only organic products. Therefore, each morning I would have the same organic egg-white vegetable scramble that I ate at the bar counter. I would then write it in my detailed food journal, where I recorded everything: food, water intake, vitamins, exercise, spa treatments, and time on the STS.

After my meal, I would put on my three-sizes-too-small bikini and head to the community pool that was directly in front of my patio. It was odd how I never considered covering up. I felt uninhibited within the condominium's gates. I did not care if fat rolls hung from my suit or my scarred abdomen and vessel-popped thighs were exposed. I was only interested in being me. I had come here to find myself and nurture my soul; this meant I had no time for self-critiquing. I needed to learn to love myself.

I practiced T'ai Chi Chih in the water. I figured if doing these postures had helped me before Texas, then following similar movements in the pool might bring me relief. Watching the soft waves lap as I slowly moved my arms in circular motions was soothing. Warmth began to circulate through my veins as my hands and feet flushed. I felt indescribable peace. T'ai Chi Chih invigorated my senses.

Once I finished my pool exercises, I would lie on a lawn chair so my body could absorb the sun's rays. Some days I would read a self-help book or write an entry in my indigo journal. Other times I would just contemplate life. Everything I did in Palm Springs seemed to revolve around bettering myself. My job was to relax so I could heal.

When I became too warm, I would retreat inside to prepare lunch. My meal was either tuna, grilled chicken, or a turkey patty that I ate with carrots and an apple. Taking my lunch onto the patio meant I could watch the tree branches slightly stir in the breeze. I was content in my simple life. I did not need television or outward distractions, because I was here to work on self-improvement. This was *my* tuning out of society.

My afternoon exercise was following Leslie Sansone's *Walk Away the Pounds*. Each day I chose her one-mile, two-mile or three-mile video. Being able to complete her program in the safety of my own home was a relief. Instead of feeling insecure, I would happily step around the living room sweating. Listening to her talk about how bodies were made to move inspired me. I even found myself conversing with her as if she were actually standing next to me. Her workouts made me feel good about myself again. Somehow, Leslie understood my limitations and worked around them.

I would then take a quick shower before leaving for the local spa. Three afternoons a week, I underwent colonic and endermologie treatments. I felt it was imperative that I rid myself of the unnatural and unhealthy pollutants that resided in my body. Both of these treatments were important tools in expediting toxin release.

Colon hydrotherapy depleted my system of harmful waste. Since I had yet to regain proper bowel function, I was unable to discard the poisons. Colonics did that for me. I would lie on a table wearing large thermal underwear that had a hole cut in the bottom. My certified technician would then insert a hose into my rectum. Distilled water ran through the hose into my colon.

While it did not hurt, it definitely felt weird. Feeling the pressure as I watched my stomach rise made me think of filling a water balloon. As the tech turned off the water—right before I thought my abdomen would explode—I viewed murky liquid flow out of the tube along with visible chunks of vegetables and fruits and whole pieces of meat. *Was it normal not to digest the food?* While I knew this should have revolted me, it was interesting to me to see waste leave my body.

Endermologie, on the other hand, loosened and softened scar tissue as it improved overall circulation. This large machine massaged the body while it rolled over the skin to create a suction that broke down tissues. The force of the suction was too strong for my entire body, so I only used the device on my lower back, upper buttocks and legs. I could not believe the drastic results. The red lines and popped blood vessels on my thighs lightened, while the raised scar tissue from the spinal cord stimulator battery lowered. Endermologie started my long inward process of accepting and loving my body again.

I visited hot mineral springs the other two afternoons. For hundreds of years, soaking in hot springs had proved to be an effective way to relieve chronic pain. These bubbling, hot waters found in the Earth's core were nature's own medicine. Being unable to duplicate the healing powers of these springs meant I had to travel to them. It took me about thirty minutes to drive up a deserted road to the spa.

There were about five other people at the spring when I arrived that first day. This made me nervous, because I did not want them to see me in my swimsuit. I looked hideous. I took a breath and reminded myself why I was here. This was not about a pageant or bikini contest. I was here to heal. Then I placed my left foot in the sweltering hot spring.

I was astonished the instant I immersed my entire body in the water, which contained high quantities of minerals like magnesium. There was an immediate decrease in my pain level. My pain dropped within minutes from an agonizing eight to a manageable six. I felt as if the invisible veil of misery had lifted from me. I was light and free. *These therapies were bringing life back to my body.*

Arriving back to the condominium rejuvenated meant I needed to try the STS machine. I had left Texas able to handle eleven seconds of treatment. Yet that was increasing by the day. It started with me lasting thirty seconds, and then one minute. Soon I tolerated three minutes, followed by five minutes. While the time improvements were small, success was success, and I had to remember the baby steps.

Dinner was usually a large salad with lots of fresh vegetables and either baked salmon or grilled chicken. Then, after an hour of reading or journaling, I would return to the pool for my late-night swim. Floating on my back, staring up at the twinkling stars and bright moon was the moment I looked forward to the most each day. I envisioned myself absorbing the energy of the planets as I thanked the Universe for its guidance and light. It was in this darkness that I found my greatest connection to a Higher Power and my Higher Self.

Although I wanted to defeat the disease and seek refuge from the pain, I had now become obsessed with losing weight and returning to my normal size. I felt like an imposter in my own skin. Even dropping almost fifty pounds did not satisfy me. I knew there were still thirty more pounds to go. My reflection startled me. Not only did I no longer recognize the image in the mirror, but I also did not want to know the person looking back at me. I felt sluggish and inadequate. I looked awful, and it upset me how my vanity somehow overshadowed my health.

Dealing with my weight was a huge challenge for me. While I had never been athletic, I also had never been overweight. This time alone was supposed to be reflective and enlightening. However, I could not cope with the excess pounds. Having visitors only brought up more of my unresolved issues.

My parents would usually spend two nights with me every couple of weeks. While I was always happy to see them, it disrupted my quiet routine and stressed me out. Having them over meant that I had to drive to the grocery store. Driving and shopping were the two activities I hated most. Putting on my seatbelt made my abdomen appear even larger. It disgusted me that I could no longer glance down and see a flat stomach.

Shopping was worse. I felt as if I was on trial in a grocery store. People would not smile or acknowledge me anymore but rather smirk at what was in my cart. Even though I only bought milk, produce, poultry and fish for myself, I would buy Pepperidge Farm cookies and ice cream for my parents. My heart would race as I placed those items on the checkout counter. Feeling the stares of other customers made me sweat. I knew people were thinking I was too big to be buying sweets.

All I wanted was to justify my weight and tell them it was not my fault. I despised being this way and just wanted to scream that I used to be pretty and beautiful. I wanted people to see *me* for who I was on the inside. Yet I knew that would never happen. We lived in a society based on appearances and first impressions. *I was the fat girl.*

My other visitor was Dylan. Dylan and I had been close friends since grammar school. He was now living in L.A., which was just two hours from Palm Springs. Since we had not seen each other for more than a year, he decided to come for a weekend. I remember being excited but very anxious. The last time he saw me, I was just skin and bones in the PCU. Now I felt like I was the size of a dinosaur.

The first words out of his mouth crushed me. "Wow, you … you are huge." My world collapsed. It was as if a piece of me no longer existed. He had seen me drooling in a hospital bed, but what shook him was my weight. I knew he did not mean to hurt me; it was just seeing such a radical transformation in my appearance scared him. The Nicole he knew was gone. Neither of us could act as if the elephant was not in the room; I was sick, and this weight only made my illness more real.

Luckily, I had the wisdom of Shelley and Maureen. Although I personally had minimal communication with them while going through withdrawal, I knew they both were sending me healing prayers. Now that I was feeling better and talking again, Shelley and Maureen were back in my life in an instrumental way; they were rebuilding my self-esteem. Together they helped me recognize the importance of a positive attitude. All these debilitating thoughts and feelings were crippling my growth. I had to learn how to focus my attention elsewhere.

They instructed me to look in the mirror three times a day and say aloud, "I love myself, I am healed, and I am beautiful." This should have been a simple exercise, and yet I struggled to repeat those affirmations. It did not feel right to say things I believed to be untrue. My love of self had conditions, and I did not feel beautiful. It was impossible for me to pretend I was better with my hand clenched and my pain extraordinarily high. I realized then that I had a lot of work to do on myself. *I really was broken.*

Both of them also encouraged me to journal about the grateful blessings in my life. Soon writing became a key component to my progress. I finally began to hold myself in the energy, light and love I wished to attract. I no longer directed my thoughts at my large body frame but began to view myself as that beautiful and vibrant size four again. Rather than hindering my progress with self-deprecating beliefs, I became proactive.

I am happy and content with my life. I am here to heal and grow. I am embracing the beauty that surrounds me. I am finally opening my heart and listening to my soul. My life affirmations are:

I am beautiful. I am healed. I am strong. I am loved. I have a very important purpose in life. I am truly blessed. I am a size four. I am special. I am filled with light, love, peace and joy. I am guided by the angels. I see every opportunity as a learning experience. I am successful. I am healed.

∞

Spending nine weeks in Palm Springs allowed me the chance to dissect the previous five years. This pain truly was the greatest thing that could have happened to me. I never would have been able to appreciate pure joy or unconditional love without such deep-rooted anguish. Without the disability triggering feelings of inadequacy, I never would have discovered my inner strength or perseverance. I finally grasped the significance of my disease. By losing everything, I had gained so much more. This disease was not supposed to be my punishment—*it was meant to be my gift.*

Palm Springs gave me the opportunity to live independently and transform. It was my place of reflection and manifestation. Yet I knew my journey to attain a pain-free life had to continue. It was time for me to move forward and take the next step to full recovery. My days living in this healing oasis were over. Now I had to return to Corpus Christi.

Chapter 26

Glimmer of Hope

Heading back to Corpus Christi was a transition for me. I missed my quiet, isolated lifestyle and found the new noise and chaos unnerving. Every street corner, restaurant and building held a memory I wished I could just forget. Coming back to the place where I almost lost everything overwhelmed me. While I should have been grateful I survived, all I felt were my past anxieties.

My former life haunted me as I felt dead walking among the living. I was out of sorts and confused from my mind being stuck in altered dimensions. I could not sleep at night, and I once again developed panic attacks. It was as if all the progress I made in Palm Springs meant nothing. I was regressing back into the black hole.

Since Mom was back in California, I had to fight these demons alone. This was difficult for me, so I spoke to Doc about my visions and depression. He believed I had signs of post-traumatic stress disorder, but he was hesitant to prescribe medications. My autonomic nervous system was still recovering from withdrawal, and adding drugs might put further stress on my body. Instead, Doc wanted to try different STS protocols to treat the disorder.

None of them appeared to help me. After a week of various treatments, I began getting worse. It seemed like the world was spinning so fast that I could not regain my balance. When the line between what occurred in the past and what was presently happening began to fade, I knew I was on the verge of a mental breakdown.

I finally cracked one evening while driving. I remember being at a stoplight when images of me connected to IV lines and hospital monitors suddenly invaded my thoughts. My vision blurred and my heart palpitated. I saw myself floating over my comatose body as Mom, Dad and Dan stood vigil. Tears streamed down my mother's cheeks as I could hear my dad clear his throat and rub his red eyes. Dan stood dumbfounded while his lip quivered. *Had I died?*

A car horn startled me out of my delusion. I began to panic when I had no idea where I was or what I was doing. Life did not make sense. *Was I in my car or was this a hallucination?*

I began to shake, paralyzed with fear. Although it was very late at night, I called Doc. Luckily, he answered.

Doc calmed me down by patiently telling me I was not losing my mind. These were normal feelings after dealing with such a harrowing experience. There had never been time for me to grieve throughout my illness. This was only happening now so I understood I had to face the pain. I had to mourn.

This made sense to me. After so many years of seeing new doctors, trying new therapies, having new procedures, and taking new drugs, I never had time to grasp the significance of what was happening. I never had a moment to breathe, let alone feel. As I started to regain my bearings, I hung up the phone.

It was then that Doc realized the severity of my condition. With my health requiring aggressive measures, he prescribed two drugs the next morning. Lexapro was an anti-depressant and anti-anxiety medication. The other prescription was a sedative barbiturate. Although he hoped my use of medicine would be short-term, he was willing to do whatever it took to calm my overstimulated nerves. Avoiding a flare-up was crucial to my recovery. He knew the sooner I could overcome this particular setback, the faster I would be able to heal.

Trying new drugs terrified me because I had never responded well to medications. I had visited many ERs in the past due to stroke, seizure, and heart-attack-like symptoms caused by drugs. I just did not want to deal with that again, being here alone. This was why I was so relieved when I only experienced minor reactions like loss of appetite, lethargy and extreme sleepiness.

Little did I know that oversleeping could be problematic too. Those first three days, I never left my bed except to use the bathroom or drink water. I was physically exhausted. All I did was sleep, continue sleeping, and sleep some more. It was as if I was a bear hibernating for winter. Nothing could disturb me. Not the phone, my alarm clock, or a knock on the door. I was cut off from the world.

I was pale, dizzy and lethargic when I returned to the living five days later. Despite feeling like shit, I had managed not to suffer from another panic attack or frightening flashback. This was good. This meant the drugs were working.

However, my current reaction of acting like a zombie troubled Doc. He felt he could not resume this therapy in good faith. Doc hypothesized that the two pills together might have led to the extreme side effects. Since he believed the Lexapro was aiding with the post-traumatic stress, he did not want to change that dose. Therefore, he stopped the other medication.

I continued taking Lexapro for a few more months. It soon became my crutch to lean on in order to cope with my past. Lexapro allowed me to be honest with myself. I no longer felt ashamed asking for help. By pulling back the layers of grief and guilt, I faced my fears and admitted to my struggles.

My only frustration now was that I had not found pain relief. I was following Doc's program to a T, and I still hurt. Soon it became hard not to question this method of treatment.

Nevertheless, Doc stayed positive. He continually told me the drugs had ravaged and destroyed the natural functioning of my autonomic nervous system. My body was still in the trenches, fighting this war. It would take time, but I would heal. What I had to do was focus on the baby steps again.

I could not deny that small changes were occurring. It was a miracle that I could even function without narcotics, and the fact that I used the STS machine twice a day was incredible. This was something I once dreamt about, and now it was my reality. Moreover, my migraines had drastically declined, and I was finally living on my own. I had the energy to exercise again, and I had started playing weekly bingo with Ruben and a few new technicians. This was the best I had been in years. I had to be proud of my progress.

Struggling with chronic pain changes a person. It changed me. As I began recognizing the significant role faith played in the coping process, I decided to start a new spiritual practice. I had always gained inner strength from reading. Learning from the experiences of others enlightened me. Don Miguel Ruiz *(The Four Agreements)* and Louise L. Hay *(You Can Heal Your Life)* were my favorite authors for that reason. Their books fundamentally changed my way of thinking about life and pain. My own perceptions shifted as I embraced a new understanding.

Each Sunday, I would spend a few hours in Barnes and Noble by myself. Drinking hot coffee, I would read self-help books that called to my soul. I had become fascinated with the teachings of Kabbalah. In fact, I could not find enough books on the subject. Enthralled by its message of love, I soon discovered that religion did not define or complete me; spirituality did.

It was while I was on this self-betterment mission that I began searching for a sacred place to sit and meditate. I could not believe it when I found the small chapel honoring St. Jude. Since I had grown up in parochial schools, I already knew much about the patron saint of hopeless cases. He was one of my favorite saints. I began spending many evenings in the back pew of the church, reading and journaling. Some nights I would merely watch the twinkling lights from the votive candles dance along the stained-glass windows. Other times I would reflect on my life path and purpose while trying desperately to move my right hand.

I remembered from Stanford that constant practice was the best way to re-train the brain to connect to the affected nerves. Although there were no visible signs of movement, I envisioned that the neural chemical charges were firing and triggering. I kept telling myself I would regain mobility and the pain would lessen. I held on to hope that my miracle would come.

Months passed quickly and December approached. It was odd to think I had been away from home for more than a year. There were many days when I became discouraged. I only wanted to be better, and yet I was still struggling. *I just needed a sign.*

Then, one night, I experienced my first breakthrough. I had just pulled out of the St. Jude chapel parking lot when Whitney Houston's "One Moment in Time" came on the car radio. For some reason, I felt compelled to move my hand. It felt like an out-of-body experience when I stared down at my fist and directed my energy into that one thought.

I immediately thought I saw a slight flicker near my thumb. Thinking I imagined the movement made me more determined to try it again. I started to grunt and squint my eyes. But this time nothing happened. My swollen claw remained perfectly still.

Thinking the twitch might have been a dream led me not to tell anyone. It was difficult not to talk about the possible tremor in my hand, but I knew it was necessary. I did not want to spread false hope or get others too excited unless I was certain. Plus, I knew myself. There was no way I would be able to handle the constant questions and probes of others.

Dealing with chronic pain affected all aspects of my life. While I knew I should have been shouting from rooftops, I opted to keep my discovery hidden. I believed verbalizing this progress would lead family and friends to assume I was better. *What if I was not? What if this improved state was temporary?* I constantly worried what others thought about me after years of the medical community questioning and holding my pain suspect. I just could not risk my support system losing faith and trust in me.

Thankfully, my secret was not private very long. Two weeks later on a Sunday afternoon, the twitching re-appeared in my thumb. I was driving home from Doc's office when I kept thinking about Louise Hay. She believed anyone could heal their life if they could look past the disease and find the root of the cause. As I repeated affirmations from her book *(You Can Heal Your Life)*, I heard Gloria Estefan's "Get on Your Feet." Once again, I felt some strong urge to move my hand.

I then watched in utter amazement as my thumb twitched. I tried it another time. Miraculously, my thumb still moved. Excited, I tried my four other fingers. But nothing happened.

While I wanted instant gratification and recovery, I knew I needed to be patient. I had to continue holding on to hope and rejoice. This was going to take time. At least I knew it was possible for me to heal.

I was going to be better.

Chapter 27

New Year's Surprises

My true miracle arrived on New Year's Day 2004. I had woken early because of a pounding headache and upset stomach. Ruben had been over the night before, and we had celebrated with too much wine and pizza. In need of some fresh air, I remember I went outside and sat down on the concrete steps that led to the second-floor apartments. There I began my usual morning routine of concentrating on my fisted hand. Yet instead of staring at an immobile hand, I saw my thumb lift an eighth of an inch when I tried extending my fingers. Then my four other digits twitched and trembled.

Seeing movement in my fingers brought me to tears. I could not believe my nerves were beginning to respond. It was a start to a new year and now a start to a new life.

As I ran inside to grab the phone, I dialed my parents, completely oblivious to the two-hour time difference. Listening to Dad's startled voice shifted my thoughts to Stanford. It was like déjà vu. He sounded the same as he did that early summer morning when I called him from LPCH to tell him I regained mobility in my hand. Thinking about the similarities made me sweat. The room started spinning as my knees trembled. I knew my next sentence would turn his world upside down.

"Daddy, my hand moved. I can lift my thumb and make my other four fingers twitch."

Then there was silence. I thought he was either speechless or still trying to comprehend the phone call. After all, it was only five in the morning on New Year's Day. I heard him clear his throat. "What do you mean your hand moved?"

I again told him how I was outside trying to lift my thumb when, to my surprise, it moved. The next sound I heard was a whistle followed by numerous questions: Was my pain gone? Had I spoken to Doc? Could I still move my hand? Images in the room blurred as I became dizzy. I sat down on the couch. The enormity of this improvement hit me like a ton of bricks: *I really was healing.*

I felt I was on cloud nine. My nightmare had ended, and I wanted to share my excitement with everyone. Soon I was on the phone, calling all my friends. Some answered groggily, but most did not answer at all. I figured this was because of their long night out partying, so I just left messages. I felt like a flower on the verge of budding open. My world had light again.

Right away, I wanted to go home. While I believed I needed Doc, I felt I needed my spiritual guidance team more. Something inside me told me I had to listen to my intuition. My body needed physical therapy, and I needed a spiritual boost. Mitzi, Shelley and Maureen would be able to help me through the next phase of recovery.

My decision to leave surprised everyone, especially Doc. Although he understood why I was anxious to return to California, he wished I would stay longer. He wanted to make sure this improvement was not temporary. Despite this making sense to me, I felt I needed Mitzi now that I had regained mobility. I had been in Texas for fifteen months; it was time to do what was right for me.

We both agreed that mid-January would be the earliest I could leave. Doc planned a schedule. I would continue e-mailing and faxing him pain grids twice a week from California. In addition, I would come back to Corpus four times a year for check-ups. Although this arrangement looked good on paper, I knew this was tough for him to swallow. Here I was telling him I had to return home after he had worked so hard to get me well. I felt bad, but I could not question my decision. I had to spread my wings and fly.

Saying goodbye was terrible. I had made a family here. Maureen and Myra were like my aunts. The Gardiners had become extended family. Ruben was my second brother. Mary always made me smile and laugh. Patricia and Amber were dear friends…and then there was Doc and his family. *What do you say to someone who saved your life?*

I was at a loss for words. All of them meant so much to me. They were the ones who supported me through the pain and rejoiced with me in better times. This group looked past my disability. They accepted me for who I currently was and who I would be once again. Moving forward was bittersweet.

Sixteen days after the twitching appeared in my hand, Mom and I said farewell to Corpus Christi. I remember the town's first Starbucks opened the day we left. Having longed for a nonfat latte the duration of my stay made it ironic that the grand opening would occur as I departed. Yet it was also humorously fitting. Although I was closing a chapter in my life, the people in Corpus would still be here. Life goes on for everyone.

∞

My getting better was a momentous occasion that had to be celebrated. Therefore, Mom and I decided to take a detour on our drive back to California and visit Sedona, Arizona. Sedona was about ninety miles north of Phoenix. I heard from friends that it was a quaint and charming community, so I could not wait to arrive. It was late at night when we finally made our way up the long, winding road that led to the center of town. Seeing the lights twinkling in the trees and the artistic stores lining the streets made me even more excited for tomorrow's exploration.

The next morning, I was in awe as I stepped outside our hotel room. Sedona was beautiful. The magnificent red rock mountains and the energy of the landscape took my breath away. It was mystical and astounding. It was as if God purposely protected and surrounded this serene oasis.

As Mom and I hiked along nature trails and drove through beautiful canyons, I felt centered and whole. My senses had awakened from their long nap, and I instantly felt renewed. I was no longer tired but instead energized. To reach a peak of a cliff and be able to glance down at a majestic ravine was indescribable. It was as if the power in nature was healing me. Love resided within the rocks and sun. I was at peace. *I knew I would survive and heal because I was on the right path.*

Sedona spiritually enlightened me. I found the motivation to keep fighting, the strength to persevere, and the self-confidence to believe in myself. Just like Palm Springs, Sedona was a safe haven for me. It was a place where I felt "one" with a Higher Power. I felt truly alive, and I did not want to leave. I promised myself that someday when I healed, I would revisit this amazing city and relish my wellness.

Our last stop before home was to visit a dear friend in Orange County. I had known Kathie for many years, and she had even come to Corpus a month after we arrived to help Mom. She was the perfect visitor for us to have when my withdrawals first began. As Kathie was like a second mother to me, I did not need to wear a mask with her. I felt comfortable talking about the insurmountable pain and severe constipation, because I knew she would not judge me. She had been through her own terrible heartache, and having watched her persevere gave me hope. I looked up to her.

Visiting Kathie was exactly what my soul needed. All I did was eat lots of good food, drink amazing wine, and spend a leisurely day at the local spa. To think that I was able to be in a steam room, soak in an aromatic bath or receive a full-body massage was mind-boggling. This was the beginning of a new life, and I refused to take the little things for granted anymore.

I finally was ready to embark on my next adventure.

Walking into my old physical therapy clinic and seeing Mitzi for the first time was emotional. I think it was hard on her too. While she had been my largest supporter of seeing Doc, my returning with a new size-ten physique seemed to shock her. I remember her mouth dropped slightly as she stared dumbfounded. It took me a second to realize that the last time she had seen me, I was wearing a size two. I was a different, rounder person now. My life had drastically changed.

Mitzi initially wanted me to visit twice a week so I could ease into the program. Eventually she would increase our time together to four sessions a week as I became stronger. That sounded like a good plan to me. I would much rather be overly cautious than foolishly naïve.

The appointments were grueling. I forgot how terribly painful physical and occupational therapy could be. Mitzi put me through the wringer. I endured passive and manual stretching, range of motion, desensitization therapy, manipulations and deep-tissue massage. There were days when the burning sensations were so intense and unbearable that I had to grunt and flail my legs just to cope. Yet I would not give up. I knew I had to press on so I could gain back my life.

Having a typical type A personality was an advantage and a disadvantage. It helped me in the sense that I refused to let this pain bring me down. I was focused on getting better, and followed Mitzi's instructions to a T. However, her being a drill sergeant also hurt me. I did not know when to stop or how to handle upsets. If I did not surpass a previous measurement, I would be devastated.

In order to minimize my disappointment and document my progress, Mitzi began recording the movements and flutters in my hand. This helped me. Now I could visually see my improvements instead of relying on past recollections and reassurances of others. Having my treatments videotaped also affected my way of thinking. During those moments when the pain held me captive, I found motivation. The agony was worth it, and I had the proof. The torture might be horrific, but it would make me well.

There was absolutely no time for pessimistic thinking. If I was going to regain mobility in my right hand and live pain-free, I had to stay positive. I understood that my future was at stake. Since I was pushing my body to its limits, it was vital that I learn to be kind to myself. I needed to remind myself that I was right where the Universe wanted me to be. I just had to trust that I would eventually reach my dream.

I continued making baby steps over the next three months. Soon I was able to open my hand and grasp a Dixie cup. I then started holding the built-up pen from Stanford and doing body-resistant stretches. I was taking care of myself by following Nicholas Perricone's eating program designed to detoxify the body and reduce inflammation.

His plan entailed reducing saturated fats, refined sugars, and other high-glycemic carbohydrates for twenty-eight days while increasing protein. I drank at least sixty ounces of water and ate five small meals per day. I felt incredible. As this healthier lifestyle made me mentally and physically stronger, I asked my parents if I could work with a personal trainer.

After years of being immobile and sedentary, my muscles had deteriorated and atrophied. I knew my disease thrived on a weak immune system, so my goal was to strengthen my body as a precautionary tool. The more lean muscle I had, the less likely a future flare-up would be. I knew it was going to be difficult to lose this excess weight and lower my body fat percentage.

However, I was willing to do whatever it took to reduce my chances of having to endure another excruciating episode with the disease.

I was lucky; both Doc and Mitzi believed that endurance and weight training were important to my overall health. Their only concern was finding a trainer sympathetic to my condition and aware of my limitations. Knowing that an injury would be detrimental to my progress made them speak out about the importance of finding a knowledgeable and conscientious trainer. They wanted a person willing to research the disease. Thankfully, Kathie came to my rescue by recommending her old training studio.

Michelle and Aaron were the owners. Their body wellness center was expansive. It had three rooms with free weights and weight stacks, two rooms dedicated to cardio machines, and another room used for abdominal exercises and stretching. It was nice for me to be around a younger couple who loved each other and believed that health was more important than being thin. I even felt comfortable with their staff, since they also made an effort to learn about chronic pain. Michelle and Aaron had invested themselves in my recovery, and that made me feel special.

While Doc insisted I begin slowly, I quickly progressed. My two hours a week with no weights heavier than five pounds quickly turned into three hours a week with fifteen-pound weights. Michelle pushed me to excel through positive encouragement. On the bad days when I felt defeated, she would reiterate how strong and able-bodied I was. What I had accomplished thus far was remarkable, so I had no reason to be frustrated with my performance. I would reach my goals, but I had to be patient with myself.

The day I stopped wearing Dad's T-shirts and my extra-large sweats to the gym was my turning point. If I did not begin liking me for me, I would never attain the happiness I was striving to reach. Soon thereafter, I was able to view my scars and loose skin as treasured mementos. I understood that those imperfections were a small price to pay in order to live.

Recognizing my own inner beauty was just the beginning. Next, I became conscious of my progress. I could not believe I was really driving, dressing and feeding myself again. After spending hours trying to improve my fine motor skills, I had finally mastered coloring and writing. Changes were occurring, even if the pain and disease were still present.

When I was ready to live life on my terms, my parents rented me an apartment. This was a huge step, because it meant I was well enough to take care of myself. It was as if the chains tying me down had been unlocked. Each day I was a step closer to recovery. *I was free from the burden of my illness.*

With my life turning around, I found myself in new territory—dating.

Harbor Half: Finish Line

"Embrace this moment and relax—you just need to stay loose. Remember, this is your time to shine. Bask in the glory. Bask in the glory, baby!"

With less than a quarter mile left to run, I see friends and family members standing near the finish line cheering and waving banners.

"Way to go, Nicole!! Conquering Pain Daily!"

"Happy 5th Anniversary!"

"Thank you, Nicole: You Represent Our Future!"

"Congratulations, Nicole, On Your Miraculous Journey to Wellness!"

Viewing their proud faces helps me realize my accomplishment. I can finally say to myself that I chose health, love, happiness and life. Pushing myself to the limits, I pick up my pace and make reaching my family my final goal.

As I try to capture the meaning behind this profound experience, I glance at the large stopwatch dangling over the finish line. Just ten more steps and I will be done. Ten more steps and the journey, pain and grief will be a thing of my past. Once I cross that line, I become the resilient survivor. This is why I ran—here is my moment ... *just two more steps to go...*

Chapter 28

Love vs. Pain

By now, it was August and I had been home almost eight months. Luke was an old family friend I had not seen in years. He was funny, and I immediately felt drawn to him. Yet the unknowns scared me. I felt awkward having attention focused on me. Men had not been interested in me since my illness, so I did not know how to act around them. Moreover, I had many dating apprehensions due to the uncertainties surrounding my health.

I was hesitant to take a chance on love. I knew trying to have an intimate relationship while coping with the highs and lows of chronic pain was complicated. These past six years had been difficult, and I was still piecing together my self-esteem. I was unsure if I was mentally ready for the dating scene, since intimacy unnerved me. However, I was ready to take a risk. For once in my life, I needed to live freely.

The first few months with Luke were happy times. He would take me to dinner and the movies. We would hang out with friends, laugh and enjoy each other's company. I had butterflies anytime he touched me, and I giggled whenever he called. It was nice feeling adored. As Luke helped me burst from my cocoon, I quickly became smitten and developed a false idea of what it means to feel complete.

When I suffered my first serious flare-up in late November, I believed the world I had worked so hard to attain was gone forever. At the time, I was still struggling with severe constipation. Having irritable bowel syndrome was extremely frustrating. It was excruciating to have a bump the size of bowling ball form in my abdomen, and I hated not knowing how my body would react to foods or when I would be able to use the restroom. To put it mildly, constipation made me miserable.

I was thrilled when my gastroenterologist prescribed two medications to help the bloating and bowel functioning. Just knowing other options existed to treat this issue was a relief. Luke's friend had invited us over to his house for a small party the night before Thanksgiving. I never considered the possible side effects of these medications. Since neither of the prescriptions instructed me to avoid alcohol, I had a few glasses of wine while I watched Luke play Texas hold 'em. That was a big mistake.

Soon I felt faint and light-headed. The kitchen spun around me and I developed double vision. I decided to step outside for fresh air when I began salivating profusely. Although the cold wind felt good on my face, I knew I needed to sit. The only chair on the porch was a rocking chair, and I quickly sat down. However, the swaying back and forth made me more nauseated. When I grabbed my stomach, hoping pressure would ease my symptoms, I lost my balance. My face made direct contact with the wooden surface.

Then I blacked out.

My next memory was of Luke and his friends picking me up. Each of them looked terrified by my Quasimodo-esque appearance. I had a swollen face, a purple eye, and a scraped, bruised nose. Because I was shaking and a bit confused, his friends wanted to take me to the hospital. But I did not want to go. In fact, I refused to get in the car. I had spent too many nights in the emergency room and knew nothing good would come out of the trip. I already knew it was a reaction to the medications. It was more important for me to use the STS machine.

That night was frightening. I remember being very embarrassed as I cried and cried. Luke just talked to me and held an ice pack on my face. He kept saying I was okay and did not look as bad as I felt. The ice would minimize the swelling, and the Tylenol should help my headache. I tried to put on my brave face because I did not want him to know I was terribly concerned. *How did this happen?*

The next morning was terrible. Seeing the extent of my injury even scared me. I looked as though I had just lost a UFC fight. My left eye was blue, purple and green, and I had red scrapes on my forehead and nose. How could I go to my first family Thanksgiving in three years looking like I just had the crap beaten out of me? I called Doc and the emergency hotline for my gastroenterologist because I was unsure what to do. Both of them told me to stop the medications immediately.

Although the drugs did not warn against negative reactions due to alcohol consumption, Doc said it was never smart to mix two medications with any type of alcohol. Three glasses of wine might not bother me in normal circumstances, but it might be lethal combined with medicine. He wanted me to know I could drink but I had to be careful. My body was still sick, and the prescriptions for my stomach problems were potent.

I felt better after talking to Doc. He not only told me the protocols to run, he also went over some of the symptoms I might begin to experience. My throbbing head was to be expected, and I should be prepared to suffer a few migraines. It also might take a few days before I could breathe out of my nose. Nevertheless, Doc believed I would be fine and my face should heal without scarring. I just needed to relax and use the STS machine three times a day.

I followed Doc's advice. I ran the machine three times a day for the next week, and only left the apartment to see Mary and Michelle. By day seven, my face had healed. Believing I had beaten my first flare-up excited me. I thought I was getting stronger, but my enthusiasm was premature. Ten days after the accident, I woke up in horrific pain.

My feet, ankles and knees were throbbing so intensely that nothing could touch my legs from my thighs downward. I stacked pillows under my thighs so my lower legs did not rest on blankets. My toes felt as if they were submerged in boiling water. My ankles screamed with stabbing pains. I just felt a deep, piercing ache that would not go away.

I fell apart. I could not bathe, sleep or leave the apartment. Walking from the bedroom to the bathroom was a nightmare. While Mom and Dad took turns coming over to check on me, I did not know what to do with myself. Forgetting how a flare-up could be so debilitating, I grieved the loss of my newfound health. This was not supposed to happen. *Doc did not say my legs would hurt.* My whole world—the world I had been trying to create for years—crashed down on me.

While I knew I had to focus on getting better, I faced another complication. I was now in a relationship. Rejection was hard enough, but to feel rejected while I was the most vulnerable would be devastating. I was petrified. *What would Luke do?* More importantly, what would I do then?

A week into the madness, I had an epiphany: I realized my health should not be a detriment to any relationship. My reality was that I had chronic pain. Some days I could be happy and fine, but other days I could be sick. Those who loved me would stand by my side in sickness and in health. I had to stop apologizing for who I was. This was just "me."

I wished I could say my revelation changed Luke and me. Unfortunately, the fantasy image I had created about our relationship unraveled. Neither of us knew how to approach my pain, so we began dancing around the issue. I yearned to hear him say that everything would be okay and he would be there for me. *But he did not.* Instead, he started to withdraw as I became needier.

I think watching my body deteriorate terrified him. This was Luke's first experience dealing with a flare-up, and he was unprepared. He needed assurance and guidance that I was unable to give to him. We were like any other couple coping with obstacles. He and I had to make it through the rough times before we could even begin healing together.

While I believed in the mind-body-spirit connection, I was currently too emotional to use those practices. Right now, I could only concentrate on my pain and heartache. I kept telling myself this anguish would end. I just needed to regain control of my spirit and attitude, yet I was unsure if I ever would. How many times could one person overcome a disease before the disease finally won?

As the pain raged on and I found myself again confined to a bed, my parents and I understood that we had to return to Texas. This shook me at my innermost core. I never thought I would be visiting due to a setback. Not knowing when this nightmare would end upset me. I had lost my power. My life was again at the mercy of my Creator.

Traveling in an airport with a wheelchair was a nightmare. I had to go through various security points in Oakland and again in Houston where we changed planes. Although Mom and I were the first ones on the plane, we were also the last to leave. This meant we were scrambling to make our connecting flight. By the time we landed in Corpus Christi, my pain was off the charts and I was exhausted. I just wanted to get to the hotel so I could rest and cry.

Doc did not waste any time, and immediately ordered beat-frequency testing. Yet none of us expected my hypersensitivity would return with vengeance. It was as if this torment would never end. Again, I was unable to tolerate the STS machine. I burst into tears as the negative thoughts bombarded my mind. *What would happen now? Would it take years for me to walk? How would Luke respond? Would he break up with me over the phone?*

I started biting my lower lip to regain my composure. Doc started talking. He emphasized how difficult flying can be for those in chronic pain. The barometric pressure, vibration, and crowded space stress the autonomic nervous system. An overstimulated nervous system cuts off circulation to the limbs, therefore resulting in higher pain levels. I just needed to stay positive. This flare-up would settle down and I would be walking very soon.

While I was discouraged by my first day in the office, I tried to put everything in perspective. What Doc said made sense to me. Obviously, my body would respond negatively under such circumstances. After all, I was worried and tense, and scared as hell. I did not want a repeat of the last six years. If my thoughts were all that I controlled, I had to believe I would heal and the pain would end. **I had to hold on to hope.**

Yet staying optimistic became more difficult later that night. I suddenly began to have trouble breathing. Sharp, shooting pains besieged my chest. It felt as if a knife was slicing away at my heart. I started to sweat and my left arm tingled. My body trembled while my face flushed. *Was I having a heart attack?*

Soon I began hyperventilating, and Mom frantically called Doc. Doc's immediate reaction was to have me eat ice cream, thinking I had low blood-sugar levels. Mom rushed to the store to buy Häagen-Dazs coffee and rocky road flavored ice cream. But I did not feel any different. Even after swallowing spoonfuls of ice cream, the intense zings still pounded in my chest cavity.

She called Doc again. This time he said we needed to go to the emergency room. Although he felt there was a greater chance that an elephant was outside our hotel window, I had taken many of the drugs that had been recalled for causing heart attacks and strokes. He felt it best that we play it safe.

As Mom sped to the ER, my cell phone rang. It was Luke. Although I was glad to hear from him, it bothered me that it was almost midnight and this was the first time he had called that day. I told him we were on our way to the emergency room. His apathetic nature stunned me. Here I was telling him I might be having a heart attack, and he did not seem worried. *What did that mean? Does he not care about me?*

While upset by his reaction, I was too frightened over my own health to care. Instead, I chalked up his lack of concern to him not knowing how to act. I always gave him the benefit of the doubt. Luke loved me; he was just afraid.

The ER was a whirlwind of commotion. I remember nurses and doctors rushed to my side and lifted me onto an examining table. Watching multiple hands swarm over my body only intensified my fears. As one person took my heart rate, another checked my throat and temperature. A cold stethoscope touched my bare skin as electrodes were placed on my chest. I looked at Mom's face; she seemed panicked. I was supposed to be moving forward, not going backward.

The rest of my visit was a blur. I have memories of beeping machines, bright fluorescent lights, translucent gowns, and cold, uninviting rooms. I still smell the peculiar scent of sterile sheets and sanitized walls. However, I could not tell you what any of my doctors looked like. I do not remember how long nurses monitored me or what time Mom and I left. All I know was that I was fine. My heartbeat was normal and I had no signs resembling a stroke. Doc was right…*again.*

Over the course of the next few days, things went smoother at the clinic. My increased tolerance of treatments put me in much better spirits. I found myself wanting to drive around the Gulf and eat at restaurants. I even had a haircut and got a pedicure at my favorite salon. Although I was not walking, I felt resilient. My days of turmoil and anguish seemed to be dwindling. There was an end in sight.

After another week of aggressive testing and numerous protocol changes, I could slowly walk with a cane. I was ecstatic. With my independence returning, hope that I would be able to lead a normal life returned as well. Two days before Christmas, Doc told us we could return home under orders that I continue to send him pain grids. This was so he could make the necessary changes to my treatment. I eagerly agreed.

During the next few weeks, I saw more and more improvements. I went from needing a cane to walking with a slight limp for ten consecutive minutes. I even returned to my personal training and exercise routine. My progress was remarkable, and the pain was becoming manageable. Life seemed promising again. No matter what happened in the future, I would be able to make it. *I would always beat this disease.*

∞

Despite my improved health, my relationship was ending. Three months after I returned from Texas, Luke abruptly told me that he wanted to see other people. The break-up jolted me. I remember I had no perspective on reality as I spent four hours groveling to him to take me back. I promised I would be different and things would be better if he just gave me another month.

I was emotionally distraught, and Luke looked ill. I was sure having someone he cared about beg and plead for another chance was difficult. Luke never wanted to hurt me, but he also did not want to lead me on. His feelings were not growing or changing like mine. He kept stressing that it was not me, but it was both of us together. We just were not right for each other.

Not knowing what to do, I called Shelley from his bathroom. I was in tears. I wanted her to tell me he was making a mistake but he would realize it soon. I needed her to say that I was right fighting for our relationship. I wanted her to fix it. She did not, at least not in the way that I wanted her to.

Shelley assured me this pain would end, but I had to leave his house and go home. I did not know who I was without him. Because he was the first person I had a connection with since my hand opened, I formed my life around his. I somehow lost myself, but I would be fine without him. The Universe had a greater plan in store for me.

Though I yearned for him to call and say he had made a mistake, I knew I needed space in order to grow as a person. After having my life consumed with doctors, drugs and operations, all I wanted was to be self-sufficient and independent. I had spent years so focused on getting better that I never considered what I would do once I healed. Now that I reached the point where I needed to make decisions, I did not know how to begin. The "real world" was overwhelming. I had not finished college, and I was not well enough to work. What was I supposed to do?

This was why I clung to Luke like a leech. Since I did not have my own identity, I gravitated toward his. He had given me a purpose. Coming to the realization that I based my worth on being with him appalled me. I already knew a person could not make me internally happy; it was time for me to discover who I was. I no longer had a connection to my High Self or Spirit, and that needed to change. This was my chance to come into my own.

Knowing I had to stay busy was why I went to my favorite shop and applied for a part-time job. Working five hours, three days a week was a perfect distraction for me. The store focused on total well-being and had an eclectic collection of healing books, soaps, candles and lotions. I embraced the atmosphere.

Whenever I felt down, all I had to do was glance upwards at the many inspirational plaques. Some of my favorite quotes were: "Live well, laugh often, love much," "Miracles Happen," and "What would you do if you knew you could not fail?" It felt as if Spirit sent me here for a reason. I did not feel as alone when I was at work, and I was thankful for that.

My friends were also amazing. Meredith and Dylan called me every day to check in. I received many e-mails from Meghan, Kristin and Nadine, while Emily, Annie, Kerry and Angela rallied around me. Inviting me to movies, dinners and bars, they basically did anything to keep me occupied.

While I greatly appreciated the support, I despised these outings. Nothing could take away my sadness. I had lost my appetite and could not concentrate on storylines, and acting as if I was fine was pointless. I was a basket case.

I hated being so depressed. After enduring all that I had, it bothered me that I could allow a break-up to destroy my spirit. Most days were completely dreadful. I knew I needed to find a way to pull myself together, but I did not know where to start. I felt I had invested so much of myself into that relationship that it was impossible for me to move forward.

I began seeing Maureen and Shelley every week. With their help, I recognized my fear of participating in life. For so many years, I had to look for my own answers in order to recover. Now that it seemed like my dream for wellness was in reach, a completely new group of issues and insecurities poured out. It was as if someone opened Pandora's Box, and I had gone from fearing I would never get better to fearing I would.

I did not know what to do now that I was able to contribute to society. My pain might still have been high, but my hand was strengthening and I was improving. I knew I should have been grateful and content, but I felt trapped and despondent. *How was I supposed to enter the land of the living when I still felt dead?*

Through these sessions, I had entered a new self-discovery period. My truth opened up to me as I learned I was okay on my own. Now I truly understood there was no shame in making a bad decision, as long as I saw the larger picture. If I grew from the experience, then it was worth the pain. This was my turn to start fresh. I could not limit my dreams because I was afraid to fail **or** succeed. Life was about seizing opportunities, so I needed to trust that what was meant to be would be.

Chapter 29

Moving On

Weeks passed, and I started to shy away from the crippling thoughts of not being good enough, not being loveable, and not being worthy of a real relationship. I began to see that my past was a gift, as it allowed me to learn that I was responsible solely for myself. I never would be able to change others, so I had to release the need of wanting to "fix" everything.

Just as I had to figure out my own life, Luke had to figure out his. While I was going to give him six months to figure things out, I also promised myself to move ahead if a new love presented itself. I knew this would be difficult, but I could not keep cowering away from happiness. I wanted to be able to love and accept love in return.

As I opened myself up to the possibility of love elsewhere, I became more social. I remember I even wanted to attend the dinner party Emily invited me to. It had been raining in San Francisco that day, and as we walked down a steep hill, I accidentally slipped on the wet pavement. Instantly the pain returned. Heat radiated from my left ankle as tears formed in my eyes. I knew it was the CRPS.

I tried my best to enjoy dinner but could not take my mind off the unbearable pain searing through my anklebone. Just walking from the kitchen to the table sent sharp stabs up my leg. I hated pretending to be engaged in conversation while secretly wishing I could leave. All I wanted was to speak with Doc and use the STS machine. Wondering if I would return to my wheelchair-bound status made me sick to my stomach.

Not about to chance the disease spreading, I left for Texas three days later. I knew Doc was the only one who could help, so it would have been foolish of me to postpone the inevitable. Since this was my second trip to Corpus in four months due to injuries, returning there frustrated me. I did not understand why I kept getting hurt. This setback brought to the surface many fears over whether I would ever be free from pain. Could I really *be* healed?

∞

Although I arrived ready to fix my ankle, my broken heart added problems. Despite it being two months since the break-up, I was still devastated over the loss of the relationship. It was as if I had lost the ability to function and live. I was drowning, and no one seemed to know what to do or how to help. I felt as though I barely kept my head above water. Something was just not right.

Nights were awful. I could not sleep, with Luke and my poor health consuming my thoughts. I kept trying to break free from my unhappiness, but I was stuck. Life was not supposed to turn out like this. I was supposed to have been happy and successful after enduring withdrawal, but I was not. How could a measly break-up cause me this much grief?

While Doc believed part of my emotional pain was normal, he suspected the deep feelings of rejection, doubt and unworthiness resulted from a chemical imbalance brought on by lack of sleep. Doc prescribed Lunesta. Lunesta was a newer sedative that showed positive results in treating insomnia. I was hesitant to try another medication, since drugs and my body did not seem to mesh well. Doc felt it was necessary. I desperately needed sleep, and medicine was the only available option.

Within minutes of ingesting the medication, I knew I was in trouble. I began to feel loopy and light-headed. Tremors appeared in my hands and legs. When I stood to use the bathroom, I stumbled into furniture. Soon my body went numb and tingled. *This was not good.*

As I started hyperventilating, I dialed my parents. My words slurred together as I sobbed to Mom. I told her a clown with a big red nose and bright red costume was standing at the end of my bed, juggling yellow beanbags.

Mom tried to pacify my fears by reassuring me that the creepy clown was only a hallucination. "This is just a reaction to the drug, Nicole. Remember, your breathing always changes when you try new medicine, but you will be fine. The clown is not really in your room; it is just a hallucination. You are safe."

While her words calmed me, the clown did not disappear, and my breathing did not improve. Instead, I began to repeat, "I am safe and this will pass. There are no clowns in my room." I prayed the madness would end quickly. I was sick of feeling miserable. How many more times would this happen to me?

Six more hours passed before the drug reaction subsided. The next day, Doc tried a new drug. It was as if we were playing a game of Russian roulette. No matter how intensely Doc researched different prescriptions, at the end of the day, I was still the guinea pig. I hated that. I did not want to be tested on anymore. *I just wanted to be better.*

Luckily, the next medication worked. After one night of sleep, I went from being a weepy, frail, and despondent mess to a hopeful, refreshed, and alive person. With the darkness gone,

I could move forward with my life. I now understood that holding on to hope did not mean waiting around for the person I loved to come back. Having hope meant holding on to the feeling that *is* love, and knowing a greater love would take its place.

With a clear head, I could again focus on healing my ankle. It was astonishing how quickly I responded to treatments. In a few short weeks, the pain in my foot had subsided. I was grateful but also confused. It was hard for me not to wonder how much further I could progress if I lived here. I was at another crossroads. What would happen if I made a commitment to move to Texas for a year?

It felt like some powerful force was pulling me to stay. There were signs everywhere. For starters, I had an amazing support system already in place. The Gardiners became my second family. I lived with them, ate my meals with them, and felt comfortable sharing my pain with them. Then there were Amy, Melissa and Patricia. I had friends here who I enjoyed hanging out with. They taught me how to be silly and enjoy life. Next there was Mary, whom I felt I had known all my life. Lastly, I had Doc, who was just as invested as I was in seeing me pain-free.

This was my opportunity to live life to the fullest. All I wanted was to be able to look back in fifty years and be proud of myself for taking chances. If I was ready to live by my rules, then it was time for me to take responsibility for my destiny.

Doc was thrilled I was staying. This gave him an additional twelve months to treat me and reduce my pain level from a six to a zero. On the flipside, the news shocked my parents. They never thought this trip would turn out to be permanent. Although it was difficult for them to be far away, they understood that I had to do this. My health was more important than my proximity.

The first three months on my own were fantastic. It had always been a dream of mine to live close to the water, so finding a one-bedroom apartment overlooking the Gulf made me feel as if I had won the lottery. I did not even mind that it was located on the third floor and only had stair access. I loved being able to see over the high brush and watch the currents lap against the shore.

I began living for the moment. Each morning I walked along the beach, treading through the soft sand. Feeling the salt-filled air blow through my hair and smelling the sea aroma rejuvenated me. I was ready to move forward: in health and love.

It almost felt like these were my college years; yet, instead of attending classes, I visited Doc. I was acting like a young, carefree twenty-something-year-old for the first time in my life. Feeling as if too much time had been lost, I was trying to make up for it now. My new friends helped in this department.

Amy, Melissa, Patricia and I were inseparable. We did everything together—shopped, exercised, partied and laughed. I learned from them how to put on makeup correctly, how to style my hair, and how to live in the moment. We gossiped about our latest crushes and shared our many first-date adventures. The three of them were there for me during the good times and bad, and I felt very fortunate to have them in my life. I was finally just like everybody else; I was living normally and doing what my peers had always been doing.

Sadly, the party did not last long. South Texas's weather was erratic and unpredictable. As soon as fall approached, the climate changed, and my health dramatically declined. Highly sensitive to pressure and temperature changes, I could not handle the roller coaster ride of hot versus cold, rain versus sun, wind versus calm.

The constant ups and downs left me incapacitated. My fingers would swell like little sausages, and I would develop cankles from increased inflammation. Constipation would worsen, causing my stomach to expand and bloat. My head would spin until I felt as if I would pass out.

Yet my most troublesome problem was that I could not walk again. The radiating pain from my anklebones made driving or taking the three flights of stairs impossible. I was literally trapped in my apartment for days on end, unable to see Doc. When I needed him the most, he was inaccessible. My life had become a living hell.

I remember I would constantly call my parents, bawling. My only wish was to be pain-free. Except whenever life started improving, I always faced another setback. Each time, it became harder to pull myself together. I had been through so much but it was never enough. The pain always returned, and I could not seem to break the pattern. *It never went away.*

Mom and Dad knew no words could change my situation, so their job was to support me. Most of the time, Mom and Dad were quiet as they listened to me vent about not being strong enough to continue. Only when I sounded like I was ready to give up did Mom or Dad engage in the conversation. Then my parents became my cheerleaders. They would reassure me that I *would* heal and that I had the inner power to keep going.

I found myself living in a semi-fantasy world once the weather cleared. With my aches and pains dissipating, I would return to my usual routine of visiting Doc and seeing friends. It was strange how quickly I would forget my previous pain…until the next weather front arrived and my nightmare began again. I was always living on the edge, afraid at any moment that my world would crash on top of me.

$$\infty$$

With my health swaying back and forth, I began to develop a persistent tremor in my right arm. It started out as a tingling and numbing sensation before progressing to rapid, uncontrollable twitches. My whole life was impacted by this nagging tremor. I could not sleep because my arm flailed about wildly. I could not exercise because I had lost my balance. I even had trouble showering, getting dressed, cooking and driving.

I saw Doc every day, desperate for answers and a remedy. This was my fifth flare-up in a year, and I was losing patience. I did not know how much longer I could fight the same fight. Doc tried every possible sedative, muscle relaxant, barbiturate, seizure and tremor medication in order to help me. He even began a rigorous testing schedule to determine my best beat frequency and protocol placement for the STS machine. Yet the unruly, painful spasm persisted.

As the pain intensified due to my tightening muscles, I feared I would soon regress to an invalid. I did not understand why this was happening. *Why would a Higher Power allow me to make such progress only to lose it all over and over again? How could I start a life when I could not escape my past?* I wanted to scream and cry that this was not fair; this was just not fair.

With my health spiraling out of control, Doc had no choice but to send me to a neurologist. Although he felt this was my disease flaring, he still had to rule out other serious ailments such as MS and early-onset Parkinson's disease. I was terrified to meet with a neurologist. Not only did I not know what to expect, I feared the worst. Something had to be wrong for a tremor to last more than three weeks.

The neurologist acted like any typical doctor who thought he was superior to the general population. He appeared pretentious and annoyed that I was wasting his time. It was obvious by the snide glances he made while he examined my arm that my case meant nothing to him. I was just another number on his tally of people to see that day.

As he was not one to make conversation, he rushed through a list of tests I would need to take and the rules I must abide by. He had ordered blood work, an MRI of the brain, and an EEG. I was also told not to fly home for the Christmas holiday because being on an airplane could cause my brain to hemorrhage. Then he was gone. I felt cheated. While I realized that he did not know me, I wanted him to *act* as if he cared. Like my story mattered to him.

I left his office in shock. Devastated, I headed to the MRI imaging building and blood center to complete the necessary tests. My mind was in a fog the whole drive as I thought about how I would tell Dad that I could not come home for Christmas. I was tired of being the reason my family suffered. How could I ruin another holiday?

My left hand trembled as I dialed home. It killed me that I was the official bearer of bad news. All my parents did was worry, and now I had to call with more problems. Would there ever be a time where I would be able to tell them *great* news? I was sick of being sick and did not want to feel unworthy anymore. This had to stop.

Hearing Dad's voice made my heart ache. He sounded like he was in good spirits, and I knew this update would crush him. I broke down in tears as I tried to talk. My family deserved better than this and so did I. *When would my pain end?*

Dad was more concerned with what the neurologist said than me needing to stay in Texas for the holiday. My health was the issue, not flying home. They would make arrangements so I would not be alone. However, at this point, he only cared about my safety and my emotional well-being. He wanted to know that I was all right.

Once I hung up the phone, I immediately called Amy. She had become my rock in Corpus Christi, and I confided in her a lot. What I needed right now was for her to tell me that everything would be okay. I had to know if she thought I was tearing my family apart, because I currently felt like the bad sheep. Basically, I needed Amy to be strong for me. She was.

She empathetically told me I was going to be fine. My parents were not angry; they only wanted me better. While she understood that I would rather be in California, having to stay in Texas was not the end of the world. What was important was that I took care of myself and found out what was wrong.

It felt good to hear her re-affirm Dad's message. I just needed to know that I was not letting anyone down—that I was not a failure. Dealing with my pain these past seven years had changed me. I now doubted myself and needed constant reassurance from others. I was searching for validation.

Since Dad would not be able to arrive until Christmas Day, Amy's sister invited me to her house for Christmas Eve. This was such a blessing. Instead of being alone in my apartment crying, I spent the evening with a family who genuinely loved each other. Being in a house decorated with candles, garlands, lights, and a large tree encircled with gifts was magical. It actually *felt* like Christmastime.

When I arrived at the airport the next morning, I was shocked to find Mom, Dad and Dan. Dad had kept telling me he was coming by himself, so it was a great surprise to see them all waiting at baggage claim. Suddenly a weight dropped from my heavy shoulders. I had my family and they would help me heal.

Christmas was low-key. We went to our annual afternoon movie, and Dad cooked Omaha steaks that he brought from home. The day was perfect. It really was true that home was where the heart is. Being home was just a feeling, a feeling I felt whenever I had my parents and brother nearby.

Dan left two days after Christmas. His high school friends were home for the holidays, and he wanted to make sure he saw them. I completely understood and probably would have done the same if the situation were reversed. Luckily, I had my parents, who were staying an extra few days. I was appreciative that they would be with me when I received my results from the neurologist.

While it worried me that the neurologist might find something terrible, all I thought about was what if he found nothing. Then what was wrong with me?

I found myself on edge the morning of my appointment. Dull aches encompassed my arm, while the right side of my back seared. This was the day of reckoning. As I sat on the padded examining table, my parents and I anxiously waited for the neurologist to appear. The X-rays of my brain were already resting on the lit-up screen along the wall. Although I stared at the images of my brain, trying to find any abnormalities, I had no idea what was considered normal. Was *that* swelling? Was *that* a tumor? Why was the lining of my brain thicker in *this* image and not in *that* one?

When I heard shuffling outside the room and the doorknob turned clockwise, I began to freak out. My heart palpitated as my eyesight became blurry. I knew my moment of truth was finally here.

As Doc had expected, all the tests had come back normal. I had not suffered from a brain tumor, early-onset Parkinson's, inflammation, or an aneurysm. The neurologist diagnosed a pinched nerve or a new dimension of my disease to be the main culprit behind the tremor. His suggestion was that I return to Doc.

The news was both a relief and disappointment. I was grateful that I did not have any life-threatening problem, but I was also frustrated. This twitch had been occurring for a month without any rhyme or reason. Moreover, I still did not have a concrete diagnosis that explained my pain, heartache and agony. *What was I to do now?*

While I felt numb, my parents and Doc were ecstatic that I was going to be all right. Learning that nothing was seriously wrong led Doc to devise a new program. He continued his STS treatments, while adding cranial sacral massages. Doc kept stressing that this was the disease, and I would be okay. It was just going to take time.

None of these encouraging talks impressed me or made me feel better. I was angry and overly exhausted. I hated how I could fall asleep managing my symptoms, only to wake in excruciating pain. Nothing made sense. When would this whole nightmare be over? When would my life begin without the pain and fear of another episode? When would I really be happy?

New Year's was only four days away, and my parents were on their way home. Although I had not noticed any changes in the tensing and constricting of my muscles, I continued seeing Doc while scheduling bi-weekly appointments for cranial sacral massages and hot-and-cold stone therapy. Fully committed to regaining my health, I was doing everything in my power to embrace the baby steps again.

Days later, I was thrilled when I discovered a position in bed that made sleeping possible. To me, this meant I was moving in the right direction. All it took was one improvement for me to see that there was a light at the end of this long, winding tunnel. Soon the twitches became less impulsive and forceful. As they lessened, my body felt stronger. Hope had returned, and I now believed 2006 would be my year.

Chapter 30

Changes

I did not know why I even questioned life. *When would I ultimately learn to trust that everything happens for a reason?* If I had never developed the tremors, I would have gone home for the holidays. Consequently, I never would have met Rick.

I met Rick January 2, 2006 at a downtown hamburger joint. Rick had grown up in a small Texas town thirty miles north of Corpus Christi, and now co-owned a personal training studio and tanning salon. Simply stated, meeting him was fate. He had entered my life for a reason.

Although I had never been one to tan because of the health risks, I found myself succumbing to the habit just so I could see him. The first afternoon I went to his workplace, I was nervous. Not only did I not know if he liked me, but I was also worried about tanning. I knew my pain could exacerbate if I burned, so I had slathered my body with organic suntan lotion. However, I was unsure if that would even protect me. This was a ridiculous idea. What the hell was I doing?

Walking into his place made my heart pound. Butterflies danced in my stomach as I quickly began to perspire. When I found myself at a loss for words, I felt pathetic. It was as if I was a schoolgirl trying to talk to her first crush.

As I took a deep breath and regained composure, conversation flowed readily and easily. I learned that he had played collegiate baseball but an injury kept him from further pursuing his dreams. After Googling him online, I discovered he was actually a really good player. It was nice to finally speak with someone who was honest about his past. *He was who he said he was.*

Although we began to e-mail each other throughout the day, I still only saw him whenever I tanned. It puzzled me that he never asked me out. My trips to tan soon decreased as I started to question his intentions. There was no reason to tan if Rick was not interested in me. Therefore, I decided to cut my losses.

It was the evening that Amy and I saw Rick exiting the bathroom at the local country bar that everything changed. We were inseparable the rest of the night, and as he walked us both to the car, he finally asked for my number. The next couple of weeks were exhilarating. Since Rick had taken culinary classes in junior college, he offered to cook dinner for me every night. I graciously accepted his invitation, and our relationship blossomed.

Although it was wonderful to have feelings for someone again, it did not take long before insecurities about my health resurfaced. While I knew he liked me, I also knew he was in the dark about my chronic pain. I had no idea if he truly understood the ramifications or the full extent of my condition.

Refusing to be hurt or rejected once more meant I had to be honest. I needed to be honest with myself *and* honest with him. If I did not want to lose him, I had to divulge my past. He had a right to know who I was, and for the first time, I wanted someone to know the real me.

I mustered up the courage to hand him a stack of papers as he was getting ready to return home. The pages contained credible facts about chronic pain, medical research on my disorder, and a fifty-page packet I had assembled, detailing my complete medical journey with pictures of how I looked at various points through my disease and information on the STS machine. It scared me when I asked him to read all the material and I saw his eyes widen. I did not want him to run away from me, but I also knew I had no choice.

I was tired of hiding and tired of feeling ashamed or embarrassed for who I was. If Rick wanted this to work as much as I did, learning about me would not push him away. I finally understood that I had to be forthright in order to have that real, loving relationship I so desperately wanted. I had to share my past and let him into my pain.

The whole night, I tossed and turned, thinking I had made a detrimental mistake. But then a calming force would reassure me that I had done the right thing; there was nothing to fear. If I was ready to be loved, admired and accepted for myself, then I had to put my faith in a Higher Source. I had to trust that it was either Rick…or someone greater.

I was a bit hesitant to answer my phone when he called the next afternoon. *What if he acted differently toward me? What if my pictures repulsed him?* Much to my amazement, Rick did not run in the other direction. Both of us had pasts filled with pain and heartache, and he was committed to making this work.

For the first time, I felt I had a companion who would stand by me. I could finally express the feelings I had denied for so many years. I would no longer need to fight the demons alone. In good times or in bad, we were in this together.

Two months into dating, my health took a turn for the worse. Once again, the unpredictable stormy weather left me crippled with pain. It seemed as if four days out of the week, I was unable to leave my apartment. This devastated me because we were still a new couple. All I wanted was to be able to eat at restaurants and meet his friends for drinks. I wished I could carry on conversations without tears streaming down my face. *This was not fair.* I wanted to be happy so badly.

Thankfully, Rick's love and concern for me never wavered. Even in the midst of such woes, he always told me *we* would find a way to get me better. *We* would deal with each flare-up as it arose. Whenever I became upset, he made me concentrate on our future. He always told me the two of us were a family and good times were ahead of us.

Even his upbeat and charismatic nature could not stop the disease from taking over my life. As my health plummeted, Rick willingly took on the role of caregiver, friend and lover. Now, on the days I could not walk, he would carry me down the three flights of stairs and take me to Doc's office. When the pain was too severe for me to get out of bed, he would call throughout the day to make sure I was okay. He also reassured my upset parents that I was going to be fine. Rick was my beacon of light, and I was in love.

∞

It was tradition for Rick and his buddies to visit the Frio River for a weekend of tubing each summer. Although I was excited to meet his college friends who lived elsewhere, I was slightly apprehensive about the cold rapids.

Not about to take any chances, I spoke with Doc about whether I should float. It did not surprise me when he gave me his approval, because he fundamentally believed I should be able to do what I wanted. I explained that I had already purchased expensive all-terrain water shoes to help with the slippery rocks and uneven ground. I was just unsure what else to bring. He told me to pack the STS machine, muscle relaxants, Tylenol, Band-Aids, sunscreen, a hat and glasses.

Then he gave me his final advice, "Just do not get hurt." I laughed and told him I would be fine. It was not as if these were whitewater rapids. Yet little did I know those words would come back to haunt me.

The water was peaceful the second day we floated the river. I could not help but look at the other tubers and feel liberated. Here I was, participating in an ordinary activity like everyone else. The moments I had once dreamed about were now coming true. Life was not supposed to be ruled by fear or pain; life was meant to be lived.

Then I glanced ahead and saw a quicker current approaching in the distance. I turned around to tell Rick when I felt the "whack" and "boom." An old, extended tree limb nailed me in the back of the head. The sheer force of impact turned my world black.

Rick and his friends rushed to my side. I heard them asking me many questions, but I was not listening. Instead, I went through my internal mental checklist. My limbs were mobile, and I seemed to have full range of motion in my neck. There was no added back pain or discomfort. Other than my blurred vision and impending migraine, I felt fine. I then looked at Rick's pale face. I smiled, insisting to everyone that I was okay.

But three hours later, the torture I thought I had once beaten returned. At first, I only felt sharp and erratic burning in my right arm and hand. Then the shooting pains began to jolt down my spine. I was able to stay relatively calm until my hand swelled and my joints stiffened. I was back in the dark abyss again.

It was impossible to push the negative thoughts from my head when my right hand became more and more difficult to move. I tried my best to breathe and stay composed, but being in this situation with people I did not know frustrated me more. I did not want them to see me cry, and I especially did not want them to see me revert to an invalid. As I helplessly watched my hand retreat to its old shiny and swollen position, I felt my identity taken away. The life I had been trying to make for myself seemed unattainable. This was hell.

Because it was too late to leave the river, I had to wait until the following morning to go home. I did not sleep that night. Tears fell from my eyes as I begged the Universe to stop the pulsating torment. I even cursed the world for screwing me over once more. With the stabbing angst increasing by the moment, I became jaded. I began to question whether hope existed for a brighter future. *What if my hand stayed closed or took another five years to re-open? Did I have what it took to deal with this pain anymore?*

The disease controlled my body by the time we left the river. I stared out the passenger window sobbing during the four-hour drive home to Corpus. While the pain ransacked my body, I kept looking at my distorted fist in disgust. I could not believe this was happening to me again. The brutal torment was more than I could handle.

I needed to reach Doc, but nobody had phone reception at the river. When I was finally able to call him, he instructed me to head immediately to the emergency room. Though it was more of a precautionary measure, he had to make sure I did not have swelling near the brain or a concussion. Hearing this information petrified Rick. I remember he sped to the hospital as I bawled uncontrollably.

As I arrived at the overflowing waiting room, the peculiar smell of cleaning solvents and dirty bedpans made me nauseated. All I wanted was for a doctor to help me, but there was a string of people ahead of me in line. Deep-rooted, knife-stabbing pains surged through my right hand, while a dull ache lingered in the entire arm. I shook uncontrollably as black and white dots skated around the room. I shrieked for help. "When would someone help me? When would someone make the misery stop?"

Finally, after waiting two hours in a crowded room, a nurse took me to X-rays. Then I sat in a tiny room with curtains acting as doors. As hospitals were not Rick's "thing," he started to pace back and forth. Seeing him so uneasy made me sad. Yet I was unable to comfort him. I was doom and gloom; *this disease was always going to be with me.*

Another three hours passed before an ER doctor performed a mediocre examination. I remember he listened to my heart while checking my eyes and ears. Although he asked me to tell him what had occurred, he interrupted me to explain how my X-rays were normal. It was obvious by the manner in which he told me my X-rays were normal that he did not believe I was in chronic pain. Therefore, while he wrote me a script for muscle relaxants, I refused them. There was no way I would give him the satisfaction of thinking I was here just for medication.

With the hospital having no answers, a nurse discharged me after seven long hours. Rick and I drove back to my apartment in silence. In less than twenty-four hours, I went from being independent to being reliant on others; self-sufficient to disabled; happy and in love to despondent and insecure. I was again incapable of taking care of myself. *Where had everything gone so wrong?*

That night was torture. As I lay in bed crying and wailing, Rick had to pick up the pieces of my broken life. He had to bathe, dress and feed me, while also reassuring me that I would be better soon. This was just temporary. Doc would be able to help me tomorrow.

Doc started the appointment by teasing me about how I had let him down. He had given me only one stipulation to follow at the river: not to get hurt. Yet here I was in his office, injured. Doc then smiled and asked how I was feeling. All I could say was "shitty." I just wanted my life back, but instead I was in the trenches.

While he promised me that I would regain mobility and the pain would dissipate, Doc had no idea how long it would take for me to recover. He only knew we could not afford to over-stimulate my already exacerbated nerves. By prescribing two muscle relaxants, he hoped I would be able to tolerate three STS treatments a day.

The next five days were horrendous. Rick tried his best to reschedule his morning clients, so he would just have to work in the afternoons and evenings. I could not even get in touch with my parents because they were on vacation. Having no one to talk to or calm my fears made me despondent. I was bitter and reveled in my own despair. Why could I not be normal?

Although unsure what "normal" really meant, I knew not being able to shower at the age of twenty-five was not typical. It was also not normal to need help getting dressed or to be unable to feed myself. Physical suffering did not often happen to people in their twenties. It was as if the scars of my past had returned to open wounds. I was falling further and further into the darkness. *What lessons had I still not learned?*

Seven days.

My hand shut to its fisted position for a mere seven days.

This was not only a miracle but also a testament to my overall health. *I was actually getting better.* In the past, something as detrimental as my hand closing would have lasted months or even years. I had managed to overcome the episode in a week. This was amazing progress.

I viewed this flare-up as a lesson, showing me just how far I had come. My moments of hell and extreme agony were shortening, and I was finally gaining control over the disease. Although there were still bumps in the road that sidelined me, each time I bounced back quicker. My dark hours were fading. Like a flower coming out of its bud, I had blossomed. I felt like I was beginning to beat the odds.

Happy to be moving forward, I was discouraged that my health had turned into a roller-coaster ride. Dealing with the constantly changing weather made it impossible for me to take the large steps I wanted toward healing. It still was an uphill battle for me, since my bad days still outnumbered my good days three to one.

I made getting answers my main priority at my next appointment with Doc. I could no longer live in hell for three days and heaven for one. Just as the pain teetered up and down like a seesaw, so did my spirit and emotions. This three-ring circus had to stop before I lost my sanity. Being stuck in a purgatory stance was not fair to me—or Rick.

As I spoke candidly to Doc about my frustrations over my current situation, he patiently listened and empathized. He felt I might have been doing better if I had been coming regularly to the office. I told him that was difficult to do when I could not trek down the three flights of stairs. He then carried on saying I should have never leased an apartment that was not located on the first level.

Sometimes he made me very angry. His whole goal was for his patients to live normally. As he believed quality of life was just as important as quantity of life, I could not understand why he was telling me differently now.

We both knew there was no use arguing our points, because it would not change my current state. Instead, we needed to look for answers. I told him I felt fifty times better in California than in Texas. Could living in Corpus Christi be feeding my disease? Could the weather be such a factor in my recovery?

Doc was beginning to wonder whether my nerves were highly sensitive or allergic to something in the water. Maybe my close proximity to the Gulf of Mexico in conjunction with the higher humidity and increase of mold was the culprit.

I took this as a sign. Rick spent every night on the island with me, since I was so frequently sick. Having a forty-minute commute and working late hours meant he would not get home until after nine in the evening. He was exhausted and hoping I might consider moving to a smaller town twenty miles outside of the city.

While this move seemed natural and right to him, I wanted to be sure we were both ready for such a serious commitment. This was a major step in our relationship. I knew he would have moved anywhere to lessen my pain, but for the next few years, he had an obligation to his business. This was why he felt that leaving the city limits would be perfect. His commute would be shorter, and my health would improve. Rick loved me and wanted to start our lives together.

While I felt the same way, I also felt I needed my parents' permission. Although I was recovering, I still could not work, which meant that Mom and Dad financially supported me. It just felt wrong to live with someone when I was incapable of paying my own bills. Moving in with Rick was all that I wanted, and yet I did not think I had the right to make that decision on my own. I was torn.

Speaking to them about this subject was difficult, because I felt so pathetic. I was a twenty-six-year-old woman who solely relied on her parents to survive. All the insecurities I had about not being good enough rose to the surface. *I was still a failure. I still had not accomplished anything for myself.*

Much to my surprise, Mom and Dad were thrilled. In fact, they even encouraged the move; so moving day was October 28, 2006.

Chapter 31

Overcoming Fear

It astounded me how my health drastically improved from that day forward. Overnight I seemed to be able to use the STS machine and sleep six hours at a time. Determined to beat this pain for the last time, I listened to my Holosync meditative tapes and ate only organic, non-processed foods. I began exercising on a consistent basis and even assisted Rick at work a couple hours a day. Life was good.

Wanting to do everything in my power to follow a healthy lifestyle was the reason I started drinking Limu juice. Since I had tried previous supplements like goji and noni juice without seeing any results, I had resisted trying Limu for months. However, my dear friend convinced me otherwise. Mary had been dealing with her own chronic pain issues for decades. While she was also a patient of Doc's and improving under his practice, her energy doubled after taking Limu. She felt as if she had gained back part of her life, and she really wanted me to try it for one month.

My expectations were quite low as I reluctantly gave in to Mary's trial period. I really did not believe this supplement would do anything for my pain. *I was wrong.* The changes in my health were immediate. I had two bowel movements, and my headaches decreased the first day alone. Within two weeks, I noticed I had not suffered a recent migraine, nor did I seem as stressed. I was amazed.

I began doing more research and discovered Limu juice contained a fucoidan-enriched brown seaweed native to Tonga. This natural plant contained powerful antioxidants that relieved stomach disorders, detoxified the body of dangerous chemicals, and improved liver function. It was incredible. After all the years suffering from constipation, acid reflux and inflammation, I finally had found my cure. Limu juice saved me.

My next big improvement came a month later, when I realized I was coping better with thunderstorms. Instead of convulsing from the shooting pain that traveled up and down my spine, I now only shuddered. I might not be able to exercise, but I could get out of bed and dress myself. In time, the intense stings became manageable. I even found myself able to drive the thirty miles into town to visit Doc. I just could not believe I was handling my intense pain with the STS, meditation and Limu juice. I was fighting back, and that was progress.

With my life looking up, so was my relationship. The stressful, sleepless nights were gone, just as the dreaded phone calls from Rick and my parents to check up on me were over. I started cooking again and taking care of the laundry. Not only was I cleaning the house but I was also dusting once a week. I had become domesticated, and for some odd reason, I liked that. It seemed we had made it through the darkness. The disease had stopped controlling our lives.

∞

By January 2007, I had reached a pivotal point in my recovery efforts. While I could now participate in most activities, I still had not lived a pain-free day. After dealing with chronic pain for the past eight and a half years, I could not comprehend what nothingness felt like. I knew it was great to have a current pain level ranging between a four and a five, but that did not satisfy me. My goal was to reach a zero.

Since I had gone home for the holidays, I decided to visit an acupuncturist and Chinese herbalist. Kelsey, another young chronic pain person, had referred me to Bih-Yeang Song (who we called Peter) after her own encouraging results. I hesitantly agreed to a meeting. I had been terrified of acupuncture ever since my first encounter eight years ago, when an ill-informed practitioner stabbed my right fist with needles. In fact, I had sworn off the entire practice, until now.

Being older and wiser, I had to trust my intuition. I had heard too many wonderful stories about Peter to shrug off this therapy. If I did not see him, I knew I would always wonder "what if." Because I hated what-ifs, I had to take a leap of faith.

The instant I walked into his office, I knew I was in the right place. The soothing natural tones of the walls and the quiet meditative tape playing from speakers calmed me. The waiting room had chairs with brightly colored cushions and a table neatly stacked with current health-related magazines like *Natural Solutions* and *Mind, Body, Soul*. I immediately felt welcomed and safe.

As I filled out the mandatory paperwork, I omitted much of my pertinent health problems. This was because I wanted to see what he would be able to discover through his own examination. His responses were startling. Peter easily named every issue, problem, symptom and pain I endured daily. To diagnose each specific problem, he checked the energy of my heartbeat, ears and tongue.

Inserting eight very thin needles in my arms, hands, legs, feet and face, Peter left me in a dark room to rest for twenty-eight minutes. A far-infrared heat lamp warmed my legs as I slowly drifted to sleep. With my body relaxing, I noticed I could finally breathe without feeling a weight in my chest. I felt like a different person as my pain incredibly dropped from a four to a minimal two. The transformation enabled me to break through my plateau. *I had found another ally in defeating the pain.*

That evening, I slept the soundest I had in years. I was blown away and quickly scheduled another four sessions with Peter before returning to Texas. I remember constantly asking him questions regarding vitamins, herbs and healing therapies. It was as if I was a sponge trying to absorb all information. Peter re-ignited my hopes of being pain-free.

∞

Months passed by, and soon I was stronger than I had been in a decade. I now had the stamina to wake at six in the morning and work continually through the day without paying the price. I could run for an hour on the treadmill and still be able to go home and make dinner. I even made it through a week without waking up on Saturday unable to move. My healing was happening.

As I began feeling better, I would sometimes forget to use the STS machine. Usually only a day or two would pass before I would remember. Except this time, it had been a week. I was in shock. How was it even possible for me to feel so well without treatments?

Thinking this had to be great news, I quickly e-mailed Doc. I naively thought that not using the machine was promising. I thought it meant that I was healing. I was sorely mistaken. Within minutes, I received a response from Doc, telling me to visit the office as soon as possible. Stopping treatments was not wise, and there were "things" we needed to discuss. To put it mildly, Doc did not appear to be as thrilled as I was.

The next day, we had a candid conversation. While Doc was elated that I felt so good, he reiterated the importance of daily therapies. If there was ever a severe lightning storm or if I accidentally injured myself at the gym, my nerves would go haywire. The STS kept me well by improving circulation and quieting my pain. It prevented massive flare-ups and was an important tool for keeping me fit and healthy.

I knew he was right, but it was hard for me to make the time when I felt so alive. However, my health was my main priority. If I would only eat organic foods, use non-toxic household cleaners, and avoid microwaves, then why was I not scheduling an hour to run the STS? Doc's machine enabled me the freedom to live.

By late June, I had an epiphany. In order to prove to myself that chronic pain no longer controlled my dreams, I was going to run a half marathon. These thirteen miles would be the culmination of all I had endured. I had already been to hell, and I miraculously survived the loss of limb mobility, long hospital stays, botched procedures, bedridden months and morphine withdrawals. Now I wanted to surpass all my expectations. This was my moment to live without fear, worry or shame. *Running would set me free.*

I wanted to do this not only for me, but also for everyone who had touched my life. I would run for Mom, Dad, Dan and Rick. This was for my grandparents, aunts, uncles, cousins and friends. It was in honor of Mitzi, Shelley, Maureen, Denise, Bob and Peter. I also wanted it to be dedicated to those who continued to live each day with chronic pain. While some had made great progress on their own journey, others were still lost in the depths of despair and anguish. This half marathon would be a tribute to their perseverance to carry on another day while clinging to hope that someday *they* could run their own personal marathons.

My mind was set. I was ready to start my new life—a life where everything was possible. This was my chance to show the world what I already knew. I *was* healed.

Rick was a little apprehensive about proceeding without first getting Doc's approval. He needed the reassurance that my body could handle the intense training and preparation. Since Doc was my biggest supporter, it came as no surprise when he said yes. The surprise was how shocked and perplexed he was as to why I would want to run thirteen miles.

He did have some stipulations. As long as I was training, I needed to increase my protein intake, use the STS machine twice a day, and visit him at least once a week. If I could abide by these mandates, he saw no reason why I could not conquer my newest challenge.

Rick was still uncertain. The furthest I had run outdoors was two miles. He knew I had the heart, but he feared my health might deteriorate. Running on a treadmill was far different from being outside, hitting pavement. Thirteen miles was taxing on average bodies, let alone someone dealing with chronic pain.

Was I sure I wanted to do this? Did I really think my body was ready for this?

The answer was "yes!" This was what I needed to jump over that last hurdle. Running would validate my new health and confirm that labels did not define a person. I wanted to do this more than anything else. I wanted to reach that point where I no longer had to dread the unknowns or uncertainties of the next day.

My adamancy and determination did not sway Rick. He really wanted to take this slowly and in steps. Before he allowed me to register, I had to train with him for a week just to be certain that I was 100 percent sure. While I remember that the week was grueling, it was also exhilarating. Exercising for a greater purpose allowed me to push myself further.

Now I was even more convinced that this was the right thing to do. My heart pitter-pattered as I registered for the Harbor Half taking place on October 21, 2007. With less than four months to train, I knew I was cutting it close. But I had tenacity, and nobody was going to tell me I could not do it.

∞

The Harbor Half was an annual event in Corpus Christi. This thirteen-mile course had runners traveling over the Harbor Bridge, along the causeway, and through wildlife preserve before looping back around. While the incline of the bridge itself only stretched a half mile in both directions, the steep grade added much difficulty. This was not a stroll in the park. In fact, I knew it would test my inner strength and physical stamina.

I was ready for the challenge. It was finally time for me to put the pain and grief behind me. I wanted the world to know that nothing would stand between me and my goals. Having spent the last nine years fighting, I was ready for my victorious triumph. This run would mark my final chapter to wellness.

Although Rick was still worried, he put his reservations aside and devised an aggressive program. The first four weeks of training were about getting me accustomed to running. Three days a week, I would jog on the treadmill for an hour, followed by three sets of abs, lunges, squats and push-ups. I would complete a cross-training circuit once a week. Wednesdays were my easy days to walk at an incline for a half hour and then do weight training. Then on Saturdays, the two of us would jog a mile and a half outdoors.

The schedule was tough, but I managed to push through without any major hiccups. My only issue was finding a comfortable breathing pattern. I seemed to be fine during the week when running in the gym. But on the weekends, I constantly felt as if I was gasping for air. Doc explained that a lack of vasoactive intestinal polypeptide (VIP) was the culprit. He decided to switch my treatments to lung protocols while having me massage Vicks VapoRub on my chest before training. The menthol in VapoRub affected the receptor sites in the lungs needed to make VIP. It allowed the airways in the lungs to relax so I could receive better airflow.

Although menthol had a strong smell, it seemed to work, and I was able to find a breathing rhythm that suited my needs within weeks. The commitment to running the entire thirteen miles meant I had to take care of myself and stay healthy. I increased my visits to the clinic to three times a week. Making sure I completed an hour of STS protocols each night while listening to my meditative CD was my way of nurturing my body. I was following a balanced program that incorporated the mind, body and spirit.

I started noticing problems in the second month when my body resisted outdoor running. Anytime my foot made contact with the concrete, I developed sharp, piercing ankle pains and numbness throughout my toes. It felt as if a nail was being hammered into my ankle. I tried to ignore the pain, but it was too severe. Although I was supposed to be running four miles, I would have to limp-walk after ten minutes. *What was wrong with me?*

I saw Doc right away. At first, he thought the recent storms and weather changes caused my symptoms. But switching my beat frequency and trying different STS protocols did not help the situation. He then questioned whether overuse was the culprit. I tried resting for a couple of days, but that did nothing. It was hopeless.

Discouraged, I went home to California to see Peter. While my workouts lasted longer after an acupuncture session, the pain would re-emerge two miles into a run. Then I would have to limp home in tears. I even tried five different running shoes and altered my running stride and pace, but I still had problems. With the nagging pains present, I was at a complete loss.

My inability to train soon became a huge stress on Rick's and my relationship. With a deadline approaching, our aggravations heightened. The stress of the situation made us easily agitated. Arguing over what I should and should not be doing became a common topic of discussion in our household. As I knew my limitations, I refused to overextend myself in fear of exasperating an already flared condition. All I needed was for Rick to understand that I was not quitting but *only* trying to save myself. I was doing everything in my power to heal.

Rick, on the other hand, had been an athlete his entire life. He wished I would just stop questioning his authority, motives, and training techniques. Because he understood what it took to succeed and compete, he felt I needed to make a choice. Either I run through the pain or we stop the training. We were at a standstill.

While I felt he did not grasp the seriousness of my situation, he felt I did not listen to his advice. Moreover, Rick was angry that I thought he would jeopardize my health by pushing me too far. We were coming from two very different places.

Our fighting bothered me tremendously. This was supposed to be fun. I had envisioned us coming closer together and thought we would laugh and enjoy our tandem workouts. However, all we did was bicker and argue. I wanted my loving boyfriend back, and I knew he wanted his emotionally sound, bubbly girlfriend to return as well. *What had happened to us?*

Shortly thereafter, Doc had another hypothesis as to what might be the culprit: old orthotics. Since I had been wearing the same orthotics for nearly two years, he wondered if my arch had changed from exercise and weight loss. When he took the new mold of my feet to compare with my previous arch, it was as if Doc had lifted a boulder from my shoulders.

Much to our delight, there was a significant difference between the two impressions. I had rearfoot and forefoot pronation that had mostly compensated my superior joint. While I was unsure what all this meant, Doc told me my old orthotics added to the problem. The aggravation and inflammation would need to heal, but new orthotics should make running possible again.

As Doc rush-ordered a new pair, he wanted me to curb my workouts. I was not to participate in any activity that might flare my ankle or create more pain. I agreed and promised to contact him before beginning a new training program.

This news was a blessing. Finally, Rick and I were able to come together to discuss our issues. Rick knew I was strong enough to finish the whole thirteen miles, but he wanted me to enjoy the race. I believed in Rick's training program and only resisted his instructions because I was ashamed. I hated feeling as if I let him down whenever I could not complete a run.

Sharing our deepest feelings opened the doors of communication. This was it—no more fighting. With wounds that were real and raw, we realized we needed to learn to support each other. Our entire relationship had always been built on trust, love, and mutual respect. We were a team, and we had to start acting like one again.

The next day, I felt much better. Rick had devised a new plan that required no running. If I could not complete long runs, we would focus on my developing stronger, leaner muscles. Having recently purchased a Concept II rowing machine for the gym, he jokingly informed me that this would become my new best friend. I was to start out rowing one thousand meters and increase to ten thousand meters. Hypothesizing that the energy put forward to row was equivalent to or harder than the energy expended running, Rick believed I could run thirteen miles if I had the stamina to row for forty-five minutes.

The rowing, weight training, and abdominal work were difficult but tolerable. I had to increase my protein consumption just to maintain my energy and weight. For the first time in months, I realized that being healthy was the ultimate goal. My stress dissipated, and I felt I could handle the thirteen-mile run with the new orthotics.

Yet there was another problem: the manufacturing company had made my inserts too long. While Doc had to send them back for adjustments, I began to panic. I had less than a month before the race. *What would I do if they never came?*

It would have been extremely easy to give up, but that was not an option. I knew I did not have the time or luxury of allowing my emotions to control my workouts. I needed to stay strong and focus on the work I was doing in the gym. It helped to have Rick as my coach, because he utilized my time wisely and kept me motivated. This was happening for a greater reason, and I would persevere.

Having to rethink how I would manage this run if I did not have orthotics made me remember the advice Peter gave me during our last session. After watching me stand and walk, he noticed troubles with my gait. If I could stay conscious of how and where my knees landed in comparison to my feet, the pain should naturally subside. Peter then marked my shoes with a black pen between my big and second toe; I just had to make sure the center of my knee aligned with the marking during every stride.

I tried Peter's technique the next morning as I attempted jogging on the treadmill. Surprisingly, it worked. While I still felt a slight twinge at my anklebone whenever I took a step, the agonizing pain had disappeared. I could feel a shift occur in my body. I knew everything would be okay.

$$\infty$$

As the monumental day grew closer, I began to stretch daily and eat only organic meats, fruits and vegetables. I went to bed earlier and consistently took my vitamins. I even increased my visits with Doc to four days a week. There was no way I was going to chance anything getting in the way of my dream.

A week before the marathon, Rick took me on a trial run. Trotting down the farm road near our house rejuvenated me. I stared at open fields where horses and goats roamed, while chuckling at the sweet dog that followed us along. My disparaging thoughts disappeared as I consciously paid attention to the way my feet touched the pavement. I stayed relaxed, loose and hydrated, while breathing in rhythm to my stride.

Completing ten miles in two hours was huge for me. I felt untouchable, and seeing the longhorn at the halfway mark only added to magic of the moment. This jog felt like a celebration of life. Now that I knew I had the tools, I was finally ready to soar.

Five days before the marathon, I decreased my training so my muscles could rest and strengthen. I could not believe the race was so close, especially since it had become so much larger than me. Although it symbolized my new life without limitations, it also represented hope to my friends in chronic pain—hope that they could also live the lives they had wanted to lead. I might be physically running, but they would be with me in spirit. This was for all of us. *We were not pain victims.*

My life seemed to be coming together when my parents arrived the day before the "big run." Having them present meant the world to me. Mom and Dad were such an integral part of my recovery that I wanted them to be a part of the beginning of my new life. I needed them to see that all the pain and misery we endured was worth it. I was finally happy and content. I was in love with the most amazing man and living a normal life.

Not only was this my parents' first trip to Corpus Christi for leisure, but it also coincidentally marked my five-year anniversary in Texas. Exactly five years ago, Mom and I made our way to Doc's clinic, hopeful we had found the treatment that would give me back my life. I had so many obstacles blocking my success that I was able to miraculously overcome. Somehow, I had survived.

Tears welled in my eyes as I thought about how far I had come. Here I was, happy and in love, laughing with my parents again. I was alive and I had made it. The journey out of the darkness was almost complete.

The next morning, I awoke to the beep of the alarm clock. It was five in the morning. I looked at Rick, as my stomach turned in circles. My life would change forever in less than six hours.

Today I would heal.

Harbor Half: Time

2:48:57

I look at my parents' water-brimmed eyes and smile; I did it, and this was a tribute to them. I had conquered the pain and misery. **My life will be mine from this day forward.**

Breinigsville, PA USA
18 January 2010
230923BV00003B/1/P

BUY A SHARE OF THE FUTURE IN YOUR COMMUNITY

These certificates make great holiday, graduation and birthday gifts that can be personalized with the recipient's name. The cost of one S.H.A.R.E. or one square foot is $54.17. The personalized certificate is suitable for framing and will state the number of shares purchased and the amount of each share, as well as the recipient's name. The home that you participate in "building" will last for many years and will continue to grow in value.

Here is a sample SHARE certificate:

THIS CERTIFIES THAT

YOUR NAME HERE

HAS INVESTED IN A HOME FOR A DESERVING FAMILY

1985-2005

TWENTY YEARS OF BUILDING FUTURES IN OUR COMMUNITY ONE HOME AT A TIME

1200 SQUARE FOOT HOUSE @ $65,000 = $54.17 PER SQUARE FOOT
This certificate represents a tax deductible donation. It has no cash value.

YES, I WOULD LIKE TO HELP!

I support the work that Habitat for Humanity does and I want to be part of the excitement! As a donor, I will receive periodic updates on your construction activities but, more importantly, I know my gift will help a family in our community realize the dream of homeownership. **I would like to SHARE in your efforts against substandard housing in my community!** *(Please print below)*

PLEASE SEND ME _____ SHARES at $54.17 EACH = $ $_____

In Honor Of: _____

Occasion: (Circle One)   HOLIDAY   BIRTHDAY   ANNIVERSARY

          OTHER: _____

Address of Recipient: _____

Gift From: _____   *Donor Address:* _____

Donor Email: _____

I AM ENCLOSING A CHECK FOR $ $_____ PAYABLE TO HABITAT FOR HUMANITY OR PLEASE CHARGE MY VISA OR MASTERCARD *(CIRCLE ONE)*

Card Number _____ Expiration Date: _____

Name as it appears on Credit Card _____ Charge Amount $ _____

Signature _____

Billing Address _____

Telephone # Day _____ Eve _____

PLEASE NOTE: Your contribution is tax-deductible to the fullest extent allowed by law.
Habitat for Humanity • P.O. Box 1443 • Newport News, VA 23601 • 757-596-5553
www.HelpHabitatforHumanity.org